E-Metrics for Library and Information Professionals

HOW TO USE DATA FOR MANAGING AND EVALUATING ELECTRONIC RESOURCE COLLECTIONS

Andrew White and Eric Djiva Kamal

facet publishing

Copyright © 2006 Neal-Schuman Publishers

Published by
Facet Publishing
7 Ridgmount Street
London WC1E 7AE

Facet Publishing is wholly owned by CILIP: the Chartered Institute of Library and Information Professionals.

First published in the USA by Neal-Schuman Publishers, Inc., 2006.
This simultaneous UK edition 2006.

British Library Cataloguing in Publication Data
A catalogue record for this book is available from the British Library.

ISBN-1-85604-555-2

Printed and bound in the United States of America.

Contents

List of Tables / ix

List of Figures / xv

Preface / xvii

Acknowledgments / xxi

Part I What are E-Metrics? / 1

Overview / 1
Note / 3

1   **Defining E-Metrics** / 4
Working in the Wired World / 4
    Pre-Internet Business / 6
    The Birth of the Internet and the Rush to E-Commerce / 8
    Elements of E-Metrics / 10
    The Application of E-Metrics in E-Commerce / 12

2   **Using E-Metrics in Libraries** / 19
Libraries in the Print-Only Era / 19
    Metrics in Libraries Before the Computer Age / 20

The Rise of E-Publishing and the Birth of the Internet / 22
Library Performance Measurements in the Digital Era / 24

3   **Understanding Vendor-Supplied E-Metrics / 28**
Examining Samples of Vendor-Supplied E-Metrics / 31
The Benefits of Vendor-Supplied E-Metrics / 38
Are E-Metrics Data and Methods Really
Standardized? / 39
Why Should You Build Local E-Metrics? / 42
Summary and Conclusions / 51
Notes / 52

Part II Why Do Libraries Need E-Metrics? / 53

Overview / 53
4   **Using E-Metrics for Public Relations / 55**
New Challenges for Libraries in the Digital Revolution / 55
Public Relations Q & A with E-Metrics / 57
Gate Counts vs. Net Counts / 57
Where Are Our Users? / 61
Why Are Library Resources Used? / 63
How Well Are We Serving the Unseen and Who
Are They Anyway? / 66
Where is My Title? / 71

5   **Using E-Metrics for Collection Management / 72**
The Vagaries and Constraints of Delivery and Access / 72
Collection Development Q & A with E-Metrics / 73
Why is This One Available and the Other One Not? / 73
Subscription Bundling / 74
Licensing and Access Restrictions / 77
Can We Collect in Specialized Subject Areas? / 80
Title Value from the User's Perspective / 81
Can We Coordinate Collections with Other Libraries? / 83
Coordinated Collection Development / 84
Conclusion / 87

6   Using E-Metrics for Library Administration / 88
Administrative Q & A with E-Metrics / 89
    How Much Do Electronic Collections Cost? / 89
        The "Big Deal" Revisited / 90
    How Many Staff Do We Need? / 93
        Electronic Resources Management / 93
        The Illusion of Seamless Access / 97
        The Unseen Technology of ERM / 98
        The Perils of Market Consolidation / 101
        ERM Solutions? / 102
    How Much Technology Do We Need? / 104
        The Total Cost of Ownership and the Price of
            Staying Relevant / 105
        Measuring the Value of Library Information
            Technologies / 109
        Connecting the Price of Access, Presentation,
            and ERM / 112
Summary and Conclusions / 114
Notes / 114

Part III   How Do Libraries Build Local E-Metrics? / 115

Overview / 115
Notes / 117

**7   E-Metrics and E-Resources: Designing Solutions to Capture
Usage Statistics on E-Journals, Databases, E-Books,
and Digital Documents / 118**
Analyze Basic Web Metrics in Libraries—Local Solution Level 1 / 119
    Library Web Site Analysis: General Statistics / 120
    Library Web Site Analysis: Most Accessed Pages / 122
Evaluate Vendor-Supplied Statistics / 124
    Data Collection / 125
    Data Collation / 126
    Data Analysis / 127
Explore Local E-Metrics Initiatives / 128
    Quick Review of Some Local E-Metrics Solutions / 128

CONTENTS

Intermediate Local E-Metrics—Local Solution Level 2 / 130
   Click-Through Script / 130
   What Identifiers Do We Need for Local E-Metrics? / 132
   Transaction Log Analysis (TLA) / 135
   Sample Results / 137
Advanced Local E-Metrics—Local Solution Level 3 / 143
Highly Advanced Local E-Metrics—Local Solution
   Level 4 / 145
Mini How-to / 147
Overview of the Local E-Metrics Project / 148
Notes / 153

8   **E-Metrics and Infrastructure: Assessing Servers, Workstations, and Other Technical Considerations / 155**
Consider Common Issues for Vendor and Local E-Metrics / 156
   Statistical Report Storage / 156
   External Data Integration Related to Title Usage Studies / 157
     ISXN, Impact Factors, Number of Articles / 158
     Date of First Access / 158
     Example of an E-Metrics Report with Title
       External Data / 159
     Title Price / 161
Incorporate Technical Issues Specific to Local E-Metrics / 161
   Data Sources for Data Collection / 163
     Library Web Server / 163
     Library's Catalog Server / 164
     Proxy Servers / 165
     Print Servers / 168
     Open-URL Servers / 168
   Data Processing Requirements / 169
     Using Off-the-Shelf Software / 169
     Using Open Source Software / 170
     Using Custom Designed Tools: Homegrown or
       Outsourced / 170
     Necessary Development Units / 171
   External Data Related to IP Addresses and User

Demographics / 172
    IP: Address Mapping and Subnets / 173
    User: Affiliation, Status, Category / 175
    Server for Library User Database / 176
Notes / 181

9   E-Metrics and Staffing: Creating the Team and Defining the Project / 182
Set Up the E-Metrics Team within Library Organization / 183
    Library Management / 184
    Access Services and Reference Departments / 185
    Technical Services Department / 185
    Electronic Resources Manager / 186
    IT Department / 187
Determine Librarians' Skill Set Expansion and Coordination / 188
    Public Relations for Reference and Circulation / 188
    Cataloging E-Resources / 189
    ERM Team / 189
Consider Additional "Systems" Personnel / 190
    User Access Management / 191
    In-House Programming / 192
    Library Systems Administration / 193
Establish E-Metrics Management Policies / 194
    Multiple Ways to Count a Title Use / 194
        By Visit / 194
        By Search and Session / 195
        By Unique Visitor / 196
    User Authentication / 197
        Access Barriers / 198
        Privacy Issues / 198
        Burden of User Database Management / 199
    Report Processing / 199
        Report Accessibility Records / 200
        Frequency and Format Standardization / 201
        Preservation / 201
    Title Persistence Over Time / 202
        New Information on a Title / 202

Source Change / 202
Title Subscription Cancellation / 203
Notes / 204

10 E-Metrics and the Future: Standards, Restrictions, Implementation, and Emerging Technologies / 205
Review of E-Metric Standards / 206
Open Access Initiatives / 206
Publishing Sector Market Consolidation / 207
Factor in the Technical Considerations / 208
Access Restrictions Through Licensing Agreements / 209
Preservation and Value of E-Metrics Over Time / 210
Applying E-Metrics to E-Resources and E-Services / 211
Impacts of Emerging Technologies like Federated Search Engines and Deep Linking on E-Metrics / 213
Cost of Local E-Metrics Implementation / 214
Conclusion / 216
Notes / 216

Appendices / 217

Appendix 1: Report Comparison between Two Web Traffic Analysis Software / 219

Appendix 2: Click-Through Script / 221

Appendix 3: Custom Log Parsing Script / 222

Bibliography / 229

Index / 245

About the Authors / 251

List of Tables

Table 1-1: Sample of Web Server Transaction Log Showing 4 Hits for
1 Page View 11

Table 1-2: Sample Web Server Log File Showing Additional Transaction
Activities Captured in the Network Transmission of Data 15

Table 3-1: Extract of the COUNTER Code of Practice Release 2 Glossary
of Terms—Providers of Page Views of Bibliographic Data 30

Table 3-2: COUNTER JR1 Report—Number of Successful
Full-Text Article Requests by Month and Journal 32

Table 3-3: COUNTER JR2 Report—Number of Full-Text
Turnaways by Month and Publication 33

Table 3-4: COUNTER JR3 Report—Number of Successful Item Requests
and Turnaways by Month, Journal, and Page-Type 34

Table 3-5: COUNTER JR4 Report—Total Searches Run by
Month and Service 36

Table 3-6: COUNTER DB1 Report—Total Searches and Sessions by
Month and Database 37

Table 3-7: General Elsevier Service Usage Statistics—Web
Site Performance 37

Table 3-8: Elsevier Service Network Use—Users, Network IP
Addresses, and Sessions   38

Table 3-9: COUNTER JR3—Number of Successful Item
Requests and Turnaways by Month, Journal, and Page Type from
Kluwer Online   41

Table 3-10: Downloads by Title by Month from Kluwer Online   42

Table 3-11: Page Views by Title by Month from Kluwer Online   42

Table 3-12: Basic (Library A)   47

Table 3-13: Intermediate (Library B)   48

Table 3-14: Advanced (Library C)   48

Table 4-1: Elsevier Overall Monthly Service Report   58

Table 4-2: Library B Overall Web Site Usage Summary   58

Table 4-3: Library B Most Accessed Web Server Pages   59

Table 4-4: Usage and Visitors to the Ten Most Frequently Used
Full-Text E-Journal Titles That are Part of Library C Virtual
Collection   60

Table 4-5: Additional Network Usage Patterns for the Ten Most
Frequently Used Full-Text E-Journal Titles that are Part of Library
C's Virtual Collection   61

Table 4-6: Kluwer Online Subdomain Visits by Content Category by
Month from Library A   62

Table 4-7: Library B Web Site Visits by IP Addresses and Sessions 63

Table 4-8: Examples of Accessed Sites from Public Workstations   66

Table 4-9: Examples of Printouts from Public Workstations   67

Table 4-10: COUNTER JR3 Report—Number of Successful Item
Requests and Turnaways by Month, Journal, and Page-Type from
Library A Highwire Subscription   68

Table 4-11: Examples of Use of Full-Text Journals by Departments   69

Table 4-12: Use by Department for the New England Journal of
Medicine   70

Table 4-13: Use by Selected Academic Departments for the
Journal of Psychology   71

Table 5-1: Kluwer Downloads by Title and Month from Library A   75

Table 5-2: Amount of Network Use for the Ten Most Frequently Used
Full-Text E-Journal Titles   79

Table 5-3: Use by Department for New Ideas in Psychology
through Sciencedirect   82

Table 5-4: Use by Department for Issues in Law and Medicine through
Galegroup   82

Table 5-5: Example of Summary Numbers of Interlibrary Loan
Activity   84

Table 5-6: Relative Value of a Particular Title to a Number of
Borrowing Libraries   85

Table 5-7: Relative Value of a Particular Title to a Number of
Borrowing Libraries   86

Table 5-8: Ten Most Frequently Requested Titles Not Part of ILL   86

Table 6-1: Comparisons of Two Package Agreements Licensed
in an Academic Medical Library   92

Table 6-2: Representative Changes in Bundled Licensing Agreements   96

Table 6-3: Breakdown of Annual ERM Title Maintenance Tasks   103

Table 6-4: Monthly ERM Collection Maintenance Patterns   103

Table 6-5: Amount of Network Use for the Ten Most Frequently
Used Full-Text E-Journal Titles   110

Table 6-6: Expansion of the Library Operating Hours with the
Shift from Print to Digital   111

Table 7-1: Characteristics of a Local Solution (Level 1) for Basic Web Metrics   120

Table 7-2: Summarized Report Comparison between Wusage 8.0 and WebTrends Entreprise Suite™ for the Most Accessed Pages on a Library's Web Site   123

Table 7-3: Non-Exhaustive List of Local E-Metrics Initiatives in Libraries   129

Table 7-4: Characteristics of an Intermediate Solution (Level 2) for Local E-Metrics   130

Table 7-5: Potential E-Metrics Data Captured when Using the "Click-Through" Method   133

Table 7-6: Title Usage Statistics   141

Table 7-7: IP/Visitor Usage Statistics   142

Table 7-8: Provider Usage Statistics   143

Table 7-9: Characteristics of an Advanced Solution (Level 3) for Local E-Metrics   146

Table 7-10: Characteristics of a Highly Advanced Solution (Level 4) for Local E-Metrics   148

Table 7-11: Creating the Click-Through Script   149

Table 7-12: Modifying the HTML Links for Your E-Resources   149

Table 7-13: Installing Your Transaction Log Analysis Application (TLA)   150

Table 7-14: Analyzing the Server Log File   151

Table 7-15: Local E-Metrics Solutions and Feasibility by Library Category   153

Table 8-1: External Data on Title Information and Possible Use   157

Table 8-2: Locally Generated E-Metric Report for E-Journals with Integrated External Data   160

Table 8-3: Road Map and Actors   162

Table 8-4: Elements of Infrastructure Data Collection and Data Processing 162

Table 8-5: Identifiers and Generated E-Metrics Reports 163

Table 8-6: Proxying of a Modified Hyperlink and the Resulting Entry in the Server Log 167

Table 8-7: External Data on IP and User Information and Possible Use 173

Table 8-8: On-Site and Off-Site Access Report 174

Table 8-9: Access Report with Network Subnet Mapping 175

Table 8-10: Specific Title Use by Department 177

Table 8-11: Most Accessed Titles by Department 179

List of Figures

Figure 1-1: Multifaceted Approach to E-Metrics   6

Figure 1-2: Hierarchy of Web Site Activity   11

Figure 3-1: Possible Information Access Route to Full-Text Article   29

Figure 4-1: Graph Showing Usage Comparison between
On-Campus and Off-Campus Computers   64

Figure 4-2: Graph Showing Usage Comparison between Computers
from Inside of Library and Outside of Library   65

Figure 5-1: Graph Showing Annual Usage of Bundled Nature
Publishing Group Titles   76

Figure 5-2: Graph Showing Comparison of Use of U.S. News Title from
the Publisher and a Vendor   77

Figure 5-3: Graph Showing Visual Analysis Comparing the Relative
Values of Individual Titles as Part of a Bundled Package from Ovid
Technologies, Incorporated   83

Figure 6-1: Diagram of Comparison of Post Acquisition Steps for
Maintaining Access to Print and Digital Collections   95

Figure 6-2: Diagram of Possible Points of Information Access Failures for Library Users of Digital Collections   101

Figure 6-3: Diagram of VPN Library Use for Network Authentication   108

Figure 6-4: Diagram of Proxy Server Library Use for Network Authentication   109

Figure 7-1: Comparison between the General Web Statistics from Two Web Analytics Applications   121

Figure 7-2: Comparison between the Most Accessed Pages from Two Web Analytics Applications   123

Figure 7-3: Schematic Access Sequence to an E-Resource Using a "Click-Through" Script   132

Figure 7-4: Sequence of Events When Accessing a Proxied Online Title   145

Figure 7-5: Overview of the Local E-Metrics Project   152

Figure 8-1: Traditional Pathway for a Title Request by a User   166

Figure 8-2: User's Request Interception by a URL Rewriting Proxy Server   166

Figure 8-3: Synthetic View of Possible Elements of Infrastructure for an E-Metrics Project   180

Figure 9-1: Administrative Decision Tree   183

Figure 9-2: Data Resolution for User-Centered and Service-Centered E-Metrics   197

Preface

E-Metrics for Library and Information Professionals evolves from one undisputed fact: libraries have a long history of collecting statistics. From the nineteenth century through the twenty-first, there has been a keen interest in the number of visitors, circulation data, average age of books in the collection, quantity of volumes, the number of reference questions answered, and many other areas. Over the years, these measures became standardized as ANSI/NISO Z39.7 by the National Information Standards Organization (NISO) and the American National Standards Institute and have been revised to include data about digital collections.

Computer network transactions offer enormous potential for statistical analysis. E-metrics are not simply another way of collecting library performance measures. They offer a look at an infinite variety of dimensions that easily surpass the accuracy and value of any prior attempt at quantifying operations. They can—and will—change how librarians look at their world.

So just what are e-metrics and how are they calculated? In their basic form, e-metrics are measurements of the activity and use of networked information. Their use in libraries is relatively recent and there is not one agreed-upon standard. At present, a number of groups have initiatives underway to develop comprehensive standards, including the National Commission of Libraries and Information Science (NCLIS), the Association of Research Libraries (ARL), and the International Coalition of Library Consortia (ICOLC). In addition, vendors and publishers are also developing their own methods of analysis, providing libraries with a variety of reports on the use of their subscription content.

Unfortunately, most books and articles on library statistics focus on ways to evaluate traditional paper-based services and materials by utilizing the same definitions, terminology, criteria, and elements applied to the operations, services, and processes of the past. We wrote *E-Metrics for Library and Information Professionals* to bridge the gap between past collection use management and the emerging solutions for handling virtual collections. Correctly employing e-metrics can streamline, integrate, and supplement the majority of statistical-gathering efforts.

Because of this, we focus on e-metrics as a cost and collection analysis tool for digital and virtual library collections comprised of formats like abstracted and full-text e-journals, subscription index research databases, and to some extent e-books. For the technical folks who put theory into practice, we also cover the how-to procedural tasks and considerations.

Part I, "What Are E-Metrics?" is designed to get even the novice information professional up to speed on e-metric basics and its use in libraries.

- Chapter 1, "Defining E-Metrics," provides a brief history and description of these statistics and their use in various sectors.
- Chapter 2, "Using E-Metrics in Libraries," looks at how this method of measurement has affected libraries and why it will only become more important as electronic resources grow in popularity.
- Chapter 3, "Understanding Vendor-Supplied E-Metrics," assesses the relevance of the e-metrics that many organizations already receive as part of their subscription packages and looks ahead to how these data sets might be supplemented by local projects.

Part II, "Why Do Libraries Need E-Metrics?" will interest both administrators and collection managers. We tried to anchor these discussions in the practical realm employing real-world examples of analyzed data sets from collection development, public relations, and budgetary circumstances.

- Chapter 4, "Using E-Metrics for Public Relations," shows how these measurements reveal the virtual usage of the library. It demonstrates the better awareness of user location, title selection, and retrieval methods. These are the kinds of figures that justify the need for change and improvement in an institution. E-metrics provides real, quantifiable data that can help make the case.
- Chapter 5, "Using E-Metrics for Collection Management," discusses how to leverage the data to more effectively build subject-specific collections, make decisions about coordinating collections with other libraries, and negotiate for licenses and usage agreements.
- Chapter 6, "Using E-Metrics for Library Administration," examines costs, staffing needs, and other technology requirements that can make or break a library's commitment to e-metrics.

Part III, "How Do Libraries Build Local E-Metrics?" tackles the managerial issues needed to make e-metrics a reality. These chapters explore the concerns surrounding the elements, standards, and implementation of e-metrics. They also clarify the technical concerns.

- Chapter 7, "E-Metrics and E-Resources: Designing Solutions to Capture Usage Statistics on E-Journals, Databases, E-Books, and Digital Documents," helps professionals evaluate the available, vendor-supplied statistics and identify what needs to be collected locally by the organization.
- Chapter 8, "E-Metrics and Infrastructure: Assessing Servers, Workstations, and other Technical Considerations," explores the storage, integration, and incorporation of statistics.
- Chapter 9, "E-Metrics and Staffing: Creating the Team and Defining the Project," deals with what personnel to involve in the project and how to utilize the full talents and knowledge of the librarians, IT professionals, and managers.
- Chapter 10, "E-Metrics and the Future," looks ahead to the potential uses and possible changes in standards.

Please note: We used a limited number of examples to reveal how one report can offer a different focus for a variety of end uses. For security, we intentionally obscured the identity of specific library names, network devices, and addresses in server logs and reports.

As the importance and ubiquity of statistics and virtual collections grows, so will the accurate measurement and reporting of their statistics. We hope that *E-Metrics for Library and Information Professionals* supplies ballast to the proposition that the gathering, analysis, and application of e-metrics in libraries needs to become an important part of daily operational considerations.

Acknowledgments

Although this book was written by only two of us, the information presented within is the result of years of collaboration amongst a number of creative and forward-thinking colleagues and coworkers. As is detailed in Part III of this book, library e-metrics requires contributions from a host of individuals and integrated systems working together towards a common goal. And so it is that we would like to recognize those people who helped us make this book possible.

Roger Kelly and Spencer Marsh are the two prominent people who pushed us for tangible measurements of electronic library transactions. Both librarians understood early on that the technological revolution associated with the Internet necessitated a much different approach toward envisioning the performance and value of library services and operations. It is also important to note that the various data illustrated in the numerous examples throughout the book came from the efforts of our coworkers and team members in the Stony Brook University Health Sciences Center Library. The activities and reports from Resource Management Services, Access Services, and Information Systems all ultimately contributed to our ability to create visual representations of virtual library collection and service use. Particular mention goes to Mary Chimato, Dana Antonucci-Durgan, and Ugen Gombo for helping to generate or gather data from their activities associated with circulation, inter-library loan, and electronic resource management. We are also grateful for the input and proofreading provided by Jeanne Galbraith and Susan Opisso; their extensive varied experience and comprehension of circulation and technical services helped us to better explain the interaction of e-metrics within the library as a system. Finally, we would be absolutely remiss if we did not give extra special recognition to our colleague, Joseph Balsamo. There can be little question that without his creativity and programming prowess, much of what we have been able to accomplish and present in this book would have been simply un-achievable.

Part I
What are E-Metrics?

Overview

"It is change, continuing change, inevitable change, that is the dominant factor in society today. No sensible decision can be made any longer without taking into account not only the world as it is, but the world as it will be."

Isaac Asimov[1]

At the beginning of the twenty-first century we note that we are currently living in an age of rapid and pervasive change, brought about primarily by the use of and promise found in computer technologies. The advancement of computer technologies in this present Information Age has dramatically altered the methods for disseminating information. No longer is it necessary to wait for news, current events, or research results to become accessible. Unlike the delay inherent in print information delivery, the use of computer networks and the global presence of the Internet have made information available almost as soon as it can be discovered, thought, and taken place. In this section of the book, we begin by profiling the history of this change in information access and its related impact on both commercial and library operations. We then turn our attention to the current and proposed methods that are being used to better understand and manage the technological changes taking place, thereby defining e-metrics in their historical and technological context.

Chapter 1: What are E-Metrics?: We begin this section on the definition and evolution of e-metrics by observing how companies have taken advantage of recent technological developments to establish new business and marketing paradigms. Today, the mechanisms of e-business and e-commerce require new marketing and customer relationship strategies. One way for companies to measure their success in this new marketing paradigm is to judge the value of a company's virtual business and customer transactions taking place over remote computer networks. Such measurements have been garnered by collecting statistics of various network and Web server activities. These measurements of numerous computer network and Internet access parameters and elements are collectively known as e-metrics. We close this chapter by examining some of the basic e-metrics elements and their usefulness when applied to business and management decisions.

Chapter 2: Using E-Metrics in Libraries: Measurements of library collections and services are a relatively recent concern. Prior to the Internet revolution, the measurement standards for libraries concerned themselves with statistics of library collections and their use along with library services and their level of activity. The success of these measurement standards was dependent upon the stability of print as the primary source of library inventories and activities. With the advent of electronic access to information, the major national and international reporting bodies and associations have attempted to adapt these earlier standards to the digital paradigm. Even though the term and definition of e-metrics are a construct of the modern Internet economy's business sector, libraries and publishers of electronic content have adopted the concept of e-metrics to help manage virtual library collections. As the transition from paper to electronic formats has altered the distribution of library subscriptions, a number of library e-metrics initiatives have arisen. But even these prominent e-metrics efforts from the Association of Research Libraries (ARL) Statistics and Measurements Program, the International Coalition of Library Consortia (ICOLC), and the National Commission on Libraries and Information Science (NCLIS) lack levels of standardization and detail that can best assist libraries in achieving optimum management data and reports. It will become evident in this chapter that it has now become critical for libraries to establish their own e-metrics projects to gather and report data that more accurately reflects local library activities and services.

Chapter 3: Understanding Vendor-Supplied E-Metrics: The current e-metrics reporting standards established by Project COUNTER (Counting Online Usage of Networked Electronic Resources) offer libraries much promise in attempts to capture and identify usage patterns for subscriptions to digital collections. These COUNTER-compliant reports can provide title and resource access details for subscription elements such as table of contents, article abstracts, and full-text articles. Of course, COUNTER provides a set of reporting standards which many information intermediaries and content providers have agreed to meet and improve with future enhancements. Not all vendors provide COUNTER-compliant reports, however, and some provide both COUNTER and proprietary usage reports to their subscribing library customers. Regardless of library environment, vendor-supplied usage reports require some degree of local processing and manipulation in order to fully ascertain comparative values of title and resource access. This chapter will outline how three different library scenarios may begin to approach e-metrics at the local level in order to best utilize and even supplement vendor-supplied usage data.

Note

1. Asimov, Isaac. "My Own View," *The Encyclopedia of Science Fiction,* ed. Robert Hold-stock, 1978; repr. in *Asimov on Science Fiction,* 1981.

1
Defining E-Metrics

Working in the Wired World

Libraries of the past were a physical environment that changed gradually, slowly evolving new types of collections and services, primarily in response to the development of the latest formats and information. But in a relatively short period of time the introduction and use in libraries of computers and their coinciding digital technologies have dramatically altered current library operations and collections. As advances from late twentieth-century digital technologies penetrate every aspect of today's libraries, the most dramatic library transformations continue to come as a result of the Internet. In fact, the Internet has now become the single most important and influential communication medium and its impact can be seen in almost every facet of modern culture and the global economy. The Internet now allows people to publish and access information with little latency of time and beyond the limits of physical presence. The Internet has also created the potential for capturing data and analyzing it at a pace and with a perspective unlike anything known before. As this global network develops from further advancements in computers and digital technologies, it continues to shape the way that information is disseminated and acquired, thereby becoming the major catalyst for rapid growth and change in areas such as medicine, media, scholarly research, publishing, and commerce.

Having an information-rich, real-time, multimedia medium at one's disposal offers many opportunities, but also poses some new challenges to long-established practices and operating paradigms within most sectors of the global economy. Many businesses have embraced the use of the Internet and its communication constituents—like e-mail, telnet, hypertext protocol, Internet relay chat, and instant messaging. As a result, traditional business marketing, transactions, and customer relationship processes are being revamped to take advantage of the potential that the Internet has to offer. A majority of the changes in traditional business processes have been driven by new sets of customer behaviors and expectations made possible by Internet functionality. But other portions of business operations have been altered in order to gather information on real customers that travel in the Internet's networked virtual environment. It is this desire and need for businesses to somehow create and track a personal experience within a virtual storefront that has given birth to e-metrics.

In general, metrics are standards of measurements. But Internet growth has enabled the evolution of networked and digital versions of many functions and services that had taken years to develop via non-electronic means. Currently, these operational analogs that can be implemented on or by means of a computer are typically denoted with "e-" prefixes, with the "e-" standing for electronic. Thus metrics, like mail and its electronic counterpart e-mail, now exist in a comparable digital format as e-metrics. In this new globally networked environment, there are actually two important aspects of e-metrics that both define and differentiate them from other measurement types. E-metrics refer to both the electronic format of collected metrics and to the methods used for gathering metrics through electronic means.

Perhaps the simplest form of e-metrics may be viewed as the measurement of Web site visits. Such measurements could include how many times a particular Web page is accessed, or the volume of Web page views in a given day or week. A more general and encompassing definition of e-metrics includes measuring the activity and use of networked information. This broader definition of e-metrics would account for data that reported on the number of uniquely identified Web site visitors, the total monthly searches for a particular term or phrase in a database, the amount of online purchases for Widget X, and the total volume of network requests supplied by a given Internet server during the month of May. The value of such data lies in its ability to be compiled and correlated in order to gain a better view of how people or groups interact with and utilize information or services that are accessible in networked and electronic formats.

Libraries, too, are beginning to explore the use of e-metrics primarily for collection and budgetary management. However, a thorough understanding and application of e-metrics can yield data useful in directing other aspects of library operations. Figure 1–1 illustrates the multifaceted nature of e-metrics and its relation to both library services and library collections. The top portion of the diagram delineates the types of elements that are captured and measured as part of e-metrics data. The bottom portion of the diagram shows how those data elements are then related to library functions. Due to their relatively short history, e-metrics have become somewhat simple to define but continue to be difficult to analyze. Yet, there is little doubt about the value e-metrics hold. In order to appreciate both the origins and value of e-metrics to libraries, we need to have an overview of commerce models prior to the Internet's proliferation and public

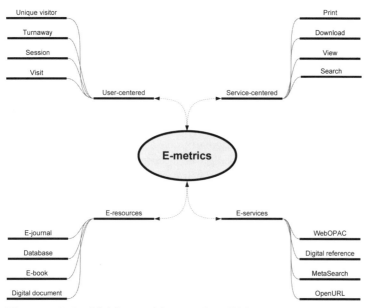

Figure 1-1 Multifaceted Approach to E-Metrics

acceptance. After examining the pre-Internet characteristics of business, we will look at the affect the Internet has had on commerce, thereby uncovering the development and application of e-metrics in the new global economy.

Pre-Internet Business

Much like library operations, the core operations and functionality of business had been static for many years prior to the introduction of the Internet. Perhaps the most essential component of pre-Internet business revolved around person-to-person communications and interactions. Business transactions between our early ancestors could be stereotyped as the barter system where, for example, one goat owned by one person could be traded for two cattle owned by a second person. Even with the advent of currencies, a business transaction still required some sort of personal interaction. The Dutch settlers in America could not have purchased Manhattan Island from the Native American Indians in 1626 without some personal discussion and negotiation, even if such conversations and business transaction documents required group participation.

The most common person-to-person business transactions still involve traveling to some location where goods are made available and exchanging currency for the purchase of those goods. Variations of this transaction model may occur when ordering goods remotely via the telephone or mail. In either case checks, money orders, or credit cards are probably used as the method of payment instead of cash currency. Analogs in library transactions are similarly bound by personal interactions and physical storage restrictions. Library materials have traditionally required an individual to journey to a library to see and use the physical item. If the library's policy dictates that items may not circulate, then the journey is all the more necessary. If items can be loaned between different libraries, the interlibrary loan operation parallels much of the mail order process of commerce.

Another possible commercial model occurs when someone comes to your residence or place of employment with the combined intention of marketing a product or service and completing a business transaction to earn a profit. But even these variants have a person-to-person component in the business procedure. There is a person that requests the goods and provides the proper amount for them, while on the other end there is a person who processes the transaction and allows for the goods to leave their stored location to become the possession of the person who paid for them. If we think of this business model in terms of library service, the modern-day bookmobiles offer a comparable door-to-door service analog in some communities.

One of the important features of the in-person business transaction is the ability of the potential buyer to investigate the item intended to be purchased. A good example of this shopping phase has been repeated for centuries when shopping for food. Chances are good that food will not sell if customers see for themselves that the food products being offered are of poor quality. The same customer behavior tends to be true when buying much more expensive items, such as cars or houses. Either of these items has historically required some kind of personal inspection by the customer before the sale is completed, partially because there is an element of personal taste and perceived functionality attached to these types of purchases. A similar type of personal inspection takes place in libraries as users browse bookshelves looking for items of interest. And whether a company sells food or cars, a tremendous amount of money is invested for advertising to inform and entice customers to company products and services. Consider the century-long success of Sears, Roebuck and Company, which began with an impressive catalog of mail-order items including products such as shoes, clothing, wagons, saddles, stoves, furniture, bicycles, and jewelry. With the production of a 532–page catalog of goods in 1895, Sears had the ability to advertise and ship its merchandise to remote rural areas of the expanding United States.

The introduction of radio and television during the twentieth century offered companies a new manner of advertising that could reach a much wider global audience of potential customers. The radio commercial offered companies the ability to remind customers of available products more frequently than paper advertising. Television advertising takes the repetition aspect of radio advertising to a new level and offers a more realistic and informative perspective of an advertised product than the mail-order catalog. The television commercial has the ability to simulate some of the visual experience that occurs during a personal encounter with a product, thereby encapsulating some of the in-person purchasing experience. In any marketing model it is important to understand both the potential customers of a given product and the target audience of the advertising project.

The Birth of the Internet and the Rush to E-Commerce

Businesses and the public had little knowledge or interest in the Internet until the mid-1990s, even though the core technologies and protocols of the Internet were developed during the 1960s and 1970s. Throughout the 1980s, the Internet was used primarily by academics and scientists. The early Internet lacked both data organization and a retrieval mechanism for networked documents as well as a corresponding application that could make communication and navigation readily accessible to a mass audience. The current data organization method was conceived by Tim Berners-Lee, a researcher at CERN, the European Organization for Nuclear Research, in a 1989 document entitled "Information Management: A Proposal." In this paper Berners-Lee outlined and expanded previously proposed concepts of hypermedia and the servers that would host this linked content on the Internet. The multiple linkages between documents and servers created a mesh or web of interconnections, which when linked globally, would equate to a World Wide Web. Although Berners-Lee also described aspects of locating these hyperlinked documents using an application known as the browser, this application still needed to be refined for public consumption. During 1992 Marc Andreessen, a college student, embarked upon the development of MOSAIC, a browser with an easy-to-use point-and-click interface to the Internet and hypertext protocols. When the progeny of MOSAIC, the Web browser known as Netscape Navigator, became publicly available in 1994, it signaled the start of a communication revolution that many businesses scrambled to become a part of.

In the early stages of mass Internet adoption by businesses, companies envisioned the Internet as another conduit for advertising to a mass audience. Most companies created "brochure-ware" Web sites, the equivalents of posting the contents of mass-mailing, magazine advertising, and in-store informational brochures on the Web in digital format. Because the Internet can make desired information accessible when and where it is needed, this corporate Web strategy allowed customers to seek out and retrieve information on their own terms. So long as the proper technological devices and network connectivity are available, use of the Internet offers the ability to pick and choose access to over 40 million Web servers, some of which host multiple Web sites and Internet domains. The other advantage of the "brochure-ware" Web site for businesses was the ability to reduce spending by decreasing the amount of paper advertising. One Internet advertisement could reach many more potential customers than that same advertisement distributed to multiple outlets in print media. It therefore appeared that it would be much cheaper and more cost effective than mass mailing and paper advertising for companies to create one Web ad that could be digitally replicated around the Internet.

But there were essentially two problems with Web sites that consisted of only "brochure-ware": their content and interface were typically static in nature and they did not provide any additional product information beyond what was already available from other sources. Companies also recognized that because the Internet offers a well of information, it could be challenging for companies to draw attention to their products when there was such a volume of advertising in one virtual place. In addition, companies needed to create methods to make money using the Internet and develop a complete electronic commerce environment. Companies concluded that e-commerce would offer greater profitability if the Internet could be used to sell directly to a customer and reduce the need to distribute products to local resellers.

Thus, the mechanisms of e-business and e-commerce required new marketing and customer relationship strategies. In order to advance beyond "brochure-ware," business Web sites acquired more interactive features that would make them more informative, establish brand recognition, retain customers, and most importantly provide the ability to complete a purchase with minimal human interaction. Today's multitude of commercial Web sites now include various combinations of product information, search engines, virtual shopping carts, personalized recommendations, secured credit card transactions, dynamically-generated catalogs of products, an item's local availability, close-up images, and 360–degree rotational product views. With Internet sites like these, businesses hoped to make the virtual shopping experience as close as possible to the in-person shopping experience, thereby using the Internet to generate income.

But as companies rushed to embrace the Internet for commerce, they soon discovered lurking in any company's e-business strategy new expenditures that had to be added to the cost of operations. Sure, full-page color advertising in newspapers and magazines can be costly. One should not overlook the astronomical costs of the single multimillion-dollar 30–second television commercial situated just before the opening kick-off of the Super Bowl. However, businesses needed to consider the price of purchasing and licensing the technology for e-commerce and securing the expertise to implement and manage it. E-commerce initiatives require software and hardware to build a digital infrastructure and are a source of recurring business costs. Companies need to take advantage of the latest features added to their existing applications and performance enhancements found in newer computer and network hardware in order to remain competitive. Like a reference librarian trying to keep abreast of new information sources in a library, computer programmers and information systems administrators need to be kept up-to-date of technological advances and require frequent training and skill upgrades. So when evaluating e-business, the question for company executives soon becomes whether or not the expenditures to support Internet commerce are outweighed by the profits such business operations can generate. Regardless of how the preceding issue is assessed, executives will still ask how companies can make their e-commerce strategy more profitable. The answers to these questions lie within the collection and analysis of the core data elements that together constitute e-metrics.

Elements of E-Metrics

Several technology components are used to generate and analyze e-metrics in order for businesses to become more efficient in their Internet strategies. Today's e-commerce Web site is built from a complex of operating systems, servers, databases, and business applications. Each of these technology elements helps to make an e-commerce Web site appear to be interactive and personalized to Web visitors. The same apparatus is used to complete secured business transactions in a virtual network space. As the content of an e-business site is accessed with a Web browser, the technology behind the scenes has the ability to log various pieces of information about the numerous Web site constituents. Analysis of the logs within the e-commerce Web site infrastructure, known as transactional log analysis (TLA), provides the raw data for e-metrics. When performing TLA, five key terms need to be addressed: *visits, page views, hits, click-throughs,* and *click rates*.

A *visit* is a virtual request made by an individual over a defined period of time to see information or contents appearing within a Web site. Any particular individual or visitor can generate a single or multiple visits to any given Web site. *Page views* are considered the action generated each time a Web visitor views a complete page on a Web site. Page views are akin to a library gate count; the gate count measures that someone entered the library while the page view measures that someone or some program viewed a Web page. Web pages are comprised of many elements, such as images, video, and audio. A single page may also be dynamically generated from a query or consist of multiple frames of separate pages. Regardless of how the single viewed page is constructed, each one of the elements observed within that page leave behind the measurement of a *hit* within the transaction log. Thus, a single page view consists of multiple hits. Figure 1–2 illustrates the relationship and hierarchy of the first four key raw e-metrics data elements.

Let us look at an example to better understand how a hit is counted. A customer requests a page called "logon.html" from a Web site, and the page contains three graphics as well as text. The Web server hosting this Web page will record four hits in its log, one for the page itself (logon.html) and four more to account for all of that page's graphics (logon.gif, logo.gif, and user.gif). Here is a small sample from a transaction log showing four hits for one page view (see Table 1–1).

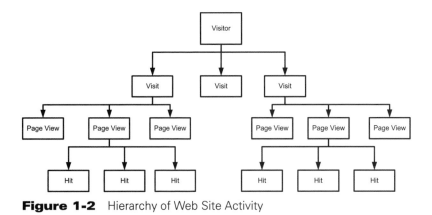

Figure 1-2 Hierarchy of Web Site Activity

While hit counts are a starting point for measuring the traffic on a Web site, they are a rather poor parameter by themselves. A similar issue is faced with library gate counts: the gate count only denotes physical entrance to a library, but does not reveal the actions taken once a user is inside the library. In order for businesses to measure customer behaviors with e-metrics, they must distill the hits into page views, which are extracted further into visits which somehow need to be traced to a single user. This means that an equation must be devised to analyze raw transaction log data and convert it to individual Web site customers. Once log analysis can identify a particular Web site visitor, further log analysis of page views and visitors can help companies ascertain many things: the effectiveness of Internet advertising, which products or offers draw in the most "browsing" shoppers to make them paying customers, which products and services are the most popular, and customer marketing and purchasing demographics. After identifying a particular Web site visitor through log analysis, it then becomes important to determine what the visitor's intentions or actions were having virtually traveled to the e-commerce storefront.

Establishing customer behavior on an e-commerce Web site is accomplished by observing customer *click-throughs*, also sometimes referred to as *clickpaths*. Click-throughs are defined as the list of all Web site pages viewed by a particular visitor as he or she navigated through the e-commerce site. If one considers the hyperlinks and graphical nature of a Web site, it is easy to understand how the

Table 1-1 Sample of Web Server Transaction Log Showing 4 Hits for 1 Page View

2003-10-02 15:25:44 192.168.163.68 - GET /logon.html
2003-10-02 15:25:44 192.168.163.68 - GET /images/logon.gif
2003-10-02 15:25:44 192.168.163.68 - GET /images/logo.gif
2003-10-02 15:25:44 192.168.163.68 - GET /images/user.gif

clickpath is generated by a sequence of mouse clicks necessary to steer one's way through a Web site. Analysis of click-throughs can reveal much information. Since clickpaths can help assess all the pages viewed by a visitor as well as the amount of time a visitor spent viewing a particular page, "click-through" navigation trails of Web site browsers can potentially be used to adjust the design and organization of an e-commerce Web site. Clickpaths are typically associated with *click rates*, or the number of clicks on a particular Web page element which bring a visitor to the company's desired link or action, for example a direct product online order. An analysis that combines data from page views, hits, click-throughs, and click rates would ultimately illustrate patterns of Web site use and functionality. And if there are certain visitor feedback elements within a Web site, user input joined with TLA could even help determine usage patterns of an e-commerce site in relation to user demographics.

The Application of E-Metrics in E-Commerce

The results from e-metrics analysis are currently applied to two interrelated e-commerce processes: Web site development and customer relationship management (CRM). We have already noted that today's Web sites contain many interactive elements besides hyperlinks, such as searchable databases, images, movies, animation, and visitor feedback forms all appearing across a variety of pages within the site. By tracking the use of these various interactive elements and the hyperlink paths activated to move amongst these Web site parts, e-metrics analysis can help determine both the ease and difficulty with which virtual visitors successfully access their desired information. This type of e-metrics data can provide useful feedback to the Web site designers, graphic artists, and database programmers so that they can modify a Web site to make it more navigable or to improve the available content virtually presented.

E-metrics can also provide performance measurements that could be further applied to procedures and policies that ultimately improve an entity's chances for establishing and building customer loyalty. It has always been in the interest of any business to improve sales and services relationships with its customers in order to have customers return to conduct more business or to recommend the company and products to others. CRM involves arranging and measuring the correlation between established customer satisfaction strategies and improvements in sales, profits, and services. The traditional tactics used to gauge CRM success have included customer surveys and product registrations as feedback mechanisms that can help a business develop offerings that appeal to customers and distinguish one business as a standout from another. However, in today's environment of global computer networks and e-commerce, e-metrics can be used to supplement older CRM performance tools by offering multiple customer data collection points as well as various data types that can be associated with individuals or customer groups.

The following hypothetical scenario will help to demonstrate the associated workings of e-metrics between site design and CRM. Suppose you are a member of a team that was responsible for managing a company's Internet business strategy. Your team is expected to recommend changes to the group responsible for the functionality of the company's e-commerce Web site. As previously outlined, today's e-commerce Web presence is comprised of information that has historically been managed by other units within the company, such as sales and marketing. The company's sales unit reports that overall Internet sales are slow and demands that changes be made to make them increase. The marketing unit is interested in knowing the number of visitors to the e-commerce site and how many of those visitors placed orders online. Additionally, both units would like to know what types of virtual customers are purchasing specific products from the virtual storefront. What data sources would your team consult in order to generate the appropriate solutions to these corporate requests?

There is a strong possibility that your company's sluggish Internet sales are the result of the structure and design of the e-commerce Web site. In the construction of a Web site, the multiple links presented on any one Web page offer a multitude of navigational possibilities. The e-commerce sites of any business must present the links and various navigation options clearly so that any potential customer ultimately becomes a paying and returning customer. Perhaps the advertising component of the Web site needs to be redesigned or maybe Web site navigation and organization is too confusing and needs to be overhauled. Then again, it could be that consumers are experiencing errors when attempting to search the online catalog of company products or are having their online transactions fail before completion.

As part of your team's analysis, you ask the Web site administrators to help you identify potential problems within the storefront functionality. The administrators locate an issue when they examine one of the Web server logs, a sample of which reads as following:

```
[Tue Jan 13 11:37:16 2004] [error] [client 172.16.112.55] File does not exist:
    /home/httpd/html/favprod.gif
[Tue Jan 13 11:42:05 2004] [error] [client 10.196.90.245] File does not exist:
    /home/httpd/html/favprod.gif
[Tue Jan 13 11:45:18 2004] [error] [client 172.31.183.52] File does not exist:
    /home/httpd/html/favprod.gif
[Tue Jan 13 11:50:17 2004] [error] [client 192.168.1.13] File does not exist:
    /home/httpd/html/favprod.gif
[Tue Jan 13 11:59:39 2004] [error] [client 192.168.1.91] File does not exist:
    /home/httpd/html/favprod.gif
[Tue Jan 13 12:20:09 2004] [error] [client 192.168.1.70] File does not exist:
    /home/httpd/html/favprod.gif
```

The logs show that there is an error accessing the particular file "favprod.gif", which just happens to be the picture of the hot item your company has on sale for this fiscal quarter. Apparently, Web site viewers cannot see this picture and might therefore avoid buying the sale product sight unseen. Other log files indicate a low click rate on an animated image located on the main products page that is accessed beyond the home page of the Web site. This animated image is supposed to draw a visitor's attention to the other special items on sale, but the logs show that the image is currently not generating the desired affect. The logs demonstrate the animated image's ineffectiveness by recording a low number of click-throughs to any of the various items on sale. If the staff responsible for site design fixed the error with favprod.gif and relocated the animated graphic to the company home page, there could be an increase in the click rate on the image with a corresponding increase in click-throughs to the sale products which would ultimately generate more product sales.

There is some additional information appearing in this sample log that is useful to the marketing group. Cursory log analysis by the Web site administrators reveals that several networked devices from a variety of physical locations (client 172.16.112.55, client 10.196.90.245) were used to visit the e-commerce site over approximately an hour's time period (Tue Jan 13 11:37:16 2004–Tue Jan 13 12:20:09 2004). Another log file from the same Web server (see Table 1–2) shows similar information, but has also captured clickpath information, revealing that two of your company's advertising partners, AdsRUs and AdLinks, were accessed prior to reaching your online e-commerce site. Both www.adsrus.com and www.adlinks.com acted as referring sites to your company's storefront, so that with a detailed transactional log analysis, your team can go back to the marketing unit and note that advertising from both AdsRUs and AdLinks have yielded visits from several network addresses. Your team will also be able to report on items such as which geographic regions produce your company's most active visitors and which periods throughout the day appear to be the most or least active times for online customers.

There is no question that the raw data of the server log can provide a quick source of e-commerce diagnostics. But statistical analysis is necessary when trying to develop profitable e-commerce strategies. While the varieties of Web transaction logs contain a wealth of data, the problem in e-commerce is that business managers are often overwhelmed with statistical numbers because digital technologies can be so efficient at capturing data. As was the case in the world of pre-Internet business, company executives and departmental managers must still spend a lot of time analyzing e-metrics statistics and business performance charts. Fortunately, the Internet and its constituent digital technologies offers new opportunities unlike ever before to observe customer behavior in an e-commerce site, collecting in-depth data that can be analyzed and used in marketing studies to stimulate new business processes and stay competitive. Recording Web transactions is only the beginning of a rather complex

Table 1-2 Sample Web Server Log File Showing Additional Transaction Activities Captured in the Network Transmission of Data

2003-10-02 12:49:27 10.191.33.7 - GET /logon.html Mozilla/4.0+(compatible; +MSIE+6.0;+Windows+98;+{Widget+Systems+Corporation};+Q342532) - http:// www.adsrus.com/T4TG5UY1AMUSICNULC55XEPS8GL6FV1EPESDTJM5FFHAXF55 5A-00001/file/start-1

2003-10-02 12:49:27 10.191.33.7 - GET /images/logon.gif - Mozilla/4.0+(compatible; +MSIE+6.0;+Windows+98;+{Widget+Systems+Corporation};+Q342532) - http://www.adsrus.com/

2003-10-02 15:25:44 192.168.163.68 - GET /logon.html - Mozilla/4.0+(compatible; +MSIE+5.5;+Windows+98) - http://www.publicco.com/new.html

2003-10-02 15:25:44 192.168.163.68 - GET /images/logon.gif - Mozilla/4.0+(compatible;+MSIE+5.5;+Windows+98) - http://store.publicco.com/

2003-10-02 15:25:44 192.168.163.68 - GET /images/logo.gif - Mozilla/4.0+(compatible;+MSIE+5.5;+Windows+98) - http://store.publicco.com/

2003-10-02 15:25:44 192.168.163.68 - GET /images/USER.GIF - Mozilla/4.0+ (compatible;+MSIE+5.5;+Windows+98) - http://store.publicco.com/

2003-10-02 15:26:27 192.168.163.68 - POST /purchase.dll - Mozilla/4.0+(compatible; +MSIE+5.5;+Windows+98) - http://store.publicco.com/

2003-10-02 15:39:56 192.168.174.36 - POST /purchase.dll - Mozilla/4.0+(compatible; +MSIE+6.0;+Windows+NT+5.1) - http://store.publicco.com/

2003-10-02 15:42:36 192.168.174.36 - GET /images/books.gif - Mozilla/4.0+(compatible;+MSIE+6.0;+Windows+NT+5.0) - http://adsite.adsrus.com/purchase.dll

2003-10-02 15:45:16 192.168.174.236 - GET /images/logon.gif - Mozilla/4.0+ (compatible;+MSIE+6.0;+Windows+NT+5.1) - http://store.publicco.com/

2003-10-02 15:45:16 192.168.174.236 - GET /images/logo.gif - Mozilla/4.0+(compatible;+MSIE+6.0;+Windows+NT+5.1) - http://store.publicco.com/

2003-10-02 15:45:16 192.168.174.236 - GET /images/USER.GIF - Mozilla/4.0+ (compatible;+MSIE+6.0;+Windows+NT+5.1) - http://store.publicco.com/

2003-10-02 15:45:24 192.168.174.236 - POST /purchase.dll - Mozilla/4.0+(compatible;+MSIE+6.0;+Windows+NT+5.1) - http://store.publicco.com/

2003-10-02 15:45:24 192.168.174.236 - GET /images/MainMenu.gif - Mozilla/4.0+ (compatible;+MSIE+6.0;+Windows+NT+5.1) - http://store.publicco.com/purchase.dll

2003-10-02 16:00:27 192.168.174.35 - GET /logon.html - Mozilla/4.0+ (compatible;+MSIE+6.0;+Windows+NT+5.1) - http://www.publicco.com/new.html

2003-10-02 16:00:27 192.168.174.35 - GET /images/logo.gif - Mozilla/4.0+(compatible;+MSIE+6.0;+Windows+NT+5.1) - http://www.adlinks.com/

2003-10-02 16:00:27 192.168.174.35 - GET /images/logon.gif - Mozilla/4.0+(compatible;+MSIE+6.0;+Windows+NT+5.1) - http://www.adlinks.com/

2003-10-02 16:00:27 192.168.174.35 - GET /images/USER.GIF - Mozilla/4.0+(compatible;+MSIE+6.0;+Windows+NT+5.1) - http://www.adlinks.com/

Table 1–2 (*continued*)

2003-10-02 16:01:07 192.168.174.35 - POST /purchase.dll - Mozilla/4.0+(compatible;
+MSIE+6.0;+Windows+NT+5.1) - http://store.publicco.com/

2003-10-02 16:02:00 192.168.163.68 - GET /logon.html - Mozilla/4.0+(compatible;
+MSIE+5.5;+Windows+98) - http://www.publicco.com/new.html

2003-10-02 16:03:28 192.168.174.35 - POST /purchase.dll - Mozilla/4.0+(compatible;
+MSIE+6.0;+Windows+NT+5.1) - http://store.publicco.com/purchase.dll

2003-10-02 16:03:28 192.168.174.35 - GET /images/MainMenu.gif - Mozilla/4.0+
(compatible;+MSIE+6.0;+Windows+NT+5.1) - http://store.publicco.com/purchase.dll

2003-10-02 16:03:42 192.168.174.35 - POST /purchase.dll - Mozilla/4.0+(compatible;
+MSIE+6.0;+Windows+NT+5.1) - http://store.publicco.com/purchase.dll

2003-10-02 16:03:50 192.168.174.35 - POST /purchase.dll - Mozilla/4.0+(compatible;
+MSIE+6.0;+Windows+NT+5.1) - http://store.publicco.com/purchase.dll

2003-10-02 16:03:50 192.168.174.35 - GET /images/Edit.gif - Mozilla/4.0+(compatible;+MSIE+6.0;+Windows+NT+5.1) - http://store.publicco.com/purchase.dll

2003-10-02 16:03:50 192.168.174.35 - GET /images/CardStack.gif - Mozilla/4.0 +
(compatible;+MSIE+6.0;+Windows+NT+5.1) - http://store.publicco.com/purchase.dll

2003-10-02 16:03:50 192.168.174.35 - GET /images/Cancel.gif - Mozilla/4.0+(compatible;+MSIE+6.0;+Windows+NT+5.1) - http://store.publicco.com/purchase.dll

2003-10-02 16:03:50 192.168.174.35 - GET /images/Checked2.gif - Mozilla/4.0 +
(compatible;+MSIE+6.0;+Windows+NT+5.1) - http://store.publicco.com/purchase.dll

2003-10-02 16:03:50 192.168.174.35 - GET /images/About.gif - Mozilla/4.0+(compatible;+MSIE+6.0;+Windows+NT+5.1) - http://store.publicco.com/purchase.dll

2003-10-02 16:03:52 192.168.174.35 - POST /purchase.dll - Mozilla/4.0+(compatible;
+MSIE+6.0;+Windows+NT+5.1) - http://store.publicco.com/purchase.dll

2003-10-02 16:03:52 192.168.174.35 - GET /images/BeText.gif - Mozilla/4.0+
(compatible;+MSIE+6.0;+Windows+NT+5.1) - http://store.publicco.com/purchase.dll

2003-10-02 16:06:49 192.168.163.68 - GET /logon.html - Mozilla/4.0+(compatible;
+MSIE+5.5;+Windows+98) - http://www.publicco.com/new.html2003-10-02 16:25:31
192.168.86.225 - GET /purchase.dll - Mozilla/5.0+(Macintosh;+U;+PPC;+en-US;+
rv:0.9.4.1)+Gecko/20020318+Netscape6/6.2.2 SITESERVER=ID=
ee5a519617eb410d903c6f16debc5608 -

2003-10-02 17:23:08 192.168.150.222 - GET /images/Edit.gif - Mozilla/5.0+(Windows;+U;+Windows+NT+5.1;+en-US;+rv:0.9.4.1)+Gecko/20020508+
Netscape6/6.2.3 - http://store.publicco.com/purchase.dll

set of processes needed to visualize and understand Web site events, usage trends, and customer relationships.

In an analogous way, libraries should consider utilizing the CRM potential that e-metrics has already afforded the business sector. Without e-metrics, libraries could investigate the correlation between library users and library collections. A review of circulation records could be used to reveal how certain categories of readers prefer certain types of books, videos, music, and subjects. While such research can currently be conducted with a library's circulating collection, what steps can a library take to uncover corresponding relationships between users and non-circulating library materials? A quick comparison between the information obtained from library print journal use studies and the data that can be captured and analyzed with e-metrics reveals the e-metrics advantage. Print journal use studies are extremely incomplete, leaving questions about what defines a print title use and presenting little chance of understanding which users use what title or how a given title is used. A more in-depth comparison of traditional print journal studies and e-metrics analysis appears in Chapter 3, pages 37–38. By applying e-metrics to digital library collection use studies, libraries have a much greater possibility of knowing who their customers are and what part of the library's digital inventory is of particular interest to them. E-metrics can also shed light on the variety and demographics of the users that libraries serve virtually.

One needs to keep in mind that while e-metrics is still not an exact science, there is little doubt that their collection, analysis, and application remove much of the guesswork involved in operating in a virtual networked environment. A more complete discussion of the new types of customer and performance information supplied by local e-metrics library initiatives appears in the book's second section, including some real-world and applicable examples of e-metrics in library administration. We will cover the multitude of technical and administrative considerations involved in the actual capture, analysis, and reporting of e-metrics in Part III of this book.

We now see the essence of e-metrics: it is data that is captured, collected, and analyzed to assess the behavior of real customers who utilize a system of virtual electronic networked resources and services. E-metrics assists e-commerce in determining the success of a Web site, from its user experience and navigation to its ability to conduct secured business transactions. E-metrics would help your company's e-commerce team know whether or not various assorted interactive Web site components are necessary or even optimized to generate the maximum amount of sales. E-metrics would offer insight for both the marketing and information technology units when determining whether or not new Web site enhancements are necessary and, if so, what enhancements to include. E-metrics also allow e-commerce to track Web site navigation, ultimately revealing significant information about the relationship between customers and products.

Now that we have had an overview of what e-metrics are and how they can be used for administrative and customer service operations in the realm of commerce and marketing on the Internet, we next need to understand their value and application to library collections, services, and processes. In order to reach this understanding of the rather complex and important uses of library e-metrics, we will put library e-metrics in their proper evolutionary context. The next chapter will not only help to develop an understanding of the history and issues that now surround library performance measures, but will clarify the reasons why libraries need to take action at their local administrative level. It will soon become clear that only by cultivating individual library e-metrics implementations can libraries and their staff acquire the best data needed to interpret the change and upheaval taking place in the new digital library environment.

Using E-Metrics in Libraries

The preceding chapter demonstrated how the Internet and its associated digital revolution have altered the nature of business and commerce. We have also seen how the Internet's new technologies served as catalysts for changes in both operational and marketing activities for companies looking to remain competitive. The resulting shift in business models, therefore, created the need for businesses to search for new management and performance measurements that could more accurately capture and represent sales and service progress. In this chapter, we will explore the similar shifting management needs of libraries by reviewing the changing landscape of library statistical measurements from both the pre-Internet and current times. Our investigation will reveal that many of the transformations occurring in libraries parallel those in the business sector. We will also observe that operational changes now affecting libraries analogously require the development, acquisition, and analysis of new and different measurement methods and criteria.

Libraries in the Print-Only Era

Like the history and activities of business, libraries and their associated operations have undergone a rather slow but stable long-term evolution. This development includes requisite procedures that were developed to gather, organize, and circulate items such as clay tablets, papyrus scrolls, codices, books, journals, newspapers, magazines, newsletters, maps, microfiche, microfilm, audio records and tape, and video film. The core of comparative library stability lies in the lengthy history of collecting physical information resources. The relatively stable set of systematic processes relevant to the core paper items of most library collections were developed over time and eventually applied to the other physical items that make up library holdings. Perhaps the best example of established library practices is the library catalog, an invention created before the first century B.C. To this day, even the online catalog of a library inventory has remained the focal point of daily library activities such as search and retrieval, cataloging, and collection development.

As part of library history, measurement systems, or metrics, were developed in order to better manage the variety of operations and services that occur inside, and even outside, libraries. Much like business and commerce, the early attempts at developing library measurements were part of internal efforts made by libraries to report on characteristics such as the amount of items in the library's inventory, the number of items cataloged or processed within a given time period, or the number of staff employed in the library. As the amount and variety of libraries increased throughout the twentieth century, these metrics became more standardized and are now used to monitor various trends occurring within numerous facets of library collections, services, and operations.

Metrics in Libraries Before the Computer Age

Library measurement standards have been developed by organizational bodies that represent both national and international associations of libraries and library professionals. Good examples of pre-Internet library measurement standards are found in the combined efforts of the National Information Standards Organization and the American National Standards Institute. In 1968, the collaborative work of these two organizations yielded a set of library metrics known as ANSI/NISO Z39.7. These two national associations created definitions and measurements for many aspects of library collections, services, and operations within American libraries. Within the United States, two additional library measurement initiatives were established through the National Center for Education Statistics (NCES). One branch of NCES, the Integrated Postsecondary Education Data System (IPEDS), examines the progress of academic libraries as part of its directive to collect data on the activities of American postsecondary educational institutions. Another branch of NCES, the Federal-State Cooperative System (FSCS), collects data on nearly 9,000 public libraries identified in the United States through various State Data Coordinators. The FSCS Public Library Data project has been collecting data from public libraries annually since 1989. The various library statistical measurements reported to ANSI/NISO and NCES essentially have a common core of categories and definitions.

Analogous developments and establishments of library metrics have been part of ongoing efforts in the international community of libraries and library professionals. A working group of individuals, identified as TC46/SC8 within the International Organization for Standardization (ISO), has a similar set of

"International Standards for Library Statistics" ISO 2789, first becoming a rati-fied document in 1991. Additional work conducted by TC46/SC8 has also yielded the "International Standard for Library Performance Indicators" ISO 11620. These two ISO standards documents have been reviewed by numerous representatives that participate in other international organizations such as the International Coalition of Library Consortia (ICOLC) and the International Fed-eration of Library Associations and Institutions (IFLA).

The primary goal of all these standardization documents is to provide a com-mon set of measurements and performance references for libraries, regardless of library type or geographic location. The intentions and scope of these of various metrics are nicely summarized in a forward to the ANSI/NISO Z39.7 document:

> Data categories are identified for basic library statistics . . . and associated definitions of terms are provided. The following areas are addressed: report-ing unit and target population, human resources, collection resources, physi-cal facilities, finances, and service and activity measures. Basic data categories that apply to the four basic library types (academic, public, school, and spe-cial) are identified as well as additional data categories that may be collected by one or more types of libraries but not by all.

An overview of the ANSI/NISO, NCES, and ISO standards shows that there are essentially six major categories that can be identified for measurement, with each category broken down into further measurement classifications. These pri-mary categories, as delineated in ANSI/NISO Z39.7, are:

1. Reporting Unit and Primary Target Population
2. Human Resources
3. Collection Resources
4. Physical Facilities
5. Finances
6. Service and Activity Measures

Utilizing the guidelines and standards from these various standards docu-ments, a library could, for example, measure and thereby determine inventory size and scope, physical library space, reference and circulation volume, gate counts, staffing, and budgetary allocations. Such measurements could then be collected at local, state, national, and international levels and offer a variety of progress comparisons according to criteria of services, collections, staffing, and budgets. There can be no doubt that such measurement criteria and perfor-mance indicators contributed greatly to a better understanding and presenta-tion of the operational progress and services of libraries. The establishment of these various measurement standards offered library administrators and staff a toolkit by which to make future decisions and present critical status reports to those individuals and organizations that fund library collections and activities. One must also keep in mind the relevancy of these national and international standards at the time of their early drafting, ratification, adoption, and implementation. The core purpose of these particular library performance standards was to capture and measure various library activities and services that were centered on the library as a physical entity with physical storage of its collections and resources. It would not be long before the advent of digital publishing and the global proliferation of the Internet would become the catalyst for developing new library measurement standards.

The Rise of E-Publishing and the Birth of the Internet

Even before the explosive acceptance of the Internet, two important computer technologies caused a significant shift in the fundamental operations of libraries: the database and the CD-ROM. The creation of the computer database during the 1970s and 1980s allowed for the development of the integrated library management system. By replacing the card catalog with a relational database system, many library processes previously tied to paper-based management tools—such as the cardex used to track serial volumes, shelve lists, and card catalogs—were either streamlined or eliminated. In addition to automating a variety of library materials processing functions, the adoption of the computer database provided an online public access catalog (OPAC) which could serve multiple library users simultaneously and offered a more efficient search and retrieval interface into the library collections via database queries of various fields, such as author, title, subject, and format.

The move to an online database of library collections also made for more efficient and cost-effective library operations while allowing libraries to share and network their respective resources. Because the Internet was developed as a tool for research and information sharing within both the government and academia, the online library catalogs of many academic institutions became important resources on the early Internet of the late 1980s. Even before the creation of MOSIAC and Netscape Navigator, numerous online library catalogs were made publicly accessible over remote network connections to the Internet and searchable via menu-driven interfaces to hypertext Internet directories. At least in the realm of academia and research, these Internet directories offered libraries and librarians a hint of the impact that remote access to library resources would have in the very near future.

When Grolier released the Grolier's Electronic Encyclopedia on a single CD-ROM disk in 1985, it marked the beginning of a publishing revolution. Because one CD-ROM disk had the ability to store as much data as an entire encyclopedia set, publishers quickly recognized that the CD-ROM medium offered a new and effective way to distribute information that had been traditionally paper-based. This new digital media could also be used to distribute one or more previously paper-based indices, which could be searched easily with self-contained databases of the index entries. As libraries increasingly adopted the use of computers and digital technologies, these CD-ROMs could be accessed in one of two ways. The CD-ROMs could either reside on a single stand-alone computer station or could be installed to a centralized server connected to the library's local area network and shared by multiple library users inside the library's facilities.

We have already noted that academic libraries contributed to Internet development before this global network became an easily accessible communications medium. The early development of digital publishing, too, expanded rapidly with the mass acceptance of the Internet. The preceding chapter outlined how businesses recognized that the use of networks and Web hyperlinks allowed companies to create one advertisement that could be viewed by many people without concerns for printing and distribution. The same type of production and distribution model was quickly applied by publishers to magazines, newspapers, newsletters, and journals. Many publishing companies who had embraced the CD-ROM as an alterative to distributing paper media promptly ceased shipping out a multitude of paper and disks to its subscribers and moved their distribution channels to the Internet. By moving the publishing model to the Internet, publishing companies could significantly reduce operating costs; there was no longer a need to create multiple paper or CD-ROM copies of subscription content and there was no need to deliver physical items to subscribers. For the publishers' customers, there was also little or no delay in receiving updated information, since published content could be revised and refreshed practically in real time and could be immediately viewed over remote networks.

This shift in the distribution and access methods of published information marked a major historical change for libraries as well. Until this point, the evolution of libraries was based primarily on their function as physical portals to stored information. For many centuries, the physical presence of both library collections and services was its foundation and, as a result, both aspects of libraries were confined to the library's physical space within a room or building. Analogous to older business models, access to the library's inventory and associated services had been dictated by physical availability and proximity. There were, of course, some operations, such as interlibrary loan, which functioned beyond the physical library borders, but these processes were still transactions that occurred under the purview of library partnerships and negotiations.

Today, the operating paradigms of libraries have changed to reflect the proliferation of computer and information technologies. The latest developments in modern society and advances of the past two decades have been catalysts for e-library growth. As a result, libraries now have a large and ever-expanding assortment of e-resources and virtual services, which may supplement or replace well-established physical offerings. Because of these computing developments, libraries must now focus on their virtual online collections and services even as they maintain physical environments and operations.

Library Performance Measurements in the Digital Era

If we reconsider the various measurement and performance standards previously established by ANSI, NISO, and ISO, there are certainly several criterion categories and subcategories that continue to remain relevant in the current digital library environment. Even with evolving virtual library collections, it is still important to keep statistics on the number of staff, the library's budgetary expenditures, the hours of operation, the size and scope of the library's collection, and the adequacy of the physical facilities. In fact, it will be shown in the following chapters that digital collections can make it increasingly important to continue monitoring these library service aspects and collection attributes.

Libraries can no longer just rely on national and international standardized measurements, for these were developed at a time prior to the mass library adoption of computer and networking technologies. There are still statistical surveys that account for a library's digital acquisitions in the reporting of subscription totals, including electronic full-text journals, electronic reference sources, and electronic books. Similar reports of locally-held computer files, such as CD-ROMs, are also part of library collections surveys and measurements. Associated costs for access subscriptions to these networked resources can also be easily included in various library fiscal reports and budgetary plans. However, the use of library digital collections needs to be assessed with methods and criteria that are very different from those applied to physical library collections. Libraries have now observed the need to investigate new methods for visualizing certain facets of their virtual services and virtual collections, in the much the same way that business needed to find ways of capturing the virtual activities taking place at virtual storefronts. These new library performance metrics are primarily the result of the shift in library collection emphasis that has further caused a redefinition in the types of services that libraries can provide. Consequently, the current focus of library e-metrics must be on those service and activity measures that have been the most altered by the new publishing and access paradigms.

Some of the major national and international library organizations, standards bodies, and digital publishers have begun to address the recognized need for new measurement standards by developing and funding a number of e-metrics projects. All of these projects attempt to define new performance criteria for virtual library collections and services. Perhaps the earliest and most influential set of results from these e-metrics projects is found in the 1998 document "Guidelines For Statistical Measures Of Usage Of Web-Based Indexed,

Abstracted, And Full Text Resources," generated from the efforts of International Coalition of Library Consortia (ICOLC) representatives. This document contained several important standards for e-metrics data elements, including:

1. Number of Sessions (logins)
2. Number of Queries (Searches)
3. Number of Menu Selections
4. Number of Full-Content Units
5. Number of Turn-Aways
6. Number of items examined

These various ICOLC definitions and standards recommendations were constructed as measurement guidelines that could then be agreed upon by libraries as well as the vendors and information providers of electronic content. The ICOLC further advised the information providers to utilize these data element definitions in their vendor-supplied e-metrics reports to their customers and subscribing libraries. The standardized definitions and measurements derived from this ICOLC project have since served as the foundation for other e-metrics efforts made by other institutions.

In the United States, the National Commission on Libraries and Information Science (NCLIS) has been actively pursuing the need for e-metrics in public libraries. One particular NCLIS e-metrics project, entitled "Developing National Data Collection Models for Public Library Statistics and Performance Measures," was funded in 2000 by the United States Institute of Museum and Library Services (IMLS). Like the ICOLC e-metrics guidelines, the NCLIS e-metrics project sought to define "a core set of network statistics that public libraries can and should collect as part of their routine annual reporting of service use to state library agencies."

Similar e-metrics standardization efforts continue to be conducted by the Association of Research Libraries (ARL). The goal of the ARL e-metrics work has been "to develop standard definitions for measures that libraries could use to describe: (a) the e-resources they make accessible, (b) the use made of the resources, and (c) the level of library expenditures." Since June 2000, there have been more than 50 ARL member libraries that have contributed to the project, which included use measurements for networked library resources and related computer infrastructure. The primary data elements used in the ARL e-metrics reports are analogous to those of the ICOLC Guidelines:

1. Number of electronic reference transactions
2. Number of logins (sessions) to electronic databases
3. Number of queries (searches) in electronic databases
4. Items requested in electronic databases
5. Virtual visits to library's Web site and catalog

Many of the recommendations and findings from the ARL e-metrics project have since become incorporated into Project COUNTER, an initiative which will be touched upon a bit later. Very similar digital library performance criteria as that found in ARL e-metrics studies has been proposed in the latest 2003 revision of the ISO 2789 document. This updated version of the document now includes the following core datasets that are recommended for digital library performance measurements:

1. Number of sessions
2. Number of documents downloaded
3. Number of records downloaded
4. Number of virtual visits

These ISO e-metrics datasets are again mirrored in the 2003 revision of NISO Z39.7. The current NISO data dictionary for electronic library collections identifies the need for use measurements of full-text content from commercial services and the library OPAC in terms of sessions, turnaways, and virtual visits. The current draft standards in Z39.7 for electronic collections e-metrics are also founded on the recommendations of both the 2001 ICOLC Guidelines and ISO 2789. In addition to the proposed ISO standards, other e-metrics initiatives have been developed by other European and international organizations. The most prominent of these international e-metrics missions is the EQUINOX Project, supported by the European Commission as a two-year project from November 1998 through November 2000. As with the aforementioned activities of the ICOLC, ARL, NISO, and ISO, the EQUINOX Project has focused on identifying a set of electronic library performance indicators and defining the appropriate datasets that would be needed to determine such digital library metrics. These include:

1. Number of sessions on each electronic library service per member of the target population
2. Number of remote sessions on electronic library services per member of the population to be served
3. Number of documents and entries (records) viewed per session for each electronic library service
4. Percentage of information requests submitted electronically
5. Number of library computer workstation hours available per member of the population to be served
6. Rejected sessions as a percentage of total attempted sessions

Once again, we see a similarity between the EQUINOX performance indicators and the dataset definitions advocated in the findings of ISO, NISO, ARL, and ICOLC. But EQUINOX had a couple of shortcomings. Most of the performance indicators defined by EQUINOX are dependent upon the capturing methodologies of the subscription suppliers for the initial receipt of per session or per document usage data. Part of the viability of EQUINOX would have been affected by the lack of vendor-supplied reporting standards prior to the development of Project COUNTER. In addition, unlike the other e-metrics projects, EQUINOX had an additional goal of identifying and developing a mechanism by which the defined and captured e-metrics data could be reported and consolidated in a large-scale client/server networked computer environment. EQUINOX was eventually envisioned as a complete system that would be most appropriate for those libraries with enough infrastructure staff support in the areas of information technologies.

Like libraries, digital publishers and e-content vendors also have an interest in e-metrics standards. Publishers and distributors of online information resources could utilize e-metrics to determine user volume and title interest in order to better plan for marketing and production of new titles, subjects, and services. Project COUNTER (Counting Online Usage of Networked Electronic Resources) is one international attempt being made by the publishing industry to deliver a standardized set of e-metrics reports for computer network-based journals and databases. COUNTER utilizes many of the e-metrics data elements commonly recommended in the electronic collections services standards of the NISO and ARL. Begun in 2002, COUNTER is now endorsed by a number of significant publishers and information sciences organizations, including the Joint Information Systems Committee (JISC), NCLIS, NISO and ARL. The standardization efforts of COUNTER and participating publishers and intermediaries is assumed to provide libraries and their staff with a common set of data elements that will appear in all of the COUNTER vendor-supplied reports. By participating as a member in the COUNTER project, electronic resource publishers and providers are suppose to be able to generate and provide e-metrics reports that show comparative use of journal and database offerings across multiple digital publishing and access points.

The next chapter will investigate in more detail the types of vendor-supplied e-metrics reports, focusing primarily on COUNTER-compliant ones. As we proceed with our overview of vendor e-metrics developments, our goal will be to determine the variety and definitions that surround these reports, the degree of accuracy and consistency to which Project COUNTER reporting standards are met by some of the information content providers, and the benefits and limitations found in the usage data delivered by the publishing industry. We will also close Part I of the book with some preliminary discussion on how different types of libraries may begin addressing the broader concerns associated with e-metrics in general, leading to some conclusions on what basic library resources need to be present in order to get the most out of their e-metrics analysis and procedures.

3

Understanding Vendor-Supplied E-Metrics

In this chapter we consider the pros and cons of information present in vendor-supplied e-metrics reports. As a prelude to Part II of this book and its concentration on the application of usage data to various library management processes, this chapter will investigate the components of both COUNTER-compliant and non-standard vendor e-metrics reports. Further examination will uncover both the strengths and limitations of vendor-supplied e-metrics, thereby establishing a foundation for pursuing some supplemental alternative e-metrics solutions that can be established at the local library level.

As was demonstrated in the historical development of library e-metrics outlined in the previous chapter, the COUNTER Project evolved from the international needs of librarians, publishers, and information content intermediaries to standardize both the definitions and delivery of usage statistics of online information resources. Libraries and subscription customers should have a clear understanding that the formation of COUNTER-compliant report standards "provides vendors/intermediaries with the detailed specifications they need to generate data in a format useful to customers [so that they may be able] to compare the relative usage of different delivery channels." Therefore, the objective of COUNTER activities is to assist various information providers in complying with a set of measurement and report standards that offer a common evaluative vocabulary by which libraries and content subscribers can further determine online information resource use.

The latest release of the COUNTER Code of Practice states that its purpose "is to facilitate the recording, exchange and interpretation of online usage data by establishing open, international standards and protocols for the provision of vendor-generated usage statistics that are consistent, credible, and compatible." The governing body and participating members of COUNTER continue to

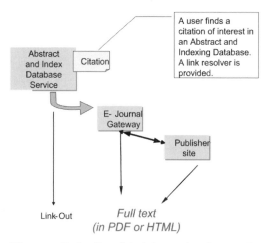

Figure 3-1   Possible Information Access Route to Full-Text Article

investigate the statistical and reporting needs of both the information providers—be they publishers or third-party information intermediaries—and libraries as subscription customers. COUNTER is not currently focused on es-tablishing new e-metrics measurement definitions, instead concentrating ener-gies on the improvement of existing data definitions codified by organizations such as NISO and ARL. In an effort to further standardize the capture and re-porting of e-metrics, COUNTER has specified several data collection protocols and created well-defined report formats. Additional refinements in the COUNTER standards will evolve from anticipated auditing guidelines detailed in the upcoming version of the COUNTER Code of Practice.

There are two pieces of information that need to be established up front be-fore analyzing vendor-supplied e-metrics. First, one should keep in mind that the reports that are generated according to COUNTER standards are achievable because in the new digital publishing environment, vendors control and own the subscription content and technology infrastructure that delivers it. A larger discussion about the implications of such control and its impact on library col-lections, operations, and services appears in Chapter 6. Second, it should be un-derstood that the content providers, as well as the report generators, are represented by one or more of the entities identified and defined in the follow-ing table (see Table 3–1) extracted from the current COUNTER Code of Practice.

In order to comprehend the reasons for accounting for the wide variety of content providers, one needs to consider the infrastructure that makes it possi-ble for any given reader to actually access a full-text of interest. The marvelous ability of the Internet and hyperlinks can allow access to information through a chain of hyperlinks that can be hosted and redirected from numerous possible Web sites as well as abstract indexes and databases. The diagram in Figure 3–1

Table 3–1 Extract of the COUNTER Code of Practice Release 2 Glossary of Terms—Providers of Page Views of Bibliographic Data

#	Term	Examples/formats	Definition
3.1.1.1	Service	Science Direct, Academic Universe, Wiley Interscience	A branded group of online information products from one or more vendors that can be subscribed to/ licensed and searched as a complete service, or at a lower level (e.g. a collection).
3.1.1.2	Publisher	Wiley, Springer	An organization whose function is to commission, create, collect, validate, host and distribute information online and/or in printed form
3.1.1.7	Host	Ingenta, HighWire	An intermediary online service which stores items that can be downloaded by the user
3.1.1.8	Gateway	SWETSwise, OCLC ECO	An intermediary online service which does not store the items requested by the user, and which either a) refers these requests to a host or vendor site or service from which the items can be down loaded by the user, or b) requests items from the vendor site or service and delivers them to the user within the gateway environment.
3.1.1.9	Vendor	Wiley, Oxford University Press	A publisher or other online information provider who delivers its own licensed content to the customer and with whom the customer has a contractual relationship
3.1.1.10	Aggregator	ProQuest, Gale, Lexis Nexis	A type of vendor that hosts content from multiple publishers, delivers content direct to customers and is paid for this service by customers

illustrates one such possible information access route that ultimately leads to the retrieval of a full-text article.

Examining Samples of Vendor-Supplied E-Metrics

Now that the core objectives of COUNTER standards have been discussed, we can begin examining the current report standards defined by the COUNTER Code of Practice for the presentation of vendor-supplied e-metrics. In the draft of the COUNTER Code of Practice Release 2, there are currently seven defined reporting standards for use of electronic subscriptions. These are:

- **JR1** = Journal Report 1: Number of Successful Full-Text Article Requests by Month and Journal
- **JR2** = Journal Report 2: Turnaways by Month and Journal
- **JR3** = Number of Successful Item Requests and Turnaways by Month, Journal and Page Type
- **JR4** = Total Searches Run by Month and Service
- **DB1** = Database Report 1: Total Searches and Sessions by Month and Database
- **DB2** = Database Report 2: Turnaways by Month and Database
- **DB3** = Database Report 3: Total Searches and Sessions by Month and Service

In order to have a better understanding of the definitions and measurement standards that constitute COUNTER-compliant reports, we will examine samples of some of these COUNTER outputs. Table 3–2 illustrates a sample of the JR1 report, showing the use of a package of Elsevier titles that are part of an academic research library's digital collection.

The purpose of the JR1 report is to summarize the number of monthly requests for full-text articles contained within a specific subscription title. A request is an equivalent of the page views described in Chapter 1, the distilled results of the "GET/logon.html" hit transactions captured in the Web server log files. A full-text article is defined in COUNTER as "The complete text, including all references, figures, and tables, of an article, plus links to any supplementary material published with it."

The JR2 report defined by COUNTER offers libraries another view of how subscription titles have been accessed. Table 3–3 offers a sample of the JR2 report, showing the use of a package of Ingenta Select titles that are part of a biomedical research library's digital collection.

This report summarizes the number of monthly and annual turnaways for full-text articles contained within a specific subscription title. Turnaways are defined in COUNTER standards as rejected sessions defined as an unsuccessful log-in to an electronic service due to exceeding the simultaneous user limit

Table 3–2 COUNTER JR1 Report—Number of Successful Full-Text Article Requests by Month and Journal

Journal	Jan	Feb	Mar	Apr	May	Jun
Academic Radiology	0	0	0	4	4	1
ACC Current Journal Review	0	0	41	0	0	0
Accident Analysis & Prevention	8	2	3	12	5	0
Accident and Emergency Nursing	0	2	1	1	3	0
Accounting, Management and Information Technologies	0	0	0	0	0	0
Accounting, Organizations and Society	0	0	0	1	0	0
Acta Materialia	118	97	119	78	94	110
Acta Metallurgica	0	0	0	0	0	0
Acta Metallurgica et Materialia	0	0	0	0	0	0
Acta Oecologica	3	13	28	1	1	0
Acta Psychologica	4	6	1	7	9	0

allowed by the license. A more detailed discussion on the vagaries and impact of licenses and access rights is covered in Chapter 5. For purposes of this report, the full-text turnaways are counted when a user accesses the abstract page of an article but does not have the rights to continue and access full text. If a user views the abstract page and has subscription rights that allow full text access, but does not download the full text, this is not counted as a turnaway.

One of the more detailed COUNTER-compliant reports is the JR3 report. A sample of this report standard is seen in Table 3–4, which illustrates the use of a package of Highwire titles that are part of a bio-medical research library's digital collection.

This report summarizes the number of monthly item requests (page views for "A uniquely identifiable piece of published work that may be original or a digest or a review of other published work") for various elements of a specific subscription title. Unlike the JR1 and JR2 reports, the JR3 report contains multiple entries per title. For each journal title, there are monthly and annual totals for network requests of the journal table of contents (TOC—"A list of all articles published in a journal issue"), article abstracts ("A short summary of the content of an article, always including its conclusions"), full-text articles accessible as PDF ("Article formatted in portable document format [PDF] so as to be readable via the Adobe Acrobat reader; tends to replicate online the appearance of

Table 3-3 COUNTER JR2 Report—Number of Full-Text Turnaways by Month and Publication

Publication	04-Mar	04-Apr	04-May	04-Jun	04-Jul	04-Aug	04-Sep	04-Oct	04-Nov
Total for all publications	159	124	83	112	112	114	96	135	153
AIDS Care	1	0	2	2	12	0	2	1	4
AIDS Education and Prevention	0	0	0	0	0	0	0	0	0
AIDS PATIENT CARE and STDs	0	0	0	0	0	0	0	0	0
AIDS Research and Human Retroviruses	0	0	0	0	2	0	0	0	0
ANZ Journal of Surgery	0	0	0	0	0	0	0	0	1
Acta Anaesthesiologica Scandinavica	0	0	0	0	0	0	0	1	0
Acta Dermato-Venereologica	1	0	5	3	1	0	1	2	3
Acta Obstetricia et Gynecologica Scandinavica	0	1	0	0	0	0	0	0	0
Acta Odontologica Scandinavica	0	0	0	0	0	0	0	0	0
Acta Oncologica	0	0	0	0	0	0	0	0	0
Acta Ophthalmologica Scandinavica	0	1	0	0	0	0	0	0	0

Table 3-4 COUNTER JR3 Report—Number of Successful Item Requests and Turnaways by Month, Journal, and Page-Type

Journal Name	Page Type	04-Jun	04-Jul	04-Aug	04-Sep	04-Oct	04-Nov	Calendar YTD
Academic Emergency Medicine	Table of Contents	6	5	8	4	5	3	74
Academic Emergency Medicine	Abstracts	3	8	13	4	3	18	80
Academic Emergency Medicine	Full-text PDF Requests	12	8	32	11	15	71	169
Academic Emergency Medicine	Full-text HTML Requests	14	18	37	11	21	66	264
Academic Emergency Medicine	Full-text Total Requests	26	26	69	22	36	137	433
Academic Psychiatry	Table of Contents	1	0	3	4	2	1	26
Academic Psychiatry	Abstracts	0	0	1	3	0	1	12
Academic Psychiatry	Full-text PDF Requests	0	0	2	5	2	2	18
Academic Psychiatry	Full-text HTML Requests	1	0	4	5	4	3	32
Academic Psychiatry	Full-text Total Requests	1	0	6	10	6	5	50
American Journal of Clinical Nutrition	Table of Contents	6	14	1	8	6	7	102
American Journal of Clinical Nutrition	Abstracts	6	7	3	8	17	24	119
American Journal of Clinical Nutrition	Full-text PDF Requests	10	32	13	24	29	24	306
American Journal of Clinical Nutrition	Full-text HTML Requests	7	16	11	16	26	34	249
American Journal of Clinical Nutrition	Full-text Total Requests	17	48	24	40	55	58	555

an article as it would appear in printed page form"), and full-text articles accessible in HTML ("Article formatted in HTML so as to be readable by a Web browser"). The number of full-text total requests appearing in the report is equivalent to the number requests made for full-text articles in both PDF and HTML formats.

The last COUNTER report standard for journal title use is the JR4 report. Table 3–5 offers a sample of a JR4 report, showing the use of a package of Highwire titles that are part of a bio-medical research library's digital collection.

This report summarizes the number of monthly and annual searches ("A specific intellectual query, typically equated to submitting the search form of the online service to the server") for a specific subscription title made available from a service "A branded group of online information products from one or more vendors that can be subscribed to/licensed and searched as a complete service, or at a lower level (e.g., a collection).

In addition to capturing use of individual journal titles, COUNTER standards also define reports that account for library use of subscription databases. Table 3–6 offers an example of one such COUNTER-compliant report, a sample of the DB1 report, showing the use of the MEDLINE research database that is part of a bio-medical research library's digital collections.

This report summarizes the number of monthly and annual searches and sessions ("A successful request of an online service. It is one cycle of user activities that typically starts when a user connects to the service or database and ends by terminating activity that is either explicit [by leaving the service through exit or logout] or implicit [timeout due to user inactivity]") for a specific subscription database. ("A collection of electronically stored data or unit records [facts, bibliographic data, texts] with a common user interface and software for the retrieval and manipulation of data.") COUNTER compliance also provides analogous reports for database use as for journals. A DB2 report is similar to the JR2 report, while the DB3 report is analogous to the JR4 report.

Now that we've uncovered some of the definitions and outputs of COUNTER-compliant reports, we should also view a couple of the non-COUNTER vendor-supplied reports. A sample of a report from Elsevier, seen in Table 3–7, captures at a greater level of detail how various service Web site features and contents are accessed and utilized.

A report such as that seen in Table 3–7 illustrates how vendors can develop and deliver proprietary reports that reflect the use of service and subscription options. Since Elsevier is currently one of the largest and most prolific subscription content providers, it is in their interest to create reports that not only satisfy the needs of their subscription customers but that also address some of the marketing and product development strategies within the publishing corporation. For example, tracking the use of Elsevier's alerting features and personal reader profiles could ultimately assist Elsevier in improving or removing these options with future technological and service modifications.

Table 3–5 COUNTER JR4 Report—Total Searches Run by Month and Service

| | | | | | Searches Run | | | |
Journal Name	04-Jun	04-Jul	04-Aug	04-Sep	04-Oct	04-Nov	Calendar YTD
Blood	90	75	117	132	93	84	1,298
The British Journal of Psychiatry	5	25	3	25	18	15	160
Chest	78	132	123	49	111	71	1,077
Circulation	58	67	74	33	61	41	805
Circulation Research	5	8	11	21	18	15	208
Clinical and Diagnostic Laboratory Immunology	0	2	2	1	5	0	24
Clinical Chemistry	4	15	7	5	15	3	128
Clinical Microbiology Reviews	6	2	5	3	2	12	76
Emergency Medicine Journal	7	3	12	8	3	3	51
Endocrine Reviews	13	12	13	11	13	15	143
Endocrinology	44	28	25	26	38	45	409
Eukaryotic Cell	0	4	2	4	0	1	17
Experimental Biology and Medicine	18	7	2	3	3	3	100

Table 3–6 COUNTER DB1 Report—Total Searches and Sessions by Month and Database

Abstract Database	Metrics	Jun 2004	Jul 2004	Aug 2004	Sep 2004	Oct 2004	Nov 2004	YTD Total
MEDLINE	Number of Searches	15	62	48	47	21	34	442
MEDLINE	Number of Sessions	10	28	22	27	13	16	219

Elsevier also offers its subscription customers another non-COUNTER-standardized report, as seen in Table 3–8, that provides the monthly summary of network activity to the ScienceDirect services measured according to users, sessions, and Internet network addresses.

As with the report seen in Table 3–7, the special non-COUNTER data found in the report shown in Table 3–8 is helpful for both the subscribing library and Elsevier. Both entities can use the report to determine the volume and variety of network activity that is being generated at the library's end of the access infrastructure, ultimately arriving at the host networks, servers, and Web pages of Elsevier's numerous journal titles and databases.

Table 3–7 General Elsevier Service Usage Statistics—Web Site Performance

	Month						
Metrics	Nov 2003	Dec 2003	Jan 2004	Feb 2004	Mar 2004	Apr 2004	May 2004
Requests for all pages	156,616	110,233	53,993	75,603	82,500	66,656	62,208
Number of Personal Profile users	11	6	18	13	21	4	7
Issue alert usage	8	1	4	8	8	0	10
New issue alerts	0	0	0	0	0	0	0
Personal Journal or Book Series list	7	5	2	0	21	1	0
Document delivery	0	0	0	0	0	0	0
SD Homepage	1126	2295	1118	1618	1931	1559	1162
Journal list	2437	2138	1213	1853	2181	1967	1578
Journal Homepage	46405	27998	10531	13738	14603	11850	10636
TOC page	19912	13828	7609	9888	10769	8176	8885
Search result list	4238	3647	2920	5297	5899	4385	3327

Table 3–8 Elsevier Service Network Use—Users, Network IP Addresses, and Sessions

Metrics	Nov 2003	Dec 2003	Jan 2004	Feb 2004	Mar 2004	Apr 2004
Number of users— detailed	3,821	3,626	3,169	4,406	4,670	4,023
Number of user sessions	9,552	8,645	8,650	11,269	12,018	10,323
Number of distinct IP's	1,651	1,545	1,404	1,925	2,003	1,837
Average session duration (hh:mm:ss)	0:06:33	0:06:36	0:06:06	0:06:15	0:06:17	0:05:55

The Benefits of Vendor-Supplied E-Metrics

A more detailed analysis of these vendor-supplied reports and their application to library and collection management will be covered in the following three chapters that comprise Part II of this book. However, now having a general overview of what these reports do and can look like, we still need to gain a general understanding of their overall value to libraries. For starters, both COUNTER-compliant and other vendor-supplied e-metrics offer libraries a baseline measurement of subscription journal and article access. Such measurements provide libraries with broad comparisons of title and database usage patterns; for example, which titles are the most or least popular with their user constituency. For libraries that subscribe to multiple journal titles from a single service, the COUNTER-compliant reports permit a library to view, download, and manage usage data for the entire service platform and individual titles and products contained within the single service. Of particular value within the COUNTER reports are the breakdowns of journal access, as seen in the JR3 report standards (see Table 3–4). Consider how much more detail about title use appears in the e-metrics of the JR3 report than what can currently be achieved with the typical library print journal usage studies. Not only does the JR3 report capture a title browse—equivalent to counting the removal of a print journal from the library bookshelves—but it also captures full-text article access by multiple format types. So the JR3 report actually indicates different levels of journal title and article use, something that is very difficult to determine for library print collections.

Most of the vendors who participate in the COUNTER Project and provide some or all of the COUNTER-compliant reports have made their reports available via some type of integrated Web-based system that requires some level of authentication, typically ID and password access, to generate and obtain the reports. As has already been demonstrated in several examples above, the vendor reports show various monthly activities, although some other proprietary reports provide detailed views of daily or weekly usage trends. In addition to the table formats illustrated in our report examples, many of the vendors also provide, in the form of charts or graphs, graphic representations of title and database use activities. Libraries that are interested in doing further analysis and comparison of COUNTER reports and title use across multiple content distributors have the ability to view and save the reports in a variety of data output options, such as HTML, delimited text files, or formats easily imported into spreadsheet applications. Other proprietary or customized reports from vendors may allow for additional flexibility in data analysis and comparisons.

Are E-Metrics Data and Methods Really Standardized?

After reflecting on the preceding survey of national and international, library- and vendor-initiated e-metrics measurement studies, and examining samples of COUNTER-compliant usage reports it may appear that a rather well-defined common set of e-metrics data elements exists for both libraries and publishers. There seems to be broad international agreement on the need to record virtual network sessions to digital library titles, failed network access to these same resources, and the number of items accessed or viewed during a given virtual network session. However, the methods for capturing these assumed e-metrics data elements are never specifically detailed in any of the numerous e-metrics initiatives. Some suggestions of e-metrics data capture techniques do appear in the current ISO 2789 (2003) specifications:

> Communication on the Internet may be described as stateless and transaction-based. Some significant parameters of these transactions will be recorded by each Web server. Dependent on individual settings, the statistical information will be gathered in one or more "log files." In their standard setting, called "Common Log file Format" (CLF), seven basic parameters are recorded. Among these are: the requesting IP address (unique Internet Protocol number attached to each Internet computer), authentication information, a time stamp, the transfer success status and the transfer volume. The CLF can be extended by two more parameters, i.e., the referring link and the computer's browser and operating system. Log files therefore only collect statistical data on transactions between Internet computers; time-based data (e.g., search time, time of document or resource exposure) can only be assessed if Web log-mining tools are being operated to analyze site or server traffic.[1]

We have already seen some samples of the CLF in our review of e-metrics history and have interpreted some of its elements and use in e-commerce performance (see Chapter 1, Table 1–2). Similar to those e-metrics operations of commerce, ISO 2789 (2003) recommends that e-metrics for digital library collections be gathered from log analysis of library OPACs, library Web servers, and the remote supplier Web servers of subscription electronic collections. Thus, the findings of the 2003 ISO study appear to point libraries and vendors in the proper direction for e-metrics data acquisition, since these methods have also been used by the business sector for obtaining its e-metrics data.

However, ISO 2789 (2003) raises some additional questions about the quality and accuracy of e-metrics data by acknowledging several shortcomings to the current sets of internationally proposed e-metrics guidelines. For example, ISO 2789 (2003) states that although there are a number of software packages and companies that can assist in extracting information from these various Web server logs, "the quality and precision of statistics for Web-based electronic collections will vary in a number of areas."[2] Such variation is the result of how one defines Web site use. How does a library distinguish Web page use for the purposes of maintenance or use by automated search engines "spiders" and "bots" for the purposes of remote indexing from actually library user use?[3] Even Project COUNTER does not appear to address such counting inconsistencies generated by the activities of automated entities, instead identifying "usage by a crawler or spider" as "misuse" of information access.[4]

ISO 2789 (2003) also explains that because many of these electronic library collections are hosted on remote servers that are outside the control of the individual subscribing library, libraries must depend primarily upon digital publishers and e-content vendors for obtaining performance measurements of e-resource use. ISO, however, recognized that as of 2003 there was still quite a bit of variability in the ways that e-metrics data elements were defined and communicated in vendor-supplied reports. An investigation of reporting procedures from two different information service providers, Elsevier and Kluwer, will underscore the problems identified by ISO.

Elsevier's study of Web server logs generated as CLF uncovered technological shortcomings that need to be considered in order to generate more accurate reports. In their documentation of a study conducted to determine an appropriate method for analysis of raw Web server logs, Elsevier developed a series of decision-rules for filtering from the raw Web server logs those records that do not refer to real and intentional end-user behavior. In keeping with those practices described in the discussion of page views and hits in Chapter 1, Elsevier concluded that "[a]fter applying the filters, the Web server log files should contain only successful and intentional requests. This filtering should remove: (1.) All images and other server generated log records. (2.) All log records with a return code other then 200, 301, and 304 for certain Web sites."

But further inquiry at Elsevier revealed "that the peak in the occurrence of identical requests for PDFs (same IP/user requesting same URL) occurs at the 30 seconds time-interval between two identical requests. After 30 seconds only a very limited number of double clicks will be removed. Identical requests for all HTML pages occurred within 10 seconds." The study goes on to conclude that additional filters need to be applied to the CLF analysis, so that both all identical requests occurring within the 10 seconds time interval and all identical requests occurring in the 30 seconds time interval for requests for PDF files only should also be removed from the CLF as part of the filtering process.

Obviously, Elsevier has attempted to rectify certain limitations inherent in the process of capturing and analyzing data in Web server logs in CLF, and thereby properly improve their reporting mechanism. However, another information service provider, Kluwer Online, while not explaining their data capture and analysis procedures, has some issues in their own reporting formats and data definitions. The following three figures (Tables 3–9, 3–10, 3–11) provide three different reports that analyze usage patterns of two titles from the Kluwer Online gateway. These three reports have been narrowed in their scope so that all three illustrate various access types for the same two titles, American Journal of Community Psychology and Annals of Clinical Psychiatry, over the same four month time frame. It is curious to observe how the number of monthly full-text article requests in the first report sample (Table 3–9) is equal to the number of monthly title downloads in the second report sample (Table 3–10) which in turn is also equal to the monthly number of title page views found in the third report sample (Table 3–11). If one were to only consider the data found in these reports, one would have to assume that Kluwer's definition of Item Request, Download, and Page View must all refer to the same access activity.

Table 3–9 COUNTER JR3—Number of Successful Item Requests and Turnaways by Month, Journal, and Page Type from Kluwer Online

Journal Name	Page Type	4-Jul	4-Aug	4-Sep	4-Oct	4-Nov
American Journal of Community Psychology	Table of Contents	0	0	0	0	0
American Journal of Community Psychology	Abstracts	0	0	0	0	0
American Journal of Community Psychology	Full-text Article Requests	0	6	1	1	1
American Journal of Community Psychology	Full-text PDF Requests	0	6	1	1	1
Annals of Clinical Psychiatry	Table of Contents	0	0	0	0	0
Annals of Clinical Psychiatry	Full-text Article Requests	0	0	0	0	1
Annals of Clinical Psychiatry	Full-text PDF Requests	0	0	0	0	1

Table 3–10 Downloads by Title by Month from Kluwer Online

Journal Name	7/1/04– 7/31/04	8/1/04– 8/31/04	9/1/04– 9/30/04	10/1/04– 10/31/04	11/1/04– 11/30/04
American Journal of Community Psychology	0	6	1	1	1
Annals of Clinical Psychiatry	0	0	0	0	1

Table 3–11 Page Views by Title by Month from Kluwer Online

Journal Name	7/1/04– 7/31/04	8/1/04– 8/31/04	9/1/04– 9/30/04	10/1/04– 10/31/04	11/1/04– 11/30/04
American Journal of Community Psychology	0	6	1	1	1
Annals of Clinical Psychiatry	0	0	0	0	1

However, some confusion arises with the Kluwer reports when one looks for the various measurement definitions found in the report user guide. In this document, the following definitions are provided:

- **Page Views.** A page view is any request for a page resource (HTML or PDF). For full text PDF pages this number represents the number of downloads.
- **Downloads.** A download is any request for a full text article. A full text article could be in HTML or PDF format depending on the user request and the format type available for that article.

After reading these definitions and applying them to the reports sampled above, one is left wondering if item requests are considered a broad access type category and downloads a subset of these item requests. One must also question if a page view of PDF articles is the only definition of a download or if the download can also include access to full-text HTML articles. So it must be concluded that while Project COUNTER offers one common platform upon which vendors can standardize, there are still many vendors who have yet agreed to these standards. Until all of the digital publishing industry adheres to complete e-metrics report conformity, there still remains variability in the definitions and terminology of vendor-generated e-metrics data elements.

Why Should You Build Local E-Metrics?

Thus far, we have seen that the analysis of vendor-provided usage reports still requires a certain amount of effort from the subscribing library. There can be little doubt that standards present in the COUNTER reports help in establishing a benchmarking environment for digital collections, but clearly these standards, when fully met, can only go so far in developing a coherent picture of e-resource value and collection relevance. COUNTER was developed in part because it was believed that libraries are unable to develop their own self-contained library systems to measure total use of electronic collections. COUNTER standards are set at a low level so that many publishers can participate. The "one size fits all" approach of the COUNTER-compliant reports has become a de facto standard which cannot address the types of reporting criteria that may benefit the wide variety of library environments and needs.

To better judge the importance and impact of e-resource titles and formats within a library's collection, thorough decision-making processes would necessitate that library staff spend a significant amount of time in data manipulation prior to finalizing administrative and collection development reports. Such requirements are dictated by the fact that not all vendors provide reports and not all vendor reports conform to COUNTER standards. In addition, it is quite possible that licensing agreements and bundled packages of resource titles create duplicate subscriptions to a single title, making it more important to merge and then summarize vendor usage reports for more accurate comparisons. Ultimately, any library seeking to utilize optimally the vendor-generated e-metrics reports needs to obtain, manipulate, massage, and store a vast quantity of usage data. All of these steps in the analysis and application of e-metrics for library administration and collection development can only be accomplished at the local library level. Even the proper comparative and historical analysis of COUNTER-compliant data will still entail the creation of a local library data repository, a technological requirement that would also be part of a local library e-metrics solution.

COUNTER-compliant reports at the moment can not provide the level of time-sensitive usage patterns because the library is dependent upon the vendors to generate the reports. This is unlike what can happen with a local library e-metrics solution, where reports could be generated on demand. Having a local e-metrics solution avoids the issue of which information distributor is generating the usage reports; is it the publisher, the subscription agent, or the content provider who captures the statistics and creates the report? Currently, under COUNTER standards, the content provider that delivers the actual requested text to the user is the entity that captures and counts the full-text requests. However, both Elsevier and Highwire COUNTER reports are generated by a third-party Web analytics company, such as IBM or MicroStrategy. Ovid, Silver Platter, and Kluwer e-metrics and Web analytics are also outsourced for processing and production to IBM.

Perhaps a more important shortcoming of vendor e-metrics report offerings is the level of detail and variety of data representing individual local library activities that can never be captured on the vendor's end. Current e-metrics accumulated and distributed by publishers and vendors provide only a few more pieces of information than what had been gathered from well-established print use studies. Like a print use study, vendor e-metrics report on the number of times a title is used. Some reports can additionally indicate the number of refused network sessions, while others can provide raw counts of successful searches and downloaded documents by type (HTML, PDF, RTF). But all of these report types are merely measuring the volume of network activity, without any correlation between titles and the local library user population. Some studies have been undertaken in an attempt to find correlations between unique user counts and the number of full-text document downloads or the number of unique IP addresses used for information access over computer networks. Certainly new computing technologies make it even more possible and imperative to know, for example, that particular electronic titles are primarily of interest to and used by individual subsets of the patron population. But unless a library was willing to provide vendors with access to the library's patron lists, there would be no way to determine resource use by patron types or user categories from vendor-supplied e-metrics reports. In an age in which there are increased concerns about individual rights of privacy and confidentiality, it seems hard to imagine that any library would opt to release patron names to vendors. Yet the management and customer service value that can be gained from knowing the virtual collection use by patron demographics is extremely significant.

Maybe one way for libraries to better understand the inadequacies of vendor-supplied e-metrics reports is to consider how much more data and statistical information can be acquired with existing technologies. If we reflect on how e-metrics is being used to make important management and marketing decisions in the business sector, we observe that business e-metrics analyzes processes from the customer's point of view. In other words, business e-metrics captures and represents how products are utilized by customers. Only with more detailed information gathered about the relationship between a company's product selection and its customer base can more informed and educated administrative decisions be made.

There can be little question that in today's rapidly changing digital environment libraries are facing a crucial need for reliable e-metrics to manage the online portions of their collections. As part of the electronic resources selection/de-selection process, libraries need to consider a variety of values, including annual cost and collection relevancy. However, these parameters when applied to digital collections are sometimes difficult to determine. Libraries should also make their collection management decisions knowing more than just the frequency of title use as provided in vendor-supplied e-metrics reports like COUNTER. The critical nature of e-metrics becomes even more apparent in times of financial restrictions and shrinking budgets: several large libraries in the United States estimate that they spent 20 percent of their budgets on electronic materials the year 2001, with the prospect of licensing agreements and subscriptions costs for Web-based content to increase annually. Given the current global economic environment, libraries are now forced to become even more selective of their subscriptions to electronic content.

The survey of existing e-metrics standards illustrates that, to a certain extent, e-metrics details are being defined to match usage criteria previously applied to traditional library print materials and services. In many ways, the methods of capturing print use data was a lot simpler but also far less accurate than what can be accomplished with e-metrics. Also, the potential latent in well-thought-out e-metrics projects can offer a depth of usage information that goes far beyond the types of data and statistical analysis that libraries have been conducting with their traditional print environment. Imagine how knowing the demographics of e-resource use could be applied towards making informed decisions when reviewing continued or canceled license agreements. Other types of more detailed usage statistics from e-metrics could also help libraries understand the true value of aggregate and bundled subscriptions, a vendor-instituted practice that is becoming increasingly prevalent.

But if the digital publishers and vendors can only provide e-metrics that show primarily the number of times a given title is used or the number of successful searches conducted on a remote database, how could your library know:

- the amount of virtual library activity that is generated by individuals who never physically enter the library;
- how the library is used when its is physically unavailable;
- the best reasons for adding new staff or retraining current employees;
- why access to a particular digital collection item generates a "turnaway" for a patron session;
- when and why you should upgrade installed technologies and infrastructure supporting digital collections?

So as libraries struggle to develop methods for determining the relevancy and costs of their various remotely-hosted electronic subscriptions, one can easily raise the question: "Can publishers deliver the kind of information that libraries need for improved collection development and library administration?" Vendor-supplied e-metrics reports like those meeting COUNTER standards still focus on limited statistical data. Building a self-contained local library e-metrics solution could provide performance indicators that would lead to better understanding of the collections economic value as well as assist in determining outcome measures for use and services. Studies have shown that vendor and local statistics on e-resources have been found to reveal very similar usage patterns.[5] However, while COUNTER-compliant reports do provide raw session numbers, it would be even more beneficial to identify use by various user communities. The application of e-metrics to library management needs to address both the need to know for internal decisions, such as collection development, and the need to know for external decisions, such as increased financial resources. The development of a local e-metrics solution shifts the collection development process back into the hands of the library, particularly with respect to bundled packages and the "Big Deal."

After considering the variability of measurement criteria and definitions still present in vendor-supplied e-metrics reports, it becomes apparent that there is still work to be done in order to make COUNTER and other vendor-supplied e-metrics reports more accurate and standardized. But even if for a moment we disregard such reporting variations, there is still a remaining question of how the information found in vendor-supplied reports equates to or supersedes other well-established traditional library performance measurements? Currently, both measurements of physical and virtual library performance are inherently limited in their ability to determine the connection between library user actions, which can be easily recorded, and library user intentions, which are more difficult and abstract to ascertain. If we reconsider the comparison mentioned earlier between the standard print journal use study and the COUNTER JR3 report (see Table 3–4), we noted that, to a certain extent, the JR3 report can do a better job at capturing user intention in virtual title use because of its ability to measure more individual title elements and granular actions applied by readers to those elements. But even with the level of detail found in the JR3 reporting standards, it is still the responsibility of the local library to determine how the information present in the other reporting types, both standard and proprietary, can be interpreted for comparisons between physical and virtual library use.

The temptation is to equate the vendor measurement standards appearing in e-metrics reports to measurement parameters of the past. For example, one could argue that the number of searches performed on a subscription database may serve as a replacement value for the number of in-person reference queries. Another option is to interpret the number of accesses to a library's Web site homepage as an activity indicator equal to gate counts. Such comparisons have become increasingly important in justifying why libraries need greater amounts and varieties of collection, staff, technology, and ultimately financial resources in order to continue providing quality and relevant services. These administrative and public relations concerns will be addressed in the following three chapters with examples of how to apply both vendor and local e-metrics to the administrative decision-making and communication process.

What should and will become apparent in the following three chapters is that there is no one-to-one relationship between the measurements of virtual activity and physical services. In fact, the problem with measuring page views and gate counts is still the same: there is no ability to fully visualize with these measurements what the user's intention is with any given library service or information resource. However, it can be demonstrated that the establishment of self-contained local library e-metrics solutions and projects can provide greater understanding of digital collection use, thereby allowing libraries to better apply e-metrics to the various management and operational decisions that the modern library now faces. And as was previously explained, even if a library could not develop its own self-contained e-metrics solution, effective cost and use comparisons needed for collection development purposes would still require a number of local library processes in order to fully analyze and comprehend the data appearing in various vendor-supplied e-metrics reports.

The remaining two sections of this book will address the management and technical issues involved in developing a local library solution to the two larger concerns associated with e-metrics:

1. How does my library apply e-metrics data to various administrative and collection procedures and policies? Answering this general concern will be the objective of the Part II chapters in this book.
2. How can my library create a system that provides a greater understanding of the relationship between digital collection use and patron activities and interest? The Part III chapters will focus on the various technical and staffing criteria that can be applied to varying degrees to building such a system.

In answering these two general concerns, we will compare how the library internally addresses both e-metrics that are strictly captured, generated, and delivered by vendors and those that can be similarly acquired and processed at the local level. Of course, the degree to which any modern library can operate is dependent upon both its technical infrastructure—including computers, servers, and network architecture—and the number and type of skilled staff within the organization. To better match proposed local library e-metrics project solutions and methods with variations in library technical and staffing environments, we will consider three general library operational scenarios, categorized as a Basic Library (Library A), an Intermediate Library (Library B), and an Advanced Library (Library C). The charts appearing in Tables 3–12, 3–13, and 3–14 outline the criteria for such library classification.

Table 3–12 Basic (Library A)

Infrastructure	Available IT Support	Available IT Skills and Expertise	Available Technical Services Resources
Online Catalog	Little support	Minimal troubleshooting	Multi-function librarian
Web server	External or		
Staff Workstations	Contractor	Minimal technical support	

Table 3–13 Intermediate (Library B)

Infrastructure	Available IT Support	Available IT Skills and Expertise	Available Technical Services Resources
In addition to Library A: Proxy server	Systems librarian Systems administrator	Some onsite troubleshooting Some onsite technical support Local Systems administration Some in-house programming	In addition to Library A: E-resource Specialist Cataloger Collection Manager

It should be noted that our designations of library types are not based upon the physical size of library facilities, collections, or staff. However, it is more likely that physically smaller libraries with relatively limited or specialized collections will find an affinity with the Library A environment, while physically larger academic, research, or consortial libraries may relate more closely with the resources available in Library C's scenario. By defining such general library configurations, we intend to demonstrate that almost any library can recruit the resources necessary to develop a local e-metrics solution with some degree of success.

Table 3–14 Advanced (Library C)

Infrastructure	Available IT Support	Available IT Skills and Expertise	Available Technical Services Resources
In addition to Library B: Database server	In addition to Library B: Database manager	Good or excellent troubleshooting and technical support	E-resources manager for licensing and accessibility management
Other servers (print server, portal, Open URL)	Web master Analyst-programmer	In-house systems administration, programming, database design and management Good technical documentation Good project management	Catalogers for data input and maintenance in the library catalog Acquisitions specialist for cost info and analysis Collection development manager

Throughout the following two book sections, we will consider the how's and why's of e-metrics within your local library. All examinations and examples in Parts II and III will take into account two broader issues:

1. What should a library consider in utilizing either or both vendor-supplied and locally acquired e-metrics?
2. How should a library prioritize such considerations depending upon the locally-available library resources?

The rest of this chapter, then, is devoted to establishing the basic guiding principles for our three library types in their attempts to acquire, manage, and utilize e-metrics for library and collection administration. Even with what has been underscored as limitations and inaccuracies in vendor-supplied usage reports, Libraries A, B, and C can all benefit to varying degrees by applying these reports to internal organizational and collection development decisions. Regardless of which library category you find to be most closely representing your home library, both COUNTER and non-COUNTER usage reports offer regular monthly and annual benchmarks of digital collection use, provide a fairly limited selection of easily-managed report formats, and contain some level of data quality control. All three types of libraries will also be required to store, extract, manipulate, and archive some or all of the vendor-supplied reports, processes and procedures that will require some elements of project management and collaborative teamwork amongst a variety of skilled individuals. A more detailed discussion on both the project planning and staff integration necessary for all e-metrics types is addressed in Chapter 9 of this book.

Having seen the advantages that vendor-supplied e-metrics offer all library types, why then would any library need to take additional steps in e-metrics processing and analysis beyond what is already provided by the digital publishing and content delivery industry? Another way to frame the question is: How would the three library types go about deciding what can be accomplished with vendor-supplied e-metrics and what additional data may be available within the confines of local library resources? If your library resources and environment are similar to that of Library A, vendor-supplied e-metrics, primarily those that are COUNTER-compliant, will provide at least some level of standardized e-resource use measurements. Yet, by purchasing off-the-shelf Web analytics software and performing CLF analysis of the raw server logs stored on both the library's Web OPAC and Web servers, Library A could at least acquire some level of standardized raw usage data for those digital resources that lack vendor-supplied COUNTER-compliant or detailed usage reports. Some of this supplemental data gathered at the local library level could also be used to clarify or supersede standards and technical limitations inherent in vendor-captured e-metrics reports since the library will have to at some point develop its own set of access measurement definitions.

In our division of library types, Library B is a bit more self-sufficient than Library A. Because Library B has more control of both its technology infrastructure and its staffing expertise, this type of library could modify and customize some of the technology infrastructure that supports user access to digital collections. By utilizing a few simple alterations, this library type could similarly use off-the-shelf Web analytics software to gather data that can parallel some of that appearing in several vendor-supplied usage reports. Taking such a local implementation approach to e-metrics can assist a library in generating standardized usage data for all digital resource subscriptions, including e-journals, e-books, and databases. This type of technical solution, detailed in Chapter 8, could be used to formulate a local use standard set of definitions that further establishes constancy of access counts across resources and vendors. Such standards can then be used to account for usage trends of resource titles, URLs and hyperlink sources, as well as resource formats.

By possessing both a mature technology infrastructure and a full complement of experienced and knowledgeable staff, Library C environments can choose to pursue more complex local e-metrics solutions. Library C has the ability to integrate raw local e-metrics data with a combination of other various local data repositories and in-house analysis programming to acquire and generate reports that go far beyond the potential found in a Library B e-metrics project. Library C can in fact (1) generate reports that truly relate user categories to resource use, (2) can visualize the amount and patterns of local library network activities that constitute digital collection use, and yield information about preferred methods of access, and (3) can compare such use across branch and consortial levels. Such reporting capabilities assist Library C in placing digital collection use measurements in greater context so that the raw page view counts and turnaways available from vendor-supplied reports are further supplemented with data captured and analyzed at the local library level to measure outcomes and better understand user intentions.

What will become clear in the examples, analysis, and solutions that constitute the remainder of this book, is that there are, in fact, many important reasons why establishing some measure of a local library e-metrics project is important. The chapters in Part II will show you the benefits that can be reaped by establishing local e-metrics procedures and combining them with existing and future vendor-supplied data. The chapters in Part III will provide instruction on the process and considerations needed to execute local e-metrics solutions from start to finish.

Summary and Conclusions

We have so far examined both the history and definition of e-metrics for library performance measurements. The evolution of library e-metrics is far from complete, leaving many unanswered questions about data gathering methods, standardization, and specific data elements. Regardless, the application of library performance measurements in general and e-metrics in particular is internationally acknowledged as an important tool for library management. E-metrics will continue to become increasingly useful for negotiating the complexities of acquiring and managing virtual library collections. As many Web-based subscriptions become available only from publishers or content aggregators as part of bundled packages, libraries will find it more difficult to know the cost and true value of individual titles in the package. Unfortunately, most libraries today can only obtain e-metrics data and reports from the very publishers and aggregators with whom they have licensing contracts. While some of these vendor-supplied e-metrics reports can be helpful in determining a subscription's value, various aspects of local e-metrics implementations can provide even more detailed and critical data to the collection management process. Because greater levels of e-metrics factors are present in data gathered from local library efforts, e-metrics showing local usage patterns of individual titles could assist libraries in gleaning the relative value of individual titles from packaged subscriptions, thereby supplementing the information found in such vendor-supplied data.

Obviously, the standards questions that have required enormous and continuous efforts of many individuals from many countries and institutions cannot be solved alone by the authors of this book. However, throughout the rest of this book we will present the application and capture of e-metrics that utilize the data elements identified by other entities but that are now defined, acquired, and analyzed at the local library level. Part II will show how e-metrics data elements that are consistently delineated by local library policies can be employed to answer several difficult questions that the modern library must address. The third section of this book will discuss the related difficulties associated with e-metrics capture and analysis, including the various measurement parameters and criteria under consideration for locally established e-metrics projects. As the focus of the next book section, we can and will demonstrate that once these locally-acquired performance and service measurements are assigned certain definitions and standards, e-metrics collected at the local library level can be analyzed and applied to numerous important facets of library management and operations.

Notes

1. ISO 2789, 2003, p. 36.
2. ISO 2789, 2003, p. 36.
3. ISO 2789, 2003, p. 36.
4. Customer categories for Usage Reports, www.projectcounter.org/code_practice .html#section4.
5. Duy and Vaughan 2003.

Part II
Why Do Libraries Need E-Metrics?

Overview

In this next section of the book, we examine the value of pursuing e-metrics projects at the local library level. The three chapters of this section will demonstrate the varied and enhanced library management and administrative decisions that are best made with detailed reporting available from combinations of vendor-supplied and individual local library e-metrics initiatives. We will see how such reports have become increasingly important to overseeing numerous library developments and adaptations initiated by the complications associated with digital publishing, networked information access, and user expectations.

Chapter 4: Using E-Metrics for Public Relations: With the increased public awareness of the Internet, libraries are now expected to enhance their traditional physical paper collections with full-text journals, articles, research databases, and books in digital formats. Library patrons also enjoy the freedom offered by Web-based content, accessing resources from a variety of locations through remote networks at all hours of the day and night. Libraries are attempting to redefine and reposition their collections and services in the realm of digital information access. Many have begun to question the functions and services of libraries. Should libraries be done away with or should staffing and operating hours be cut? In this chapter we pose a series of rather generic questions asked from both an administrative and user perspective and offer answers with support from real-world e-metrics analysis conducted at the local library level.

Chapter 5: Using E-Metrics for Collection Management: This chapter will underscore why libraries are now facing a crucial need for reliable e-metrics to manage the online portions of their collections. Of course, libraries have been conducting various collection management procedures with their traditional print materials for years. However, such procedures are not that applicable to the extremely complicated selection/de-selection process for electronic resources. Many Web-based subscriptions are only available from publishers or content aggregators as part of bundled packages, making it difficult to know the actual cost and essential local library value of individual titles in the package. Issues of value are also interrelated to licensing and access control policies dictated by resource providers. Now that the library collections environment has shifted from an archival model to a virtual access model, libraries need to consider a variety of title and package values, including annual cost and collection relevancy. Computer technologies now give libraries an opportunity to make their digital collections management decisions knowing more than just the frequency of title use. But these additional use parameters are sometimes difficult to determine, especially when most libraries today can only obtain electronic subscription usage reports from the very publishers and aggregators with whom they have licensing contracts. While these reports can be helpful when determining a subscription's value, there are still some limitations inherent in such vendor-supplied data. Once again, we investigate the importance and application of e-metrics to navigating the complexities of digital collection development and to answer the seemingly simple question: "Why doesn't the library have title X?"

Chapter 6: Using E-Metrics for Library Administration: Much of the perceived freedom electronic library collections provides for patrons comes at a price to libraries: larger percentages of library budgets are being allocated to electronic materials acquisition, with the prospect of licensing agreements and subscriptions costs for Web-based content to increase annually. Given the current global economic environment, libraries are now forced to become selective of their subscriptions to electronic content. Library administrators must also confront the management complexities of digital collections. It now takes more time to review, evaluate, process, manage, and trouble-shoot library virtual collections. These complex and interconnected issues of staffing, operating hours, facilities, and services are considered via another series of questions again answered with supporting evidence provided by library e-metrics capture and analysis.

Using E-Metrics for Public Relations

New Challenges for Libraries in the Digital Revolution

Today, with increased public awareness of the Internet, libraries have supplemented traditional physical paper collections with full-text journals, articles, and books in digital formats. Such virtual library collections of subscription content are made available around the clock through remote networks in a nearly seamless fashion. But there is more library staff effort necessary beyond providing patron access to such digital collections. Although the acquisition of digital content does not require physical material processing procedures, it does call for other processing and accounting methods different from those of traditional print collections. Libraries must now cope with both issues of delivery and management of their emerging digital library resources.

We closed the previous chapter by proposing three different broad categories of library environments. As a review of what can easily be seen as variations in library technical and staffing environments we offered three general library operational scenarios, categorized as a Basic Library (Library A), an Intermediate Library (Library B), and an Advanced Library (Library C). Tables 3–12, 3–13, and 3–14 (pages 47–48) reiterate the technical and staffing criteria for establishing such library types.

In the new digital information environment, all three library environments must figure out how to apply the measurement standards of the past to the library of the future. However, continued retention of and reliance upon the various metrics established for pre-Internet era libraries may in fact yield some very disturbing numbers, justifying some disastrous administrative reactions. Pundits in the media have rather recently predicted the demise of the library as an institution, citing examples of how all of the world's books will be digitized, thus eliminating the need for libraries and their numerous shelves of dead tree remnants. Others foresee an Internet with enhanced capabilities to index its unfathomable amount of electronic content, making it possible to search and retrieve anything one could ever imagine, thereby making the role of the librarian obsolete. Unfortunately, there are a number of library measurements that can be used to support these hypotheses. Libraries, administrators, and accrediting bodies can easily see by reviewing low gate counts that there are in some cases fewer individuals physically entering libraries. Analysis of the annual numbers of reference "ticks" could indicate that the amount of mediated reference searches and reference questions has decreased in many of today's libraries. Other libraries can readily demonstrate a sharp decline in the number of circulation transactions as indicated in their periodic statistical reports.

Slumps in library metrics such as these can be easily misunderstood and misinterpreted. One can probably appreciate (and may have experienced first hand) how a library board of directors could mistake a down-turn in these various traditional performance measurements for indicators of poor library service to patrons. In addition, the various measurements that have recently exhibited dramatic declines contrast sharply with the rapid budgetary increases needed to sustain new digital library collections. During financially tough times, such a disparity can be confusing to administrators, especially to those who are not involved in daily library activities.

Declining numbers in circulation and gate counts combined with larger library budgets could cause library boards, institutional administrators, government entities, and the public at large to wonder about the function and necessity of libraries. Communities that contribute financially to their public libraries through state and local taxes would be equally disturbed when viewing such numbers. Many library users might perceive that there is little or no fiscal need to support libraries when much of the population believes all the information resources they need are accessible for free from the comfort of their home or office.

Now you may be thinking at this point that such perceptions and beliefs could be easily dispelled with the rational explanation that past library metrics have shown rapid and dramatic decreases in response to the availability of digitally-based information and the use of computer networks. But what evidence can you present that would support your explanation to administrators? As was demonstrated in preceding chapters, e-businesses can to some extent use statistical data of virtual visitors and their activities in order to justify many policy and procedural decisions. Libraries, too, can utilize analogous measurement results to help steer future directions for several aspects of collection development, user services, and operations.

It seems clear that as more published and accessible library content is delivered in electronic formats over computer networks, more of the statistical measures that depend upon the physical presence and services of the library will become secondary data that support the more important e-metrics results. It also emerges that as the importance of the library in the digital publishing world becomes less visible to the remote virtual user, it becomes more important to find ways to reveal how the library has actually increased its value in the online environment. To demonstrate how one can support the library's position through the application of local e-metrics to administrative functions, we will examine some hypothetical administrative-level and public relations questions about the effects of the digital paradigm on the future of libraries. After each question or group of questions, we will provide samples of how all three library categories could utilize real-world e-metrics, both vendor-supplied and locally acquired, to answer these potential inquiries. It may appear to the reader that there are a preponderance of academic and research titles in most of the local e-metrics examples provided in association with the three different library scenarios. Such title focus is the outgrowth of local e-metrics implementations that currently reside within the academic and research library environments. At the time of this writing, very few local e-metrics models exist for public and corporate libraries.

Public Relations Q & A with E-Metrics

Gate Counts vs. Net Counts

Question: The annual reports show that the library's gate counts are down this year. Why aren't people coming in to use the library?

Answer: Fewer people are entering the library because libraries have made more of their collections and resources available in digital formats that are accessible from remote computer network locations. In the past, libraries functioned as physical portals to stored information. We can still see the physical library consisting of reference and subject specific areas, card catalogs, and book stacks, all available during operating hours and confined to the library's physical space within a building or room. And for many libraries, the other level of confined physical access had been polices not to circulate items such as encyclopedias, magazines, and numerous reference indexes. But as the publishing sector transitions to digital distribution models, many of the important and popular reference and journal titles have become online subscriptions. Once the title is hosted in an online format, a library can actually serve many users at the same time without having them physically enter the library. With online formats, users need not worry about whether they will have to wait for someone else to finish using the item in question and the library will not need to purchase, process, and house multiple copies in order to satisfy user access.

Library A can address the concerns of declining gate counts by presenting some of the vendor-supplied usage data for digital collections. Table 4–1 provides a sample of a proprietary report from Elsevier that shows monthly

Table 4-1 Elsevier Overall Monthly Service Report

	Month					
Metrics	**Jun 2004**	**Jul 2004**	**Aug 2004**	**Sep 2004**	**Oct 2004**	**Nov 2004**
Number of users – detailed	3,346	3,619	3,560	4,297	5,430	5,725
Number of user sessions	9,134	9,647	8,682	10,385	12,681	12,951
Number of distinct IP's	1,417	1,518	1,458	1,681	2,116	2,054
Average session duration (hh:mm:ss)	0:06:12	0:06:04	0:05:48	0:05:41	0:05:50	0:06:08

amounts of network activity on their Web site generated by the users associated with the subscribing library customer. What can be easily observed from this report is that there is a high volume of network sessions that increase monthly. The report also indicates that there are a wide range of networked computing devices that are used to access remotely the Elsevier content.

Library B has opted to supplement the previous vendor-supplied report with one that was generated within the library itself. The staff of Library B performed a transaction log analysis (TLA) of the library's raw Web server logs to develop a report seen in Table 4–2. We can see that Library B's Web site has re-

Table 4-2 Library B Overall Web Site Usage Summary

	Report Range: 08/01/2004 00:00:05 – 10/26/2004 01:42:56	
Hits	Entire Site (Successful)	223307
	Average Per Day	2566
Page Views	Page Views (Impressions)	223180
	Average Per Day	2565
	Document Views	0
Visitor Sessions	Visitor Sessions	46252
	Average Per Day	531
	Average Visitor Session Length	00:07:17
	International Visitor Sessions	0%
	Visitor Sessions of Unknown Origin	100%
	Visitor Sessions from United States	0%
Visitors	Unique Visitors	9519
	Visitors Who Visited Once	4782
	Visitors Who Visited More Than Once	4737

Table 4–3 Library B Most Accessed Web Server Pages

Pages		Views	% of Total Views	Visitor Sessions
1	Library B Home Page - www.libraryb.org/	53539	22.93%	27817
2	Electronic Journals - www.libraryb.org/ resources/e-journals.html	22332	9.56%	12838
3	Databases - www.libraryb.org/ Research resources/databases.html	7784	3.33%	5038
4	Electronic Books - www.libraryb.org/ resources/e-books.html	1874	0.80%	1478
5	Library Services - www.libraryb.org/ services/	739	0.31%	617
6	What's New? - www.libraryb.org/ new.html	716	0.30%	582
7	Web Resources - www.libraryb.org/ resources/web-resources.html	730	0.31%	575

ceived a large amount of visits (223,307 in the span of almost 3 months), with an average of 531 daily visitor sessions.

Another detailed and more important piece of information extracted from this same log is a list of the library's most visited pages, seen in Table 4–3. Because this report uncovers layers of access within the library's Web site, Library B can begin to determine and assign certain comparative values to access points and virtual resources. Analogous to the COUNTER JR3 reports seen in the previous chapter, this report list assists Library B in revealing a degree of user intention once having virtually accessed the library Web site. The report clearly shows that the Home Page is the most visited Web page of the site. This result is to be expected as this page functions as the gateway to a number of other more important and useful pages within the site. The report shows that the next three most frequently accessed pages of the Web site are those pages providing access out to subscription e-resources. Further analysis shows that journals appear to be more popular as a resource format than databases and books. To gain an even better understanding of digital subscription use, Library B would still have to perform additional analysis with this data, incorporating the actual number of titles subscribed to and integrating the data from vendor-supplied reports.

Library C has a bit more expertise and infrastructure on site than either Library A or B. By using a more advanced local e-metrics solution, Library C can generate a few data samples that show the amount of network use for the ten most frequently used full-text e-journal titles that are part of its virtual collection (see Table 4–4). In paper formats, these journal titles are part of this

Table 4–4 Usage and Visitors to the Ten Most Frequently Used Full-Text E-Journal Titles That are Part of Library C Virtual Collection

Title	Total usage	Unique visitors
Nature	9877	950
The Journal of Biological Chemistry	7331	536
New England Journal of Medicine	6795	1072
Cell	6679	655
Proceedings of the National Academy of Sciences of the United States of America	6144	633
Science	5146	602
Biochemistry	2860	286
Journal of Immunology	2634	219
Journal of the American Medical Association	2630	542
Lancet	2547	454

library's non-circulating collection, yet we can see that the volume of use for these titles in online format is rather large. Table 4–4, which is only a sample of a much larger report, shows the volume of use and number of users who accessed particular titles during a calendar year.

This chart clearly shows quite a bit of title usage and virtual user activity, even though the reduced gate counts provide information that may initially seem counter to a high volume of library users. Besides underscoring that these titles are used frequently, Table 4–4 also notes that there are hundreds of individuals who use any one specific title throughout a year.

Two other important aspects of library use are indicated by Table 4–5, which shows additional usage information about the ten popular titles. Table 4–5 illustrates in the second column that large amounts of individual users are conducting library access of any one title from a sizeable number of network-attached computer devices. The last two columns of the table even present data indicating that title use is occurring over computer networks when the physical library is closed for operations and access. Two aspects of these after-hours visits need to be considered. The data does not tell us if such visits would have been physical trips to the physical library rather than virtual visits. However, the data does indicate that the library is providing virtual services that increase its value and accessibility by enabling visits occurring during periods when the physical library is inaccessible. Even though the off-hours access is comparatively less than that taking place during regular library operations, this data still exemplifies how in the current networked information environment, gate counts cannot capture all that a library provides in services and access.

Table 4–5 Additional Network Usage Patterns for the Ten Most Frequently Used Full-Text E-Journal Titles that are Part of Library C's Virtual Collection

Title	Unique Network Addresses	% of Use During Open Hours	% of Use During Closed Hours
Nature	1541	88.01%	11.99%
The Journal of Biological Chemistry	979	88.77%	11.23%
New England Journal of Medicine	1360	94.07%	5.93%
Cell	1084	85.52%	14.48%
Proceedings of the National Academy of Sciences of the United States of America	1010	89.16%	10.84%
Science	918	88.73%	11.27%
Biochemistry	516	89.58%	10.42%
Journal of Immunology	342	90.62%	9.38%
Journal of the American Medical Association	670	92.66%	7.34%
Lancet	594	91.60%	8.40%

Where Are Our Users?

Question: I can see now from these charts that there is quite a bit of title use and virtual library activity, but where are all these networked library visitors coming from?

Answer: To answer this follow-up question, each of our three model libraries will have to consider additional report types. Library A again refers to one of the proprietary vendor-supplied reports seen in Table 4–6 for another perspective of network access traffic to subscription resources. The Kluwer Online service reports that the monthly network activity total for the Library A subscription to a variety of Content Categories (full-text article downloads, single article sales, and table of content views) originates from the ".org" sub-domain (listed as Organizations) of Internet network addresses. In this specific instance, Library A is a non-profit organization and its respective network is registered within the global directory of Internet network addresses under the ".org" category. Upon viewing this report, Library A could assume that the volume of network activity accounted for originated from its own internal library computer network. However, such an assumption could be erroneous as

Table 4–6 Kluwer Online Subdomain Visits by Content Category by Month from Library A

	1/1/04–1/31/04	2/1/04–2/29/04	3/1/04–3/31/04	4/1/04–4/30/04	5/1/04–5/31/04
Content Category	350	698	723	683	540
Unresolved	30	178	160	174	123
ISPs	1	0	0	0	0
North America	319	520	563	509	417
US Subdomains	319	520	563	509	417
Organizations	319	520	563	509	417

this data, while indicating a volume of network activity, does not however reveal particularly useful information about the physical location of networked users.

Having already processed its Web server logs, Library B answers this question about user physical location by analyzing log data and generating a report that currently provides greater detail than the Kluwer Online report. Table 4–7 captures the variety of Internet network addresses that indicate the origin of Library B Web site visits. The value in this report is both its level of detail, distinguishing between individual network addresses, and its ability to be further integrated with additional data sources to build even more comprehensive e-metrics reports.

Using the reporting type illustrated in Table 4–7, Library C addresses this network location question by performing TLA against the logs from its proxy and remote access servers. The results from such analysis are then integrated with data that can better identify actual physical locations or localities from network address ranges. The following two graphs provide more detailed information about where network access to the ten most active Library C e-journal titles originates from. Figure 4–1 shows that these same ten e-journal titles are accessed almost equally from devices that are part of the organizational network and from devices that are not part of the organizational network. The computers in the library are contained within the organization's internal network and are therefore included in the count of organizational accesses. However, Figure 4–2 shows in striking contrast how the overwhelming majority of virtual access to these online titles takes place from computer devices that exist outside of the library's internal computer network.

These graphs also help to answer the question as to why the library's gate counts have declined as library users conduct their library business beyond the boundaries of the physical library. Clearly, there are many journal titles that are highly used by a large number of individual users over the period of a year and can continue to be so because they are in digital formats that serve multiple simultaneous remote users. Such data therefore shows that even though the

Table 4–7 Library B Web Site Visits by IP Addresses and Sessions

	Organizations	Hits	% of Total Hits	Visitor Sessions
1	192.168.175.237	18124	1.03%	272
2	192.168.164.18	9156	0.52%	232
3	10.0.116.136	502	0.02%	230
4	10.0.116.11	552	0.03%	229
5	192.168.162.118	1199	0.06%	225
6	10.0.116.14	516	0.02%	219
7	172.16.1.16	843	0.04%	216
8	192.168..174.211	17487	1%	216
9	192.168.174.215	13484	0.77%	203
10	172.25.115.134	1914	0.10%	190
11	172.16..100.11	398	0.02%	184
12	172.16.100.14	377	0.02%	180
13	192.168.174.187	12638	0.72%	178
14	172.25.116.11	361	0.02%	166
15	172.20.100.73	316	0.01%	166
16	172.20.6.133	2045	0.11%	165
17	172.26.116.14	372	0.02%	165
18	192.168.175.113	14086	0.80%	165
19	192.168..86.102	9140	0.52%	161
20	192.168.86.213	1141	0.06%	158
Subtotal For Companies Above		104651	5.99%	3920
Total For the Log File		1756393	100%	47062

physical library has low gate counts, there is still quite a bit of virtual service that the library is providing to remote networked users.

While the preceding questions addressed concerns of declining gate counts and circulation statistics, there are, however, many libraries that have seen increases in their gate counts in conjunction with declines in circulation statistics. Typically, these rising gate counts have been the result of libraries providing Internet access from computer workstations housed inside the library. Administrators and management boards of libraries experiencing these types of trends may ask the following:

Why Are Library Resources Used?

Question: Our reports indicate an increase in gate counts, but also show a decline in our circulation numbers. We have recently seen an increase in the number of people waiting to use computers in our library and are assuming that our visitors come into the library primarily to use the computers and not so

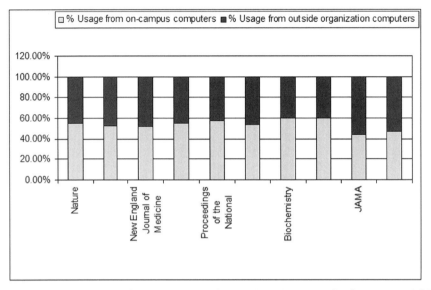

Figure 4-1   Graph Showing Usage Comparison between On-Campus and Off-Campus Computers

much the books and other materials. Is there anyway for us to know what the people are using our computers for?

Answer: As we have seen, the transmission of packets over computer networks can reveal quite a bit of information. Answering this question will probably require the technology and staffing resources more comparable to that found in Library· C than in Libraries A and B. Table 4–8 provides a snapshot of local e-metrics data taken from public computer use inside Library C during a week in January. Such data would be impossible to acquire using the current national and international e-metrics specifications and are only made available by a library's internal e-metrics efforts. The chart lists the twenty-five most frequently-accessed Web sites from a cluster of twelve public Internet workstations inside Library C. In general, the data clearly indicates that these workstations are used primarily for accessing a variety of information sources relevant to the various personal and research activities of the library's host institution. However, the chart reveals that these computers were also used for e-mail access (webmail.libraryc.org), updated weather and sports results (www.weather.com and sports.espn.go.com), as well as online auctions (search.ebay.com, cgi.ebay .com, and thumbs.ebaystatic.com). The table also assists in identifying the amount of cumulative time spent viewing the contents of these Web sites. From this report, one would deduce that many individuals are using these twelve public workstations to check on reports because

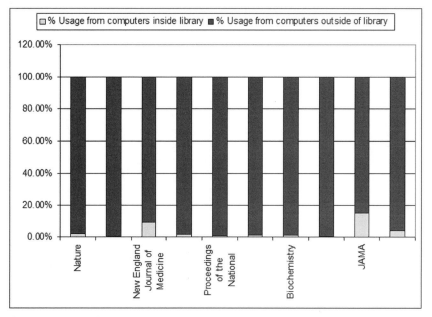

Figure 4-2 Graph Showing Usage Comparison between Computers from Inside of Library and Outside of Library

of the amount of data transferred (23.944.782) from and time spent (13:18:43 minutes) on visits to reports .organizationc.org.

Local e-metrics printing statistics offer another source of usage patterns for library computing facilities. Table 4–9 provides a small sample of e-metrics data gathered from printing activities occurring from the same twelve Internet workstations referred to previously. This report indicates not only that there are certainly many word processor documents that are being printed from these stations, but that there are viewed Web sites of enough interest to initiate the desire for hardcopy print outs of information from these sites. Tracing back the URLs from these visited and printed sites reveals additional library user interest in sources of medical information (for example, www.ilru.org/mgd-care/consumerinfo.htm being a site about Managed Health Care). Although these statistics cannot completely detail the level of user satisfaction and application of the information viewed or printed, the combination of library workstation and printer usage does provide another view of computer use and library user behavior.

Our next hypothetical question is once again motivated by the observation of declines in pre-Internet library services.

Table 4–8 Examples of Accessed Sites from Public Workstations

ACCESSED SITE	BYTES	TIME SPENT
www.libraryc.org	35.870.643	0:03:42
informatics.organizationc.org	29.781.478	22:39:28
catalog.libraryc.org	25.129.684	0:21:09
reports.organizationc.org	23.944.782	13:18:43
www.imdb.com	9.981.379	0:05:47
www.cnn.com	8.051.260	0:00:34
webmail.libaryc.org	7.702.053	0:28:50
blackboard.university.edu	7.023.942	0:09:07
thumbs.ebaystatic.com	6.664.795	0:08:49
cgi.ebay.com	6.201.724	0:14:49
www.university.edu	6.170.250	0:22:34
vip.rongshuxia.com	5.722.457	0:27:29
home.mdconsult.com	5.298.656	0:09:53
search.ebay.com	5.214.653	0:11:56
www.weather.com	5.171.756	0:01:29
gateway1.ovid.com	4.632.731	0:13:03
sports.espn.go.com	4.547.752	0:05:17
cache.unicast.com	4.309.952	0:00:59
www.bananarepublic.com	4.185.970	0:03:19
hospital.university.edu	4.156.851	1:36:17
www.google.com	4.102.193	0:03:15
image.weather.com	3.949.429	0:02:56
www.phonecards4sale.com	3.746.600	0:00:48
archopht.ama-assn.org	3.309.926	0:04:05
www.kaptest.com	3.291.462	0:01:23

How Well Are We Serving the Unseen and Who Are They Anyway?

Question: I can now understand why there may be fewer people entering the library and that this could account for other declining numbers appearing in periodic reports. But if there are fewer individuals physically entering the library, how do we even know who is even bothering to still use the library through computer networks? Is there any way to know if we are properly serving our user base when they primarily use virtual services and collections from remote locations?

Answer: Depending upon library category, it may only be possible to answer one part of this question. In all probability, Library A will have to depend solely on information available in vendor-supplied reports, thereby only having the ability to answer to a certain degree how well it may be serving remote users. Table 4–10 illustrates an extract of a COUNTER JR3 report detailing the several

Table 4–9 Examples of Printouts from Public Workstations

Workstation	Document Title	Pages
04	Microsoft Word - mso6621B.doc	6
06	Microsoft Word - mso2B369.doc	5
06	Microsoft Word - msoC26EE.doc	9
06	Microsoft Word - msoD9ABB.doc	12
06	www.uhmc.university.edu/prevmed/mns/mcs/ 2/sched/Boundaries_S	2
06	www.uhmc.university.edu/prevmed/mns/mcs/ 2/sched/Boundaries_S	4
06	Microsoft Word - msoB28EA.doc	1
06	Microsoft Word - msoEBCD4.doc	1
01	Microsoft Word - Document in Microsoft Internet Explorer	1
01	Microsoft Word - Document in Microsoft Internet Explorer	2
01	Microsoft Word - Document in Microsoft Internet Explorer	2
07	www.iha.org/gloss.htm	4
07	www.ilru.org/mgdcare/consumerinfo.htm	16
07	www.halftheplanet.org/departments/health/marriage_penalt	2
01	catalog.medlibrary.university.edu:4350/ ALEPH/6EJS6ED8I4IPTK	2
02	jama.ama-assn.org/pro.PDF	4
12	external1.nbme.org/ciw/servlet/usmle_application?action	2
12	external1.nbme.org/ciw/servlet/Step1Step2ApplicationSer	2
12	external1.nbme.org/ciw/servlet/Step1Step2ApplicationSer	2
12	external1.nbme.org/ciw/servlet/usmle_application?action	2

journal title elements that have been accessed by Library A users. This report provides Library A with information that can be used to determine if its users are to some extent satisfied with the digital collection choices. By looking at the total number of full-text request in Table 4–10, we see that *Emergency Medicine* is more frequently accessed than *Psychiatry*. The report also shows that use of Emergency Medicine goes beyond mere browsing of journal contents as full-text requests for both HTML and PDF formats exceeds the number of TOC and Abstract views.

Like Library A, Library B could also refer to COUNTER and other vendor-supplied reports for views of broad title usage patterns. However, because Library B has more technical and staffing resources at its disposal, additional information could be acquired through the TLA of the local library Web server and proxy logs. Library C, on the other hand, has access and control to other data which could be further integrated in order to see more important relationships between users and titles. Libraries, unlike many corporate businesses, have a relatively finite customer base. The best example of this known entity is the borrower or patron database housed within a library's integrated management system. Databases such as these can contain contact information about individuals, an individual's

Table 4–10 COUNTER JR3 Report—Number of Successful Item Requests and Turnaways by Month, Journal, and Page-Type from Library A Highwire Subscription

Journal Name	Page Type	04-Jan	04-Feb	04-Mar	04-Apr	04-May
Emergency Medicine	Table of Contents	11	7	15	6	4
Emergency Medicine	Abstracts	14	7	9	1	0
Emergency Medicine	Full-text PDF Requests	0	0	6	9	5
Emergency Medicine	Full-text HTML Requests	18	12	39	16	12
Emergency Medicine	Full-text Total Requests	18	12	45	25	17
Psychiatry	Table of Contents	5	2	2	0	6
Psychiatry	Abstracts	0	0	0	7	0
Psychiatry	Full-text PDF Requests	4	0	0	2	1
Psychiatry	Full-text HTML Requests	8	3	0	1	3
Psychiatry	Full-text Total Requests	12	3	0	3	4
American Journal of Clinical Nutrition	Table of Contents	11	19	12	16	2
American Journal of Clinical Nutrition	Abstracts	13	8	12	20	1
American Journal of Clinical Nutrition	Full-text PDF Requests	41	48	42	35	8
American Journal of Clinical Nutrition	Full-text HTML Requests	34	35	38	30	2
American Journal of Clinical Nutrition	Full-text Total Requests	75	83	80	65	10
American Journal of Geriatric Psychiatry	Table of Contents	2	7	7	7	2
American Journal of Geriatric Psychiatry	Abstracts	1	0	1	4	1
American Journal of Geriatric Psychiatry	Full-text PDF Requests	2	5	8	0	2
American Journal of Geriatric Psychiatry	Full-text HTML Requests	14	3	15	9	5
American Journal of Geriatric Psychiatry	Full-text Total Requests	16	8	23	9	7

Table 4–11 Examples of Use of Full-Text Journals by Departments

DEPARTMENT	Virtual Library Visits	% Total Visits	Unique Visitors	% Total Unique Visitors	Visits per Visitor
Allied Health	46175	8.98%	791	9.17%	58.89
Medicine	41824	8.14%	664	7.70%	49.63
Nursing	26284	5.11%	646	7.49%	41.37
Social Welfare	12981	2.53%	445	5.16%	29.27
Dentistry	2489	0.48%	142	1.65%	17.6
Totals	**129753**	**25.25%**	**2688**	**31.16%**	**48.27**

group affiliations or category, and borrowing policies applied to certain user groups. This patron information can also be used by Library C to determine demographic use of library resources, thereby offering another perspective of library user behavior.

Table 4–11 shows another e-metrics report generated from local library analysis of the use of full-text journal subscriptions in Library C. This report of locally-captured e-metrics data helps to determine the volume of virtual library activity generated by a specific sampling of library users who can be assigned categories based upon organizational units within the library's host institution. The rankings and percentages in this table reflect comparisons of use from 261 departments within this institution, 8,626 uniquely identified virtual library users, and 513,967 annual virtual library uses. From the sampling shown in this table, we can see that users associated with the Allied Health department virtually visit the library more so than their counterparts in the other observed organizational units. Additional analysis of this data would need to consider the total number of employees in these departmental units, the breadth and depth of the library's virtual collections, and possibly the research and business subspecialties within the sampling of organizational units.

However, data like this only provides a partial picture of the way virtual library resources may be used. What if libraries could see the usage patterns of a particular title according to user categories? The next two tables show with Library C's local e-metrics data gatherings how this same selection of user categories uses two specific titles in different ways.

Table 4–12 confirms what most collection librarians or subject selectors would easily predict given the subject material of this title: for this collection particular to Library C and user categories, the individuals employed in the department of Medicine make up the largest user base for the online version of the *New England Journal of Medicine*. Not only is this unit the most active department using this title, the use patterns are more than double that of the other sampled units in terms of both virtual visits and number of unique users.

Table 4–12 Use by Department for the New England Journal of Medicine

Department	Visits	Unique Visitors	Visits Per Visitor
Medicine	882	126	7
Nursing	247	50	4.94
Social Welfare	207	51	4.06
Allied Health	183	54	3.39
Dentistry	14	4	3.5

Contrast this report with a similar report, found in Table 4–13, that analyzes the annual use of the *Journal of Psychology*.

Table 4–13 demonstrates that individuals from the Allied Health and Social Welfare departments find the *Journal of Psychology* more useful than those in the department of Medicine. The Dentistry unit does not appear in Table 4–13 because there were no e-metrics indicating departmental use for this title from that unit. Local e-metrics data such as this offers insight into the interests of user groups, further supporting decisions required for the development of library services and collections. The information exhibited by these three tables (Tables 4–11, 4–12, and 4–13) can prove to be of great assistance to a library's collection development and reference units. Observing the usage of libraries by user demographics could ultimately help a library "get in touch" with the needs of its remote customer base.

Upon viewing such important data, someone may question the process of identifying individual users in the context of library user privacy. While there are admittedly a number of privacy concerns that have developed as outgrowths of current trends in both government and technological policies and procedures, there are ways to design local e-metrics library systems that disassociate individuals from the statistical measurements. The data presented in these tables are therefore akin to the statistical "ticks" kept for reference questions or sign-up sheets implemented as a system to control and track library computer use. We must keep in mind that the intent of these statistical systems and e-metrics is not to infringe upon individual rights, but rather to provide information that assist in the management of processes and operations within the library.

The local library e-metrics examples provided so far reveal that there is another facet of library user activities that extends beyond the inherent limitations of physical library facilities. These examples have also pointed out that library staff, administrators, and the general public need to reconsider the importance of past performance measurement standards if all are to better understand this virtual environment of library services. One can still determine library productivity and value from reports that outline the volume of library use. But the traditional measurements of walk-ins, items circulated, reference questions, and

Table 4–13 Use by Selected Academic Departments for the Journal of Psychology

Department	Visits	Unique visitors	Visits per visitor
Allied Health	58	18	3.22
Social Welfare	58	17	3.41
Nursing	42	18	2.33
Medicine	21	4	5.25

hours of operation need to be viewed along with measurements that capture the functions and opportunities present in the digital networked world. The explanations offered by the data in Table 4–12 and 4–13 have touched upon the application of local library e-metrics in collection development policies and procedures. It is in this context that our next hypothetical question, frequently the bane of many library collection development staff, needs to addressed with thoughtful discussion.

Where is My Title?

Question: I am under the impression that most of what is important to have access to is already available online. And there appear to be many free sites for information. The library's Web site even points me to many of these free reference sites. I also see that the libraries are connecting to one another to provide better online information services. With all of this information available, why doesn't the library own an online version of *Title X*?

Answer: There are many factors that need to be considered in maintaining library collections in this new digital environment. Perhaps it is best if we present the complex answers to this seemingly simple question in their own chapter.

5

Using E-Metrics for Collection Management

The previous chapter demonstrated how e-metrics gathered and processed both by vendors and at the local level of an individual library could help to explain certain measured and anecdotal changes in library operations. Yet the trends captured by these new measures of library functionality may spawn additional questions about the management of library collections in this digital era. In this chapter, we will continue our exploration of e-metrics applications by focusing on their use in library collection development policies and procedures. As in the previous chapter, we will examine a set of hypothetical questions which will in turn be answered with information gathered from real-world e-metrics analysis of individual library data. Each answer will also continue to present some of the options that our three library environment scenarios may choose as tools for addressing the problems posed in each question.

We closed the prior chapter with the fundamental collection development question: "Why doesn't the library have *Title X*?" This query typically comes from a library user, but could easily come from an administrative level within or outside the library's staffing structure. In the past, this question was answered with a combination of explanations that included concerns of budget, collection focus, and library user constituency. While these three elements are still pertinent to digital collections development, there are now several other factors that must also be taken into consideration.

The Vagaries and Constraints of Delivery and Access

Digital technologies have changed the delivery of subscribed information for both publishers and libraries. Like the traditional pre-Internet business transactions outlined in Chapter 1, distributing and authorizing use of information via a physical item was historically a rather simple operation. A subscriber would pay the publisher or distributor for access to the published content and the publisher or distributor would send the requested content to the subscriber. When offering paper-based information, publishers provided regular access to weekly, monthly, and annual issues of journals with paid subscriptions. The provisions of these subscriptions meant that user access to the subscribed title was only limited by its physical receipt, processing, shelving location, and circulation status within the library. If only one physical copy of a title was actually processed by the library and it was in circulation to a single library user, other users did not have access to the content.

However, the Internet electronic publishing and distribution models became catalysts for new subscription and access methods. As was demonstrated by the new advertising model adopted by e-commerce, once published content is migrated to a digital format, it can be accessed remotely over computer networks and can be used by multiple simultaneous readers. The move to electronic publishing and network-hosted subscriptions over the Internet thus offers greater availability of content as a result of the fundamental alteration in publishing creation and distribution models. As a consequence of the publishing industry's need to accommodate to these newer operating paradigms, publishers and distributors have been investigating new subscription arrangements. Under such a publishing model, the access limitations no longer exist due to availability of physical items. In the new digital publishing world, access limitations now become a matter of both policies and technologies.

Unlike paper titles, electronic titles are now accessed largely under licensing agreements, akin to a purchasing and access model established by computer software manufacturers. Information access dictated by such licensing models has stimulated an environment that is far more complicated and costly to navigate for libraries and their staff. Our investigation of these collection management complexities continues with more hypothetical questions that stem from the simple initial question: "Why doesn't the library have *Title X*?"

Collection Development Q & A with E-Metrics

Why is This One Available and the Other One Not?

Question: I frequently require information on topic *Y* and need access to a specific set of titles that cover that topic. I can see that these titles are available on the Internet. How come the library doesn't offer these titles with all of the others offered online? And why does the library subscribe to titles that are of little interest to the majority of users?

Answer: The adoption of e-resources in libraries demands that libraries consider new criteria when evaluating the value of online subscriptions. Bundling and access restrictions, two recent licensing initiatives established by e-publishers and distributors, are very important parameters that have a significant impact on a library's ability to develop its collections.

Subscription Bundling

Bundling—one licensing practice that has become prevalent—forces subscribers to pay for a group of titles, some of which are desired by the subscriber and some of which are not. It is a marketing and business model that is analogous to a practice in the auto industry. Cars are now sold with preconfigured option packages. For example, it is now nearly impossible to purchase a car that has only air-conditioning but not an automatic transmission, six-speaker stereo, and power door locks included. Similarly, it is becoming increasingly difficult for libraries to acquire a single individual title from the electronic publishing industry. Libraries are more likely to purchase access to a package of multiple titles, either because there often is no other way to gain access solely to the desired title or because subscription pricing to an individual title is less cost effective for libraries than that of bundled packages.

Bundling may be offered by title aggregators at the level of title, yearly coverage, and format. For example, a distributor may develop a subscription plan that requires the subscribing library to receive current print issues of a title, while only the prior year's issues are provided in electronic format. This bundling scenario could also be reversed where the previous issues are only available in print with the current month's issue available in only digital formats. Other bundling configurations could be structured so that from a bundled package of 100 titles, 25 of them are only available in print for older issues and online for the prior 3 months, while 25 others are only available in digital formats from two years prior to the current issue, and the remaining 50 titles have previous issues available online as far back as the last decade.

The predominant bundling structure is not so much formulated at the format level as it is at the number and subject scope of titles in a package. There is an increased probability that the title your users and library are interested in comes as part of a bundled package that includes a significant number of titles that have little relevance to an individual library's user base or collection focus. Publishers have so far justified these bundling practices by creating a pricing structure that makes it appear to be overall more cost effective to purchase access to unneeded titles along with the sought-after titles. In addition, through the bundling approach, the same title may be available through licensing agreements from two different distributors, but a library would be unable to avoid the title duplication because the title is part of a package of many offerings and cannot be separated from the other subscriptions in the distributor's bundle.

Table 5–1 Kluwer Downloads by Title and Month from Library A

	1/1/04– 1/31/04	2/1/04– 2/29/04	3/1/04– 3/31/04	4/1/04– 4/30/04
Journal of Biomolecular NMR	0	0	21	7
International Journal of Primatology	87	180	125	176
Journal of Autism and Developmental Disorders	8	7	4	53
Annals of Biomedical Engineering	0	8	27	14
Breast Cancer Research and Treatment	3	2	17	19
Cancer and Metastasis Reviews	0	4	18	1
Molecular and Cellular Biochemistry	7	8	7	11
Neurochemical Research	1	3	5	4

Bundling fundamentally makes it difficult for libraries to satisfy the needs and interests of local communities and library patron populations. Bundling typically results in a library gaining access to titles that are not truly applicable to its user base nor that fit within its collection profile. The practice also inhibits a library's ability to subscribe to titles that may logically fit within locally-established collection development policies or to adjust the policies in order to suit other specific changes. Therefore, as bundling becomes a more prevalent content distribution model, it becomes increasingly important for libraries to determine the value of individual titles acquired in licensing bundles in order to truly calculate the overall value of title packages. Using e-metrics, we can actually determine the amount of use of individual titles within a bundle, thereby gaining a clearer picture of the true value of bundling agreements.

The table seen in Table 5–1 is an extract of a larger vendor-supplied report of full-text PDF article downloads from a package of Kluwer journal titles subscribed to by Library A. Of the titles viewed in Table 5–1, the *International Journal of Primatology* is clearly the most heavily accessed title within the bundle package.

A comparison by package title of annual article download totals appearing in this report can provide Library A with a better sense of which titles in the bundled licensing agreement are of more value and greater interest to the library's user base. Such comparisons can also assist in determining which titles or subject areas are more relevant to current and future collection development of digital subscriptions.

Library B can call upon its ability to capture local usage measurements from its proxy server. Figure 5–1 shows a sampling of Library B's local e-metrics data, concentrating on the annual usage of a selection of titles that are part of this

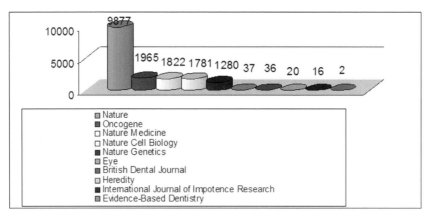

Figure 5-1 Graph Showing Annual Usage of Bundled Nature Publishing Group Titles

library's bundled subscription from the Nature Publishing Group. The numbers atop each one of the cylindrical columns in the graph denote the actual number of visits to the individual titles sampled. Even just a glance at the height of the cylindrical columns in the graph clearly illustrates that not all titles in a subscription bundle are of equal interest to this library's user base. The chart also demonstrates that titles such as *International Journal of Impotence Research* and *Evidence-Based Dentistry* may be of negligible value to this library's collection and could be considered for cancellation if they were not part of a bundled package.

Not only is it important for libraries to be able to ascertain the value of individual titles within a particular subscription bundle, but is also crucial for libraries to visualize the value of the same title made available from different content distributors. Figure 5–2 illustrates how with a local e-metrics solution, Library B is able to draw a comparison of use of the *U.S. News and World Report* from both the publisher and as part of the Gale Group Incorporated InfoTrac subscription bundle. Library B's user base appears to prefer accessing *U.S. News* in its format as presented directly from the publisher. Reasons for this preference could include variations between the ways that content is presented by two different vendors: Web site presentation, article and keyword searching functionality, and access to archival issues. User preference could even just simply be influenced by the order in which the two different access points to the title are presented on the library's Web site and online catalog, so that the InfoTrac source is accessed less because it is listed as a second entry point in the OPAC.

The feedback seen in this type of important e-metrics data could be applied by Library B to help redesign the presentation layer for public access to its subscription titles. In this particular instance, Web site and OPAC modifications along with additional e-metrics capture and analysis could further reveal the reasons

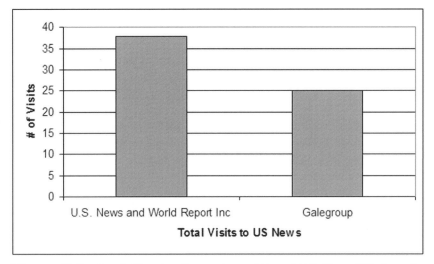

Figure 5-2 Graph Showing Comparison of Use of U.S. News Title from the Publisher and a Vendor

for such user access preferences. For example, Library B could alter the positioning of the hyperlinks to *U.S. News and World Report* so that the InfoTrac source was listed first as opposed to second in both the library Web site and OPAC. E-metrics data captured over a given time period after such changes could show the same type of usage preferences, indicating something more about the information's source interface, or perhaps point out that Library B's public presentation has a significant impact on its users information seeking behavior.

Licensing and Access Restrictions

In addition to the collection development limitations inherent in bundled subscriptions, libraries need to account for licensed access restrictions when evaluating title acquisition. Consider for a moment how information access was restricted in libraries before the advent of computer networks. Items within library collections could be restricted by policies defined at the library level. Even today, certain titles determined to be reference resources are therefore deemed to be part of the non-circulating collection. Other examples of non-circulating items could be special collections and current periodical issues. Various formats could also have access limitations, i.e. records and videos can only be borrowed for seven days. Additional circulation policies can be implemented according to user categories and borrowing privileges. For example, children can only take out four books at a time or institutional faculty can borrow items from an academic library for the duration of the college semester. However, when libraries subscribe to information in digital formats that are no longer managed and housed at the physical library, new and different access policies can be set by the entity that stores that information remotely.

Earlier, we mentioned that access to electronically-published resources require licensing agreements. These end-user license agreements come in many varieties and contain numerous stipulations and restrictions. Many licenses, taking into account that libraries need to serve a varied and potentially geographically dispersed group of users, accommodate the remote access capabilities of global networks by providing site-wide or institutional licensing. Other agreements are less flexible, limiting access according to group definitions or subsets of a library's user community. Some contracts prevent access to those affiliated library users who attempt subscription access from devices and networks outside the local range of network addresses within the physical library or institutional facilities. Another stipulation may disallow access to "walk-ins," those non-affiliated library users who may be visiting the physical library premises and using computers on a network that is approved for access under the institutional license.

Constraints such as these can also be used by publishers and distributors to develop various pricing arrangements for access. For example, some licenses limit the number of simultaneous networked user sessions from a particular subscribing organization or confine networked access to only a specific number of computing devices within the library's facilities. Under these types of agreements, the cost of access increases should the library require additional access beyond these explicit numbers. One recent trend from distributors is to abandon site-licenses in favor of a license priced according to the precise total number of potential on- and off-site users at a given library.

When one begins to consider the variety of access restrictions that exist for electronic subscriptions, it once again becomes easy to see how important it is for libraries to determine the value of a particular title. Locally-acquired e-metrics can help libraries determine use of digital titles, thereby deciphering which combination of access and pricing options for a particular title would be the most beneficial to the library and its users.

In the previous chapter, we illustrated with a few e-metrics reports how more library users are accessing data outside the physical library. Table 5–2 provides a combined view of the amount of network use for the ten most frequently used full-text e-journal titles that are part of Library C's virtual collection. Three important usage trends are captured in Table 5–2. First, users access any given title in this selection of 10 from a wide range of networked computer devices. Second, users access these selected titles almost equally from their organizational environments as they do from their home or remote research study locations. Finally, when provided with opportunities to access library-based information over computer networks, users overwhelmingly choose logically to take advantage of the convenience of remote access to these titles from non-library devices.

Table 5-2 Amount of Network Use for the Ten Most Frequently Used Full-Text E-Journal Titles

Title	Unique Networked Devices	% Use from organizational computers	% Use from outside organizational computers	% Use from computers inside library	% Use from computers outside of library
Nature	1541	54.91%	45.09%	2.21%	97.79%
The Journal of Biological Chemistry	979	52.46%	47.54%	0.60%	99.40%
New England Journal of Medicine	1360	51.42%	48.58%	9.30%	90.70%
Cell	1084	54.77%	45.23%	1.89%	98.11%
Proceedings of the National Academy of Sciences of the United States of America	1010	57.06%	42.94%	0.73%	99.27%
Science	918	53.81%	46.19%	1.19%	98.81%
Biochemistry	516	59.93%	40.07%	1.19%	98.81%
Journal of Immunology	342	60.29%	39.71%	0.53%	99.47%
Journal of the American Medical Association	670	44.22%	55.78%	15.17%	84.83%
Lancet	594	46.45%	53.55%	3.89%	96.11%

How could such information aid in collection development? Obviously, prior to electronic publishing and digital subscriptions, users clearly entered the physical library in order to access physical collections. However, the data shown in Table 5–2 illustrates how a library can extend the reach of its services by providing access to important information beyond the boundaries of the physical library structure. Suppose for a moment that the digital access to *Nature* was under consideration for subscription renewal by this same academic library, but the renewal license mandated that *Nature* in its electronic format could only be accessed from computers that were part of this academic library's campus. We can already see from the e-metrics analysis in Table 5–2 that such access restrictions associated with *Nature* would not be viewed positively by this library's user base, since this user population predominantly accesses the virtual library from devices outside the physical library. In addition *Nature* access restricted to the physical library network could be extremely inconvenient to those individuals who can only access the title from locations outside of the physical organizational network, such as researchers situated in remote laboratories or testing facilities. Certainly, the cost of *Nature* would be another factor up for consideration in this title's evaluation, but the important parameter of title accessibility would no longer be an unknown criterion in the selection decision process.

As content aggregators and publishers modify their subscription options and library budgets become less favorable for collection development, the locally-generated e-metrics graphs and table examined so far can assist in judging the overall value and cost effective way to subscribe to electronic titles. Recent developments indicate that regardless of the variety of locally-specific interest levels in different titles, subscription arrangements will be structured so that the bundled package continues to be the most affordable way to gain access to required content. Although such e-metrics data will not change the bundling policies of many publishers and distributors, e-metrics can provide libraries with better information to bring to the fore when negotiating and evaluating the value of licensing agreements.

Can We Collect in Specialized Subject Areas?

Question: In light of bundling practices, it appears that by using e-metrics you've constructed a collection development policy that assures subscription to the most-used titles and cancellation of the least-used titles. Doesn't such a policy mean that titles focusing on niche but important subjects will be dropped from the library's collection?

Answer: We have already observed how bundling, to some extent, assures that some selection of generally less popular titles will continue to be accessible. Bundled subscriptions typically contain a mixture of titles that are of great interest and importance, as well as those that would generate little revenue for the publisher were they to be offered as individual subscriptions. Yet, the economics of bundling practices can also prevent a library from subscribing to a niche title that more appropriately fits with a small segment of its local user base. Such collection deficits occur because bundling practices could force a library to commit a sizable portion of its finances to one particular package of titles, thereby leaving little monies to invest in the subscription of more selective and targeted subject areas. Under the access limitations resulting from bundling, the frequency of local library title use then becomes a tangential consideration for the survival of titles in specialized subject areas.

Title Value from the User's Perspective

Nevertheless, when selecting subscription titles on the basis of usage statistics, libraries should also account for a secondary element of use. One reason that a title could have low use numbers is because the title appeals from the start to a small segment of a library's user population. Conversely, titles that are used infrequently across a broad spectrum of library user categories could indicate that indeed the title is of little value to the subscribing library. While vendor-supplied e-metrics can help libraries determine the difference between the most and least popular titles, only locally-acquired e-metrics can provide a much clearer picture of how title usage relates to the demographics of a library's user base. We observed in the previous chapter that e-metrics will allow a library to see use per title according to patron demographics. Keeping in mind that the patron database for most libraries is finite in number and patron categories, one can calculate e-metrics title use according to the percentage of a given patron category.

To understand the value of a particular title to a library's various users, we have drilled down into the aforementioned Library C local e-metrics data to look at the user demographics for *New Ideas in Psychology*, one of the lesser-used titles from the virtual collection. Table 5–3 shows that, throughout an entire calendar year, this particular title was only accessed twelve times by a total of six unique individuals. While this is obviously a little-used title, it is also important to observe the relationship between the title's subject matter and the user groups who have accessed it. One would guess that a journal covering the topic of psychology would be of potential interest to those studying or researching in the fields of psychology and psychiatry. Table 5–3 indicates that while local users representing those specific fields have indeed accessed the title, the title is still of little local interest even to the assumed target audience.

By way of comparison, Table 5–4 shows the title use by user demographics for *Issues in Law and Medicine,* another little-used title from the same Library C virtual collection. Besides the fact that *Issues in Law and Medicine* was used even less than *New Ideas in Psychology* during the calendar year, the table shows that *Issues in Law and Medicine* was also of little interest to a more diverse cross section of Library C's local user groups.

Table 5–3 Use by Department for New Ideas in Psychology through Sciencedirect

Department	Visits	Unique Visitors	Visits Per Visitor
Clinical Psychology	4	2	2
Allied Health	2	1	2
Research Psychology	2	1	2
Chemistry	2	1	2
Psychiatry	2	1	2

Keep in mind that both Tables 5–3 and 5–4 show the importance of a title to a local library's collection and users. Perhaps a good way to illustrate the importance of observing and considering local usage patterns for electronic titles is to compare title use, title subscription cost, and the ISI Impact Factor. Such comparisons can be extremely enlightening when applying them to titles that are part of a bundled package. The integration of impact factors in e-metrics reports can be found in Part III of this book.

Figure 5–3 provides a visual analysis comparing the relative values of individual titles acquired by Library C as part of a bundled package from Ovid Technologies, Incorporated. The bubbles appearing to the left side represent titles at this library that are used less than those appearing on the right. Those bubbles located near the bottom of the graph correspond to titles that are less costly to subscribe to individually than those that are located closer to the top. The size of the bubble and the number adjacent to it stand for the value of the ISI Impact Factor. What becomes readily apparent from a view of this graph is that the value of a title cannot be judged solely on the basis of its subscription cost or its impact factor. For this particular library, the less expensive *American Journal of Nursing* title (ISI factor of 0.242) is of greater value to its user population than the more expensive and more highly-cited titles of *AIDS* (factor of 5.983) and *Spine* (factor of 2.311). Once again, the high quality of local library e-metrics that Library C is able to gather helps to reveal the comparative value of individual titles by teasing out the relative importance of a title to a library's specific patron population.

Table 5–4 Use by Department for Issues in Law and Medicine through Galegroup

Department	Visits	Unique Visitors	Visits Per Visitor
Biochemistry	4	1	4
Acute Surgery	2	1	2
Allied Health	2	1	2
Social Welfare	2	1	2

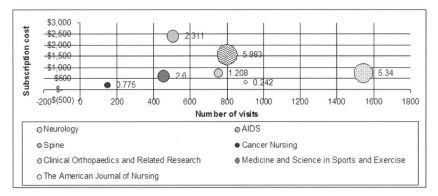

Figure 5-3 Graph Showing Visual Analysis Comparing the Relative Values of Individual Titles as Part of a Bundled Package from Ovid Technologies, Incorporated

Can We Coordinate Collections with Other Libraries?

Question: I understand that given the circumstances and state of the library's present finances, subscription and access license cancellations to certain titles might be necessary. Instead of canceling "unpopular" journals, is it possible to coordinate subscriptions to these niche and little-used journals with other libraries collaborating in an interlibrary loan system? In this way, even less-used journals would stay accessible.

Answer: While on the face of it coordinated library collections would seem to be a workable solution for public, academic, and special libraries, the peculiarities of bundling and access restrictions can inhibit and impede such coordination. In principle, coordinated library collections would mean that at least two libraries had collections that both compliment and supplement each other's holdings. For example, under coordinated collection efforts, my library should own *Title X* but not *Title Y*, while your library should own *Title Y* but not *Title X*. Our libraries therefore would avoid title duplication and save on some of the acquisition costs for the respective titles. Local e-metrics analysis based upon the demonstrated desires and usage of that particular title could provide some excellent reasons why one library should have any given title. But suppose that both Titles *X* and *Y* were only available as part of the same bundled package. We have already seen from e-metrics analysis that the "one-size-fits-all" approach of bundling practices does not truly suit a library's need to subscribe to individual titles. Even if there are a couple of different package options available from a content distributor, the licensing agreements that accompany the bundled titles most often stipulate that there cannot be any cancellation of any individual titles within the package during the length of the licensing contract. Under such conditions, it would be difficult for libraries to truly coordinate the acquisition and access to individual titles, thereby avoiding duplication and affording access to "unpopular" or "niche" titles.

Coordinated Collection Development

Even though the factors of bundling and licensing restrictions pose numerous obstacles to coordinated library collection development efforts, e-metrics analysis at the individual library level can assist in navigating some of these barriers. Several examples have already shown how local e-metrics can provide rather detailed information about the use of individual titles in a digital collection. But e-metrics can also supply information about those items that are not part of a library's existing electronic resources. Our next series of tables shows sample e-metrics reports of interlibrary loan activities occurring over a six-month period between five academic libraries that are part of the same state-wide university system. The data in these reports were captured by one of the five libraries, referred to as the Southern University Center Library, a medical library supporting the activities of biomedical research and a teaching hospital. These reports contain analyses of logs from both computer network transactions and database activities initiated by both library users and staff.

The first sampled report, Table 5–5, demonstrates the summary numbers of interlibrary loan activity. By capturing the amounts of Southern University Center Library lending activities, Table 5–5 could be used to determine what other libraries may be viable Southern University Center Library partners in coordinated collection development efforts. Table 5–5 indicates that the collection of Southern University Center Library was an important information resource to the user base of the other four institutions, particularly so for those 108 users associated with the Southern Medical Center. Table 5–5 also reveals that the importance of the Southern University Center Library collection is based on a broad scope of more than 100 titles. The minimal number of duplicate requests from this library by any one particular borrowing institution even indicates that there is an important value to any one loaned title.

Tables 5–6 and 5–7 show in greater detail request patterns of unique title lends to the other four borrowing libraries. Both tables organize local e-metrics data so as to calculate the relative value of a particular title to a number of

Table 5–5 Example of Summary Numbers of Interlibrary Loan Activity

Borrowing Library	Number of Lends	Number of Unique Titles	Number of Unique Articles	Number of Unique Users
Northern University Center	167	116	166	107
Southern Medical Center	220	148	218	108
4-year College	20	15	20	16
Northern Medical Center	58	42	58	45

Table 5–6 Relative Value of a Particular Title to a Number of Borrowing Libraries

Borrowing Library	Year	Journal Title	Citation	Patron ID #
4-year College	1998	Movement Disorders	May;13(3):617–9	1
4-year College	1997	Movement Disorders	Nov;12(6):1019–27	5
4-year College	1999	Movement Disorders	Jul;14(4):689–93	20
4-year College	1994	Movement Disorders	Mar;9(2):223–6	20
Southern Medical Center	2000	Movement Disorders	Jan;15(1):24–9	40
Southern Medical Center	1998	Movement Disorders	13():2–13	37
Southern Medical Center	2001	Movement Disorders	May;16(3):521–5	101
Northern University Center	2004	Movement Disorders	May;19(3):211–5	138
Northern University Center	1991	Movement Disorders	6(7):512–7	146
Northern University Center	2003	Movement Disorders	Nov;19(12):1413–7	49
Northern University Center	1983	Movement Disorders	1(3):174–8	146

borrowing libraries. Table 5–6 points out that over a six-month period, *Movement Disorders* was of interest to nine individuals from three other libraries. The table also underscores that even access to older issues of this title was of importance to users associated with other libraries. Similar information is observed in Table 5–7, where we see that the *Journal of Shoulder and Elbow Surgery* was requested by six individuals from two different borrowing libraries. Unlike *Movement Disorders,* older issues of the *Journal of Shoulder and Elbow Surgery* appear to have been of less importance to users at other libraries. Information such as this would help in both coordinated collection development efforts and consideration of subscriptions with access to archival volumes.

One more table of local library e-metrics, Table 5–8, shows the ten most frequently requested titles that were not part of the Southern University Center Library collection acquired through interlibrary loan by various users during a calendar year. Because most of the titles listed in this table appear to be requested so infrequently through interlibrary loan, this information can demonstrate that the Southern University Center Library collection did a fairly good

Table 5–7 Relative Value of a Particular Title to a Number of Borrowing Libraries

Borrowing Library	Year	Journal Title	Citation	Patron ID #
Northern University Center	1990	Journal of shoulder and elbow surgery	Aug;5(6):719–23	203
Northern University Center	2002	Journal of shoulder and elbow surgery	Jun; 39 Suppl 2():S22–8	301
Northern University Center	2003	Journal of shoulder and elbow surgery	Spring; 17(2):99–111	222
Northern Medical Center	1998	Journal of shoulder and elbow surgery	Nov–Dec; 7(6):555–9	156
Southern Medical Center	2001	Journal of shoulder and elbow surgery	10():380–82	187
Southern Medical Center	1997	Journal of shoulder and elbow surgery	6():11–17	187
Southern Medical Center	1998	Journal of shoulder and elbow surgery	7():586–96	295
Southern Medical Center	1998	Journal of shoulder and elbow surgery	7():205–9	295

job of meeting the needs of its local user base during that particular year. On the other hand, the table could also provide motivation for this library to consider subscribing to *Vocational Evaluation and Work Adjustment Bulletin* or coordinate access to this title as part of collection development efforts with libraries that already subscribe to it.

Table 5–8 Ten Most Frequently Requested Titles Not Part of ILL

OCLC Number	Journal Name	Number of Requests
2269274	Vocational evaluation and work adjustment bulletin.	10
25976498	British journal of nursing : BJN.	5
1514548	Association management.	3
47250252	Molecular & cellular proteomics : MCP.	3
8441044	Nucleosides & nucleotides.	3
12503251	Adverse Drug Reaction Toxicology Review	2
10169522	American Journal of Managed Care	2
13830677	American journal of health promotion : AJHP.	2
5070935	Australian veterinary journal.	2
12703310	Biotechniques	2

Conclusion

This chapter has so far illustrated that even though the transition to digital publishing has increased the potential accessibility to numerous and varied library resources, collection development and evaluation in the digital age has become a much more complicated process. The examination of collections questions has clarified how the new publishing industry subscription and licensing models for electronic titles require the development of new library tools that assist in measuring the value of individual titles. Both vendor-supplied and local library e-metrics initiatives can provide such decision making tools that can be used to determine the most fiscally sound method of information access in the face of library financial constraints, bundled subscription packages, and access restrictions. We will next use e-metrics to answer more general library administration concerns, especially those focusing on library staffing and non-materials budgets.

6

Using E-Metrics for Library Administration

The two preceding chapters have illustrated how useful e-metrics specific to your individual library can be, providing information necessary for both library public relations issues and more detailed library collection development policies. In this chapter we will review the use of e-metrics to address other library management concerns tangential, yet supportive, to collection development. This chapter will also outline some of the core technologies required for libraries to support electronic collections, the very same technologies that will form the foundation of both vendor-supplied and library-level e-metrics data capture and analysis. A more detailed discussion of the library specific e-metrics how-to, including terminology covered in this chapter, follows in the next section of the book.

The preceding chapters have focused on a number of library issues that are the consequences of recent digital technology adoption. However, the examination so far has addressed both the historical changes and misconceptions of how libraries deal with the rapid advances of digital publishing, but has not yet tackled the more fundamental issues of library workflows and needs in the digital era. Both library users and those library employees who are not preoccupied with the daily management of digital collections can easily overlook the processes, procedures, details, and problems that encompass the act of creating seamless access to library materials. Consider, for a moment, how many library users today enter libraries just to utilize the public computers that are connected to the Internet (Newsletter of University of Western Ontario Libraries 2002). Analogous to customers of the electric, water, and telephone companies, the average library user has little awareness or concern with what actually occurs behind the scenes that enables such unfettered access to information. The library user or customer expectation is that information access in and from the library is always available all the time. This notion is constantly reinforced by the mere existence of other information services. Think for a moment how quickly TV, radio, and numerous other Internet media outlets can provide news, weather, articles, diagnoses, recipes, and seemingly comprehensive Internet searches anytime from almost any radio, any television, and any computer network. Seen from this perspective, one could certainly argue that the development of computer technologies and digital library collections has altered the library's traditional role. No longer are libraries just a data and information repository, but libraries have a new position as a centralized information utility. The larger question that may be asked by or of library administrators looking to succeed as an information organization might be: "What do libraries actually need to operate and remain relevant information outlets in the current Information Age environment?" As has been done before, we will continue to investigate a series of hypothetical questions and answers that use e-metrics to more accurately represent various facets of these library operational needs and responses to the new digital environment.

Administrative Q & A with E-Metrics

How Much Do Electronic Collections Cost?

Question: Why does the library require a budget increase when it is shifting its collection emphasis more towards materials that are in electronic formats? It must ultimately be cheaper to subscribe to materials in electronic format because there is no need to do all of the physical processing and storage of electronic titles.

Answer: The rationale at the core of this question—that going digital is cheaper—is perhaps the most pervasive and pernicious one being posed to library staff and administrators in their requests for larger material and personnel budgets. To answer this rather encompassing question, we need to consider the overall impact of digital collections from three main administrative concerns: issues of cost, licenses, and access. The discussion of each administrative quandary will examine how the networked landscape has generated a level of user expectation and service that requires libraries to possess new and different assets. These assets can be divided in terms of three main categories: acquisitions, personnel, and technology.

The truth is that there are a number of operating costs that libraries must account for in the creation and maintenance of electronic materials and resources. In fact, many libraries have discovered that it can be more costly to develop and maintain digital library collections than had been the case for traditional print resources. These costs go beyond the subscription price for a given title and should include both the staffing and technical infrastructure, which are covered in greater detail in Chapter 9. But even though these expenditures are not quite as obvious as the initial subscription costs for library resources, they still need to be accounted for by library administrators. We have already touched upon some of the acquisition cost issues associated with digital collections in the previous chapter. Earlier, we saw an overview of the financial choices connected with digital library collections, particularly those alternatives contingent upon the conditions of bundled title packages and access restrictions contained in subscription licensing agreements. Let us delve a bit deeper into the issues of subscription bundles, since they are becoming the primary licensing model available from many publishers.

The "Big Deal" Revisited

If we reconsider the local e-metrics data that we examined in the previous chapter, we saw how e-metrics easily demonstrated the mixed value of individual titles within a bundled subscription package. In Figure 5–1 (page 76) we observed a sampling of e-metrics data concentrating on the annual usage of a selection of titles that are part of Library B's bundled subscription from the Nature Publishing Group. Recall that the height of the cylindrical columns in the graph quickly illustrated that not all titles in a subscription bundle are of equal interest to this library's user base. The chart also indicated that some of the bundled titles such as *International Journal of Impotence Research* and *Evidence-Based Dentistry* could be considered for cancellation if they were not part of a bundled package.

Yet other complexities of bundles still need to be addressed. In addition to locking a library into a pre-selected group of titles, bundles may also offer even better subscription pricing if the subscribing library commits to a long-term bundled license agreement that extends through multiple calendar years. What potential implications does such a pricing option have upon library budgets? Obviously, long-term contracts mean that libraries are committing over multiple years large sums of their collections budgets to a single static subset of their digital titles. But is this really a wise commitment to make?

One needs to keep in mind that the aforementioned graph shows the use patterns of a bundled package accessed by one library population. We have already indicated that it would be highly unlikely to see identical e-metrics results from another library as usage of titles will vary from one library to the other. These variations would be due to a number of parameters associated with a specific library's environment: user population, local economy, current issues, research, and news of interest during a given timeframe and associated with a particular geographic region. In other words, library use patterns can be easily influenced by the events of the time, in much the same way that the varied and numerous Internet information outlets need to reflect the news of the day. This fact can be easily demonstrated.

In the virtual world of the Internet, there are a handful of search engines that have grown to global dominance and have even been seen as competitors to libraries. The types of searches performed with these engines and the popularity of particular search terms can be seen to correlate with breaking news stories. Four of the major search engine services—Ask Jeeves™ weekly SearchIQ, Google's™ weekly Zeitgeist, Lycos'™ daily Lycos 50, and Yahoo!'s™ daily Buzz Index—currently gather statistics of popular search terms. Their statistical results clearly indicate certain global personal interests in common topics but also demonstrate a broad spectrum of subject interests, from popular personalities to sporting events.[1] Additionally, a wonderful visualization of news trends occurring globally according to the Google search engine news aggregator can be found at the Newsmap.[2] On any given day and any given hourly measurement, certain subjects have more prominence than others in the global media. This prominence even varies from one geographic region to another; the main focus of the media and the public one day in India can be different than that on the same day in France.

These same current events with their associated periodic interest trends can readily affect the collection and operation of a library in a very simple way. Public libraries can easily attest to this fact by monitoring the number of purchase requests, circulation recalls and holds, and even interlibrary loan requests for a recently published book or novel that has received critical acclaim. Analogous activities may take place in research or special libraries where the latest scientific discovery or important legal case can be a catalyst for adding new materials to a library's collection. The publishing industry similarly appears to respond to current events by altering their offerings to meet the public interest in particular topics. The tragic events of September 11, 2001 certainly provided impetus for publishers to contract for and release titles that focused on the history of the Taliban and Osama bin Laden. Similarly, the publishers catered to other popular interest of the time by offering books on both the construction and destruction of the World Trade Center Towers in New York City. How would long-term bundled licensing and subscription agreements enable a library to easily and satisfactorily meet the potential changing subject focus and interests reflected in both current events and their local library user constituency?

Given all of the other restrictions that are part and parcel of bundled title subscriptions, the assumed answer to this question is that it would be very difficult to find a package of titles that would or could potentially address the current and future comprehensive collection needs of a library. The measured proof of this assumption, however, will have to come from long-term library e-metrics studies which, like those of the Internet search engines, would really offer periodic comparisons of title use and patron interests over time. But the other aspect of bundled titles that needs to be considered is which bundle package should take priority in terms of both annual and long-term contractual agreements, therefore becoming a determinant of library budgetary allocations. The best way to judge the relative priority of long-term bundled title subscriptions is to perform some type of e-metrics usage comparison across titles and across bundles. For a library with resources analogous to that of Library A, such a task will be limited by the availability of standardized vendor-supplied reports. If Library A is subscribing to titles from an information intermediary who only provides COUNTER-compliant reports and another one who only provides proprietary usage reports, then Library A will be unable to complete an accurate comparison due to a lack of common measurement criteria generated by differences in vendor accounting and reporting procedures. To avoid this potential lack of common criteria by which to make global comparisons of e-journal use, Library B utilizes a local e-metrics capture solution by re-writing and modifying standard vendor-supplied title access URLs on its Web site. This process, which will be described in detail in Chapter 8, helps to maintain consistency of the definition for access counts across all digital subscription titles and formats. Library C can duplicate the local e-metrics processes found at Library B, later integrating data from other repositories thereby determining package value beyond network use. For example, Library C could consider the title access count as a unit of use and then integrate cost and ISI impact information as was seen in the previous chapter (see Figure 5–3).

Table 6–1 shows some local library e-metrics comparisons of two package agreements licensed by Library B. The 203 titles that make up the ScienceDirect package are part of a multi-year agreement while the 81 titles from the Ovid bundle are renewed on an annual basis. The ScienceDirect titles account for approximately 14 percent of this library's total virtual visits for a calendar year, while the Ovid titles only account for nearly 11 percent of the total virtual visits.

It would appear at first glance that the ScienceDirect package is of greater value to this library than the Ovid bundle. But these use percentages can be deceiving. The results for ScienceDirect title use need to be viewed in the context of the total number of available titles in the package. Then it becomes clear that part of the reason that ScienceDirect represents a higher total percentage of e-resource use is because there are indeed more than double the number of Ovid titles appearing in the ScienceDirect bundle. The more telling numbers for

Table 6–1 Comparisons of Two Package Agreements Licensed in an Academic Medical Library

Package Name	% of Total Visits	# of Subscribed Titles in Package	Annual Visits	Proportional Importance of Package (number of visits per title)
ScienceDirect	14.3381	203	73693	363
Journals@Ovid	10.6495	81	54735	675

determining overall bundled license value is seen in the average number of visits per package title. By dividing the number of annual virtual visits to a package by the number of titles in the specific package, we see that the Ovid license appears to provide titles of greater value to this library's user base. Additional analysis of the overall package value could be accomplished by creating charts akin to Figure 5–1 in order to determine how many titles in the package are of little interest to the library's users. Finally, with this e-metrics data, library administration needs to compare the overall subscription costs in terms of annual budget allocations.

How Many Staff Do We Need?

Question: I can see the problems associated with predicting collections budgets for the upcoming years, especially in view of the predominance of bundled subscriptions for future digital acquisitions. But there is still an increase in the library's payroll budget. While you continue to address the ramifications of the publisher's stated subscription costs, you have not yet made the case for more materials processing work. Why then would the library require more staff to manage our growing digital collections?

Answer: When viewing the impact of electronic publishing on the management of virtual library collections, several factors need to be considered. Answering this question properly will require reviewing and detailing electronic resources access and licensing issues beyond what has already been covered in earlier answers. The foregoing answer, and much of the content of the previous chapter, underscored the tight integration publishers have developed between subscription costs and licenses. There is still more of this integration and its impact on library operations that needs to be examined.

Electronic Resources Management

Recall that the previous chapter provided several examples of the variety of subscriptions and licenses associated with digitally-based library materials. We have already seen through the discussions of licensing and access restrictions that the publishers and vendors are now the primary arbiters of information access. This is the case because information that is part of a subscription or license is no longer sent to a library, but instead virtually stored and maintained by the vendors and publishers themselves. This new distribution model is the core reason why these various models can exist: the library no longer is the physical owner of these e-resources in the new digital publishing environment and may therefore no longer physically own much of its newest material. But what impact does this new mode of access have on library workflow?

We have noted that in the print environment of the past, user access to library materials was dictated by library policies of shelving, circulation, and patron status. Such policies could exist because the library physically maintained and owned hard copies of these subscription and monograph resources. For those libraries that have large monograph collections—such as libraries with a strong arts and humanities focus or individual public libraries—these access policies will still remain important components of library procedures and operations. Since the e-book has yet to achieve the popularity of the e-journal and e-database, libraries, including those concentrating on biological and social sciences, still need to concentrate to some extent on the physical processing of monographs. In this book, we have not devoted much time towards an examination of e-books in the analysis and management of digital collections in part because, as noted in the ISO and NISO standards cited in Chapter 2, e-books in general constitute much smaller library acquisitions expenditures than electronic journals and databases. Even so, this observation does not address the level of staff support that certain types of e-books may require, an issue that will be discussed at a later point in this chapter.

Still, as one may correctly assume, with increased digital collections, the library's efforts are no longer focused as intently upon the physical processing of paper materials. Instead, a library dealing with larger electronic collections serves as the main entity that centralizes both the acquisition costs and the virtual access to information. By assuming these responsibilities, the library, in one sense, acts as an information intermediary to digital content. Some of these intermediary responsibilities have already been addressed; without the library's efforts to centralize and manage the costs and licensing of subscriptions and title bundles, the costs and evaluation of these titles would be the responsibility of those specific individuals that were interested in gaining access to them.

But what about a library's additional responsibility of centralized support for user access to digital content? Although the library can spend less time on the physical processing of library materials, it can be demonstrated that it is even more time consuming to virtually process digital collections. This fact becomes clear when one reconsiders the point that the library is now only the intermediary to most digital resources.

The overall categories of steps needed to maintain consistent user access to information resources are provided in Figure 6–1, adapted from the documentation of the Digital Library Federation Electronic Resource Management Initiative.[3] This diagram shows a comparison of the broad concerns and components of print and digital collections management processes after the title acquisition decision process has been completed. The multiple steps and considerations appearing in the column for digital collections we will refer to as electronic resource management (ERM). The main goals of these ERM steps are keeping users informed of changes in subscriptions and easing user access to information.

To better understand the workflow issues represented in this diagram, let us review the data appearing in Table 6–2 which summarizes a possible contract scenario created when a publisher decides to change licensing options after a

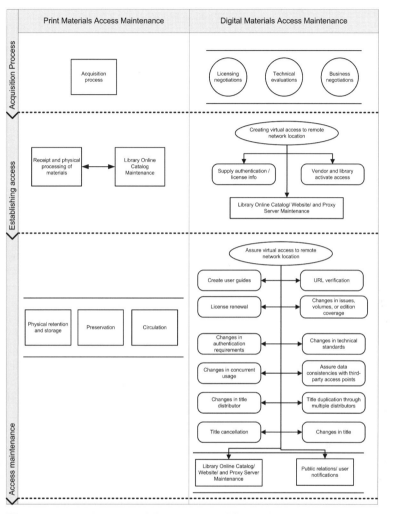

Figure 6-1 Diagram of Comparison of Post Acquisition Steps for Maintaining Access to Print and Digital Collections

one-year contract. For example, Vendor A has a package of 6 titles that are licensed to a library for one year. In this package, Titles X, Y, and Z are available online in this license for the years 1990–2003. Titles Q, R, and S are also available online, but only for the years 1997–2004. But Vendor A's license for the upcoming year will change, with a few differences from what was offered in last year's contract. The new contract no longer incorporates Title Z in the package because the vendor has replaced it with Title W covering the volumes from 1990 to 2001. Issues for Title Q are now available from 1992 to the current issue, but

Table 6–2 Representative Changes in Bundled Licensing Agreements

Title Within Vendor A Bundled License	Initial Annual Contract Agreement	Follow-up Renewal Contract Agreement
W	Not available	1990–2001
X	1990–2003	1990–2003 with new authentication requirement
Y	1990–2003	1990–2003
Z	1990–2003	No longer available; replaced by Title W
Q	1997–2004	1992-current issue
R	1997–2004	1998–2004
S	1997–2004	1998–2004

now online issues for Titles R and S start from 1998. Access to Title X also now includes a new requirement of a username and password combination to get to the title's Web site.

Had Vendor A's subscription package been delivered as traditional print materials, a library would have a lot less to worry about. In the past, when a library subscribed to only paper titles, the library staff received and processed the subscription title at the library, housed it somewhere inside the library facilities (or possibly in storage) and made it available for circulation or made it part of the non-circulating collection. These print storage responsibilities are identified in Figure 6–1 as the retention portion of the print access maintenance category. If the print title subscription was ever cancelled, the subscriber (in this case, the library) remained the physical owner of older editions or volumes of a particular title. With paper subscriptions, the replacement of Title W for Title Z would have meant that the library could still hold older issues of Title Z in its possession. A similar situation would have existed with a subscription to a paper version of Titles R and S. And of course there would be no need to require a username and password for authenticated access to a paper version of Title X.

But when a library has a subscription to resources that are no longer physically housed and processed within its facilities, the cancellation of a subscription frequently means that access to even historical and archival copies of the title is no longer available. The ramifications of this fact are represented in several parts of the digital access maintenance category in the diagram. Because these hypothetical titles from Vendor A are part of an electronic subscription, the new licensing agreement will mean for this library complete loss of access to Title Z, loss of access to older issues of Titles R and S, and a new type of access restriction for Title X. If a library agrees to the contract as it will be structured for the upcoming year, what would be the immediate impact of these contract changes? Obviously, those library users who are interested in seeing the latest and older issues of Title Z will have to find another information inter- mediary other than their own library or perhaps sign up for their own sub- scription to gain content access. Individuals interested in reading information from older issues of Titles R and S will similarly need to identify other outlets for their needs. We will temporarily postpone addressing the issue associated with new authentication requirements for Title X, for this requires a more tech- nical discussion.

The Illusion of Seamless Access

The description of the contract's impact on both library and user has so far concentrated on library collection and user needs—the two extreme issues as- sociated with this hypothetical vendor, bundle, and contract. However, the core concern of this scenario is really one of information access, a problem that is most obvious when encountered by the library user. To make this in- formation access issue less confusing, there are a number of steps that li- braries need to take, steps that occur between those behind-the-scenes activities of collection management and those more visible endeavors of public access and reference.

To clarify the relationships between the ERM steps in Figure 6–1, particularly those of the digital resources access maintenance category, let us outline some of the staff duties required to assure users seamless access to library subscrip- tions if a library were to subscribe to the Vendor A package. The holdings rec- ords created in the library's integrated management system and online catalog for Titles Q, R, and S would have to be updated to reflect changes in volume and issue coverage. The record in the library's catalog system for Title Z would have to be modified according to library policy to inform users that the title was no longer part of the library's collection. Depending upon local policy, someone may suppress the complete bibliographic record from public view or annotate the holdings record to note the title's lack of future availability. A new entry would have to be created in the system for Title W, as it has now become part of the library's virtual collection, whether the library really needs it or not, by virtue of Vendor A's bundling policy. If the same library maintains a separate Web site that isolates access to e-resources only, analogous changes need to also be made at the various virtual access points for the titles in the bundle.

While the maintenance procedures summarized so far as a response to this scenario may appear to be simple, they only outline the preliminary steps that need to be taken to manage electronic collections. It can easily become neces- sary to repeat this process for multiple titles when all of the annual vendor and publisher licenses take a similar approach to our Vendor A scenario. Even this potential annual change may not appear to be problematic enough for a library to require more skilled staff. Unfortunately, electronic publishers do not all uti- lize the model sketched in our scenario.

A library can additionally be confronted with another possible and common ERM problem; vendors, publishers, or title aggregators may continue to offer the subscription title from the license, but change the URL of that title without prior notification to the library. Typically, when this type of unannounced change occurs, the first person to discover this unexpected access switch is the user who really needs access to the resource and is directed by the library's systems to the old URL. Then the rather agitated user contacts the library via phone, e-mail, or in person, and reports that something is wrong with the access through the URL that has yet to be determined to now be outdated. As with our earlier scenario, title access points in the OPAC and library Web site will have to be updated accordingly by library staff to reflect these URL changes. But because the user can only report that access to the needed title is "broken," someone from the library has to do some research to identify why the access is "broken" and what needs to be done to fix it.

The issue of "broken" hyperlinks to digital resources presents an information access concern parallel to that of missing print titles from a library's physical collection. Frequently the search for a missing printed book or journal volume begins when a user attempts to access the particular title from its appropriate bookshelf location. When the desired item cannot be found in its designated place, the user may persist in the search mostly likely bringing the problem to the attention of someone on the library staff. At this point, the possible solutions for finding the missing title could include an extensive search throughout the book stacks and unshelved items on book trucks, or a review of circulation records to see if the item in question was borrowed and not returned. A more thorough and time consuming policy of performing periodic inventories of the print collections would be necessary in order for the library to avoid such questions and information access issues in the first place.

In the case of URL readdressing, there is a similar work-intensive solution which may avoid making the library user the first discoverer and therefore informant of URL changes. A library could have an employee do periodic verification of URLs for all of the electronic titles, either manually title by title or with some URL verification tool. But even this process can become complicated by both technological barriers and market conditions in the publishing sector. To provide an overview of these potential problem-solving considerations, we need to outline some of the possible reasons why access to an electronic subscription may be "broken."

The Unseen Technology of ERM

Besides changes in subscription or issue coverage and URL changes, there can also be changes in the technological requirements of the computing device accessing the new URL or even the existing URL. Recall that in the e-commerce world it is necessary to keep up with the latest technological advancements in order to retain a competitive edge against other e-businesses. The same conditions are also true in the realm of digital publishing. We have already seen one example, highlighted with e-metrics analysis, which demonstrated how the same title offered by two different content distributors can have different usage patterns, perhaps based upon publisher Web site functionality. As publishers attempt to enhance the user experience by adding advanced searching capabilities and real-time interactivity, they often choose to standardize access to their Web sites without accounting for the wide variety of technology and software that the Internet is capable of supporting.

Thus a user may report a "broken" library link without understanding that the particular version of the Web browser being used to access the link is no longer supported by that publisher's Web site. Similar situations may occur when the Web browser is not properly configured to meet the access specifications of the particular site in question. There may even be a requirement for additional software beyond the Web browser that is needed to access the enhanced full-text features of a specific title. Finally, the hyperlink may be considered "broken" because of one of a myriad of networking issues—an offline vendor Web server, overloaded network router somewhere on the Internet, a severed networking cable, or a wrongly-configured domain name server—that are outside the control of either the user or the library presenting the link on its system.

What has been outlined so far at the technical level should show that the possible technology variables of seamless access to electronic collections require those responsible for ERM to have a fairly firm knowledge of several computing and networking infrastructure components and their workings. We should also consider that ERM staff should adopt techniques similar to the traditional reference interview in order to better understand what a user is communicating when encountering a "broken" link on the library's system. Such troubleshooting techniques should include trying to replicate the user's access issue in another computing environment and probing the user for information about their own computer setup. But there is far more than the technological impediments that need to be addressed by the ERM staff, for they often have to inquire of vendors and publishers as to reasons why subscription access may be blocked.

Many times, denial of information access for users can be due to problems related to the remote host of the desired content. We have already mentioned that a vendor or publisher could alter a URL unannounced or change the technological requirements to access a particular Web site. The publisher's remote site could also be experiencing a technological glitch at the specific time when users are attempting to reach the requested title. For example, vendor computing issues could be due to an unannounced server or network technology upgrade. But there can also be confusion on the vendor's part with regards to the licensing agreement reached with the subscribing library. Vendor mistakes and misunderstandings of the approved range of subscribing library computer network addresses, the number of simultaneous user accesses, or the length of time for which the licensing contract is valid can all contribute to levels of library user frustration. Regardless of the difficulties on the vendors' information delivery end, it has become the responsibility of the library to function as the problem-solving entity when its users encounter issues accessing digital library collections.

There is one other unique user access problem, diagrammed in Table 6–2, related to the intrinsic difference between print and digital library collections and connected with difficulties at the vendor and publisher service level. If we reflect on the power of the Internet as a communication medium, we can readily acknowledge that the concept and implementation of the hyperlink has made it possible to access the same content from a multitude of Web sites and networks. Therefore, unlike user access to print materials, the world of digital publishing and remote network access to virtual library collections also offers a set of unique complications that arise from information inconsistencies between multiple user access points. It can be easy for library users to find a hyperlink maintained outside their library's control that refers back to a title that their library is assumed to have a subscription to. The problem is that those links externally maintained by organizations or entities not directly associated with the users' specific library may have inaccurate information as to what the library has really licensed.

For example, a Web site that provides an online database of journal citations may provide a link directly to a full-text article of a journal. A library patron could use such a citation site to reduce the amount of searching required to find information on a specific topic. The user could then click on the citation hyperlink to the full-text article which is then hosted on the journal's main Web site. But if the actual journal publisher or vendor does not acknowledge that the user is coming from a recognized library network address or that the article in question is not part of the issues or titles covered under the licensing agreement with the user's library, the user will be denied access to the full-text article. There could also be misrepresentation on the citation database site of library holdings because the title vendors and publishers have not properly informed the citation database entity of the library's updated subscription and licensing information. With each of the possible roadblocks caused by these inconsistencies in library subscription representation, the user may encounter multiple points of information access failure, notated in Figure 6–2 by the circle-line combination crossing the hyperlink contact points. Such experiences are particularly confusing to users because of the multiple access layers present but hidden from the users' view.

These particular user access problems are extremely difficult and time consuming to address in the ERM process. A combination of user education, public relations, and multiple vendor contacts are needed to properly resolve such

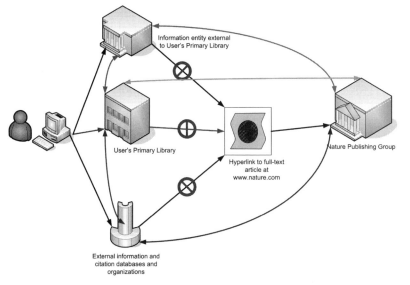

Figure 6-2 Diagram of Possible Points of Information Access Failures for Library Users of Digital Collections

complicated access issues. In order to uncover the multiple layers of access and inconsistencies, the user's library will have to communicate with both those maintaining the access and information on the title's publisher or vendor Web site and those individuals who maintain the information contained in the citation database. It is also possible that multiple information entities external to the library are providing inaccurate information about the library's digital collections, thereby creating additional work for ERM staff as they will need to contact multiple sources in their efforts to reduce the number of access errors encountered by library users.

The Perils of Market Consolidation

The Vendor A contract scenario is only one of multiple possible information access changes that libraries are attempting to manage. Recently, there has been a trend towards consolidation in the electronic publishing industry. As global adoption of the Internet and its digital technologies increases, so does the acquisition of smaller publishing companies by larger publishing houses, which in turn become more profitable content distributors and media companies. This market consolidation has so far not had a positive affect on libraries. When the number of players in the publishing market shrinks, libraries have fewer choices and channels from which to acquire subscription content and published titles. And when a library has fewer distributors to choose from, the license negotiating positions of this limited number of large distributors and publishers grows stronger.

While this discussion of electronic publishing consolidation could continue with concerns of licensing options, this consolidation also has serious implications on ERM. In fact, ERM concerns stemming from publishing company mergers can include URL changes, title cancellations, new technological requirements, modifications in title coverage, and new authentication requirements all occurring simultaneously across multiple subscription titles as a result of a licensing contract change.

Even as the acquiring company makes alterations to an existing licensing contract previously structured by their latest business acquisition, libraries wishing to retain access to most or all of the titles in their digital collections under the old contract must find methods to keep that access seamless and uninterrupted for their users. If we reconsider how a library copes with a company merger of print material publishers and distributors, there are far fewer steps required to maintain uninterrupted user access to paper collections. The slower pace of change in the print materials environment offers few occasions for a library user to be confronted with the hidden logistical issues of library acquisitions and cataloging. The paper editions of the library materials would be stored locally within the library and would continue to be so regardless of which publisher or distributor acquired future rights to the title. Compare that pace of print developments with those of vendor-controlled changes to virtual title access which themselves intertwine with the increasing complexity of both licensing and technology. In fact, the integrated inability to offer both real-time updates and access to print materials and their need for local physical storage within the library make the management of print materials a less demanding operation than ERM in terms of both staffing and skills.

ERM Solutions?

Many libraries, as well as several publishing and content vendors, are hoping and attempting to develop and sell ERM systems that will fit the new library needs that have sprung from this demanding new environment. One of the requirements of these systems is the ability to generate a new set of staffing e-metrics. Table 6–3 provides a sample of the e-metrics from a local ERM system that has been developed on-site by Library C. Even though this chart is an example of what can be done in Library C through an automated ERM solution, Libraries A and B can also track such activities through a paper-based accounting system. This library's ERM system counted 731 changes to links to this library's electronic collections of 1,800 e-journals, e-books, and e-databases during the year 2003. These changes included URL modifications and replacements, new volume coverage for journals, changes in title distributor, title additions, and title cancellations. This number does not include an additional

Table 6–3 Breakdown of Annual ERM Title
Maintenance Tasks

Add	454
Delete	80
Change	132
New or changed authentication	76

seventy-six titles that were required by the title vendors to have new username and password authentication credentials during that same year. We will still address the requirements of remote information access authentication a bit later on.

Even the current multifaceted explanation of possible user access issues that need to be accounted for in daily ERM procedures has barely enumerated all of the potential modifications that can occur over a short period of time within digital collections. Because the library is no longer a physical owner of the materials that make up the electronic collections, we should be aware that any number and combination of digital resource changes may occur at any time. If a library is fortunate, some work days will require few adjustments to the virtual access to digital collections. At other times, a library may be confronted for a week or two with a variety of access issues from several titles that represent single or multiple bundled subscriptions. Table 6–4 illustrates additional details of Table 6–3, highlighting some of the periodic randomness of ERM workflow. The high volume of title additions for the months of January and February were due to recently activated and renewed bundled subscription packages by this library at the beginning of the calendar year.

It should be noted that the amount of post-acquisition steps and effort needed to add electronic titles to a digital library collection is far less than that required to maintain existing links to remote content. For example, although the number of title additions for May in Table 6–4 is more than double that of URL and title changes, the amount of work necessary to account for those changes to existing collection resources is more than double that of the new additions. This inverse relationship is due to the number of variables that must be

Table 6–4 Monthly ERM Collection Maintenance Patterns

	Add Title	Delete Title	Change URL, Holdings, or Content Provider
January	98	5	5
February	89	9	6
March	5	1	1
April	28	1	3
May	32	9	15

investigated by ERM staff before committing the changes to public view in multiple access points.

It has hopefully become clear from our lengthy explanation that there are numerous complexities in digital library collections that require constant follow-up with great attention to details that are often times outside the physical and administrative control of the library. The difference in the staffing resources needed to manage digital collections thus becomes obvious. One only needs to compare how libraries have learned to cope with title changes, continuing sets, and cancellations of traditional paper resources to similar and additional potential modifications occurring to titles in electronic formats. It is probably necessary to hire more staff to manage the increased complexities associated with digital collections. Regardless of staff sizing for ERM, it is becoming imperative to hire and train individuals who are capable of performing multiple interrelated tasks, of following through various steps and procedures sometimes out of sequence, and of communicating with both vendors and library users so as to develop a level of public understanding that assists in eradicating the confusion that can accompany information access over computer networks.

The rapid pace of change in both the electronic publishing industry and the computer technology sector will continue to make the tasks of ERM increasingly complex. The ever-changing models for information access at both the levels of contractual agreements and technological requirements must be promptly reflected on the library's Web site as part of the ERM process. Additional needs for trouble-shooting information access issues will require far more than a passing familiarity with computer networking architectures and Web technologies. If a library wishes to avoid having any problem with the e-resources immediately noticed and reported by its patrons, the library needs to attract and train a skilled group of collection development, acquisitions, and ERM staff, both for now and the future. The collaborative efforts of such employees will enable a library to continue providing a level of seamless access to its digital collections by hiding the complex and multifaceted nature of electronic publications and computer technologies.

How Much Technology Do We Need?

Question: So far you have accounted for the costs of digital collections, both in terms of the actual license or subscription and in terms of the personnel and workflow needed to manage it. Why then does the library require an increase in its technology budget? We purchased new computer systems last year based upon the latest specifications. Also, I notice in the news that the price of desktop computer hardware has dropped dramatically over the past few years. It would seem that it is actually cheaper to purchase more powerful computers now than a year ago. What is all of this technology money needed for?

Answer: It is true that the overall cost of computer hardware in terms of both processors and data storage have decreased over a relatively short time. However, this decline in purchase costs does not account for the total cost of technology ownership. At a simple level, the use of e-books in libraries provides a particularly good example of the variety of technology costs and support services that digital library collections can require. It appears as though e-books will continue to be offered by the digital publishing industry as an alternative to the traditional paper folio with the promise of greater portability and greater storage. But the promise of the e-book has not truly been met, for even from their initial introduction and through today, there has not truly been an established standardization of the technologies used in e-book access.

The Total Cost of Ownership and the Price of Staying Relevant

Early e-book technologies included a hardware component that was designed specifically for the sole purpose of reading e-books. But now that the early e-book technology has since become obsolete, leaving those libraries that purchased that hardware with yet another specialized but somewhat outdated information format, analogous to the 8–track audio cassette, the BETA video format, and the video laserdisc. Even now, there are still multiple e-book formats and delivery systems available. Some e-books are designed to be read on small hand-held computers or personal digital assistants (PDAs). These e-books require different reading software depending upon which model and hardware platform of PDA is being used for e-book reading purposes. Other e-books can be accessed via the Internet through a relatively typical Web browser, while yet another e-book format can only be read with the appropriate computer application that is assistive to the Web browser. Some e-book vendors and publishers provide access to free content to multiple simultaneous users. Other e-book content providers have developed methods that simulate the experience of the physical printed book, assuring that only one individual at a time accesses any given e-book title.

Any library that has added e-books to their collections has certainly encountered several issues in providing user access to this specialized and varied information format. How are library staff and users trained to operate the various competing and developing e-book technologies? As these technologies change over time, how can a library incorporate newer technologies to meet the information needs of its users? How much will it cost the library to acquire the appropriate technologies to address user requirements? How many individuals and what types of skills are needed to support those various technologies? How can a library determine which technologies to invest in for now and the future?

The e-book example illustrates that in addition to hardware and software purchases, the respective costs of a library computing infrastructure are similar to that of ERM—workflow and skilled staffing. In an earlier chapter, we demonstrated with library-acquired e-metrics that there was a large volume of virtual networked library activity taking place both inside and outside the library's physical structure. But much like the phone, electric, and water utilities, it is easy to take for granted the critical components of networked access to digital information. A library's technological infrastructure acts as the very foundation of such information access. Let us consider the types of resources required to support and allow for all of this activity.

Recall that in our first chapter we noted how e-commerce needed to develop a virtual shopping experience and storefront that would enable a company to make a profit. In the commercial sector, digital technologies are implemented to stay competitive and to increase earnings. Such execution requires a sizable investment in a computing infrastructure that includes computer hardware, computer software, various operating systems, computer networking equipment, and of course electrical power. A similar type of computing infrastructure is evolving at libraries, both large and small. Like e-business, libraries have had to invest in the materials necessary to create the proper computing environment that supports access to digital information. However, the catalysts and demands on such an infrastructure in libraries differ in many ways from that of the business world.

The Library Information Access Infrastructure

We can illustrate the importance of a library's technical infrastructure by now returning to the issue of additional authentication requirements to Title X imposed by Vendor A in our earlier scenario. We should first understand why the vendor would impose such a requirement in the first place. When a publisher houses all of its current titles in a centralized network location, it has to come up with some way to guarantee that only the subscribers paying for access are the ones who actually get to view the information. And libraries should not have their subscription fees allowing access to the wrong population of non-library users. Imagine how frustrating it would be if you paid for a daily print newspaper delivery that was frequently delivered to a neighbor several houses away. As part of licensing agreements with electronic publishers and vendors, libraries and distributors have a mutual interest in assuring access to subscribed electronic content.

Two methods are typically used by publishers and vendors to establish levels of network access security. One technique offering proper access to subscription content requires a unique login with a username and password assigned to the subscriber. Another system used by vendors restricts network access to content according to the network address, known as the Internet Protocol (IP) address, of the computing device used to request the subscription. This system is typically the one used to allow for site-wide and institutional licenses. Either of these authorization solutions from the content distributor's side places an additional set of demands on libraries if they are to meet the needs of their users.

Access logins controlled by username and password can be a rather flawed authorization system because of its dependency on the "human element." One can easily forget login credentials and is therefore tempted to write down these items, increasing the potential for such private or personalized authorizations to be stolen. Admission to a subscription Web site by login can also be problematic when only one username-password set is issued for a single institutional subscriber. If a library has several hundred users, the library faces both the issue of distributing this single set of credentials to multiple users and assuring that non-authorized users do not obtain this information and then take unauthorized advantage of the library's subscription. This is particularly troublesome when this authorization method is required for a subscription license that limits the number of simultaneous user sessions.

Libraries must also create a technical infrastructure that allows access to subscription content for users who are not physically located within the library's facilities and use computing devices that are not considered part of the library's network. This information retrieval requirement is particularly important for academic research libraries that serve users who may be distance learning students or research scientists performing studies at off-site locations. From a technical perspective, the credentialed login approach is more amenable to remote users than access restricted according to network addressing. However, chances of having credentialed access "stolen" are fairly high with the ease of transferring these credentials to non-authorized users.

So with site-wide and institutional licensing contracts, two technological remote access solutions have come to the forefront. Several large institutional libraries have chosen to create a Virtual Private Network (VPN), a solution that initially gained popularity in the business sector as a network security and confidentiality solution. VPNs utilize the infrastructure of the existing public Internet, but create a virtual tunnel within the public network so that the client device at one end of the VPN is assigned a network address from the server side of the tunnel as though it was part of the library's local area network (see Figure 6–3). VPNs use encryption and other security mechanisms to ensure that only authorized users can access the network and that the data passing through the public network cannot be intercepted. The VPN solution typically requires the installation of additional software on computer devices located on networks outside the library or institutional network.

The second remote access solution commonly installed in libraries is a proxy server. Proxy servers were initially installed within businesses either to improve the retrieval times of Web pages or to act as a gateway network security solution. In both implementations, the proxy server is positioned as a network intermediary between the Internet client, such as a Web browser, and the intended target of the network request. Like the VPN, the proxy server can make the request from a network client appear as though it is coming from an authorized network address, even if the network client is situated on a non-licensed network

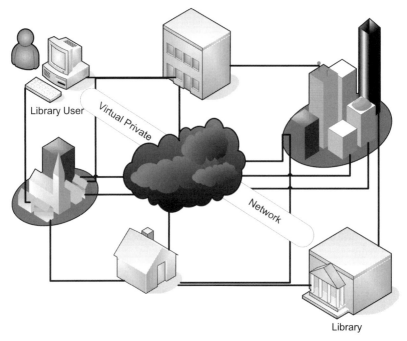

Library User

Virtual Private

Network

Library

Figure 6-3 Diagram of VPN Library Use for Network Authentication

(see Figure 6–4). Use of proxy servers on a network may or may not require some configuration on the remote user's computer device.

Whether using a VPN or proxy server solution for providing secured authentication to information resources, the subscribing library supporting remote access authentication needs to develop mechanisms that grant access to the appropriate library patrons. Such processes require the creation and maintenance of updated user lists, now typically stored in large computer databases. Depending upon the number of individual users and library type, this list can become difficult to manage. For a small specialized library—for example, a law library—the user list could consist of a few hundred entries, with infrequent needs for alterations and updates. For a large academic research library, the user list may require a large update during transitions between the various periods of the academic year of user entries generated from the university's human resources and student registrar data. For public libraries, the user list can be preloaded with information provided by local township or city government offices, but then updated as individuals move into or away from the local community.

The other maintenance point for a remote access solution is a list of network addresses—either IP, or URL, or both—that needs to be accurately accounted

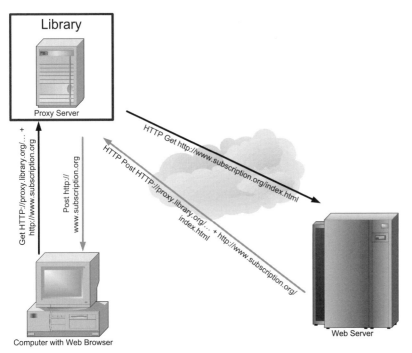

Figure 6-4   Diagram of Proxy Server Library Use for Network Authentication

for in the configuration of VPN and proxy server technologies. Such data up-keep efforts may be the responsibility of the ERM staff, but probably consist of collaborative work between ERM and computer systems administrative staff. The ERM portion of this responsibility is part of the steps and processes out-lined in Figure 6–1, but the ERM workflow also needs to intersect with that of those individuals managing the library's computer infrastructure.

Measuring the Value of Library Information Technologies

To demonstrate the important role that remote access technologies play in li-brary services, we will consider a familiar e-metrics report. Table 6–5 shows with local library e-metrics from Library C the amount of network use for the ten most frequently used full-text e-journal titles that are part of Library C's vir-tual collection. We have seen the data in Table 6–5 used previously to answer questions of library activity and licensed access restrictions. Now consider this data in terms of the value of a library's technology infrastructure. As has been pointed out before, this table illustrates that for this library, most users prefer to access these titles from a wide variety of computer networks located beyond the library's physical boundaries and computing facilities. If this library lacked the

Table 6-5 Amount of Network Use for the Ten Most Frequently Used Full-Text E-Journal Titles

Title	Unique Networked Devices	% Usage From Computers Inside Organizational Network	% Usage From Computers Outside Organizational Network	% Usage From Computers Inside Library Network	% Usage From Computers Outsideof Library Network
Nature	1541	54.91%	45.09%	2.21%	97.79%
The Journal of Biological Chemistry	979	52.46%	47.54%	0.60%	99.40%
New England Journal of Medicine	1360	51.42%	48.58%	9.30%	90.70%
Cell	1084	54.77%	45.23%	1.89%	98.11%
Proceedings of the National Academy of Sciences of the United States of America	1010	57.06%	42.94%	0.73%	99.27%
Science	918	53.81%	46.19%	1.19%	98.81%
Biochemistry	516	59.93%	40.07%	1.19%	98.81%
Journal of Immunology	342	60.29%	39.71%	0.53%	99.47%
Journal of the American Medical Association	670	44.22%	55.78%	15.17%	84.83%
Lancet	594	46.45%	53.55%	3.89%	96.11%

Table 6-6 Expansion of the Library Operating Hours with the Shift from Print to Digital

Title	Unique Network Addresses	% of Use During Open Hours	% of Use During Closed Hours
Nature	1541	88.01%	11.99%
The Journal of Biological Chemistry	979	88.77%	11.23%
New England Journal of Medicine	1360	94.07%	5.93%
Cell	1084	85.52%	14.48%
Proceedings of the National Academy of Sciences of the United States of America	1010	89.16%	10.84%
Science	918	88.73%	11.27%
Biochemistry	516	89.58%	10.42%
Journal of Immunology	342	90.62%	9.38%
Journal of the American Medical Association	670	92.66%	7.34%
Lancet	594	91.60%	8.40%

technology infrastructure capable of supporting this prolific and varied remote access external from the library, users would be forced to physically enter the library to gain access to resources, thus reducing the efficiency of the host institution's business and research activities.

We have also seen from other local e-metrics reports, as shown in Table 6–6, that the shift in library collection emphasis from paper to digital can expand library operating hours. In order for all of this network activity to take place during hours in which the library is not physically accessible, the library's computer and network infrastructure needs to be developed and maintained so that the library can continue providing an expected level of information access service even when its physical facilities are considered closed.

Such user service levels from the library necessitate certain degrees of electrical power, data storage, and hardware redundancy to avoid having users encounter computer failures. Perhaps a local community or research institution may not consider the data and services provided by a library to be as mission critical as those that make up the financial and governmental units of a particular organization or entity. Nevertheless, libraries now need to consider how their data and access infrastructure can be designed to support users at all hours of the day, every day of the year. So in reviewing a library's budget, we need to recalculate the technology expenditures by determining the importance of a library's data and services. The old definition of water and fire disasters oc-curring within the physical library storage facilities for print materials now has to be recast in terms of the library's ability to assure information access continu-ity. Many of the same business continuity plans implemented by large corpora-tions and financial institutions can and should be adapted and applied to libraries and their technology infrastructure. Such practices should consider ex-penditures in hardware, software, staffing, training, along with that needed for data backup and disaster recovery procedures.

Connecting the Price of Access, Presentation, and ERM

While our review so far has focused on the technologies of network access, we still need to consider the technologies of information presentation, including search and retrieval. Although it can be demonstrated that the issues of infor-mation delivery and subscription management are distinct in the minds of li-brary users, these two issues are very closely intertwined by their need for improved library ERM staff workflow. In terms of electronic resource access, li-braries need to reflect on the methods which can best deliver their electronic subscriptions and content to their patrons. As libraries increase their electronic holdings, new systems and search engines ought to be developed so that the public can easily find links to a wide variety of resources. A broad search of li-brary Web sites illustrates how various systems have been used in order to pres-ent this dizzying array of e-resources in a logical manner so that library patrons can find what they want quickly and efficiently. Some libraries have organized their e-journal and e-database collections by classifying them in subject or keyword-specific Web pages. Other sites offer lengthy alphabetical listings of journal and database titles. Another alternative has been to create a database, separate from the library OPAC, of e-databases, e-books, and e-journals search-able by subject and title keywords.

When one considers the number and complexity of the technological consid-erations and components, it should become apparent how far technology costs really extend. Library administrators now need to include in their budgets the price of purchasing and licensing the technology for information access and securing the proper amount of skilled staffing expertise to implement and man-age it. In the business sector, e-commerce initiatives require software and hard-ware to build a digital infrastructure and are a source of recurring business costs. Companies need to take advantage of the latest features added to their ex-isting applications and performance enhancements found in newer computer and network hardware in order to remain competitive. Good information tech-nology know-how, whether found within the company's staff or outsourced, needs to be kept up-to-date of technological advances, therefore requiring fre-quent training and skill upgrades.

The same principles of infrastructure purchases and computer support staffing need to be equally accounted for in library budgets. Depending upon the size and scope of the digital collections, the number and variety of library users, and the level of access service a library expects to provide, a library will somehow have to employ some combination of skilled computer technicians, computer programmers, as well as database, network, and system administrators. These individuals will also need continuous education in order to implement and keep abreast of advancements in computer technologies. Without doing so, a library risks falling behind the technology curve, thereby becoming an obsolete and less valued information resource as it can no longer compete and meet the needs of its user constituency.

Summary and Conclusions

The past three chapters have focused on the needs for libraries to investigate and analyze local library e-metrics. We have seen the importance of e-metrics in their application to two general categories. The first is the use of e-metrics to demonstrate the impact of the digital publishing revolution on both library operations and user expectations. The second is the analysis and application of e-metrics as guidance for the current operating paradigm shift occurring in the modern library. What the various e-metrics examples examined have underscored is the gap between the past and present. Examination of local library e-metrics clearly shows that what may be considered by some to be appropriate past library workflow, services, and resources really needs to be modified and enhanced within libraries in order to meet today's library user expectations and do business with the current digital publishing industry. It has hopefully become clear that without the use of library e-metrics at the local level, libraries will find it increasingly difficult to manage and evolve in the Information Age.

Now that it has become apparent how critical e-metrics can be to library management and operations, we can begin investigating how libraries go about the process of capturing and analyzing e-metrics on their own. The next portion of this book will take us through a series of discussions on the technical and administrative considerations that surround e-metrics implementations. As with the preceding chapters, the forthcoming examination will offer examples and diagrams of the complexities that are intrinsic to local e-metrics collection and study.

Notes

1. searchenginewatch.com/searchday/article.php/3296341 retrieved July 14, 2004.
2. Newsmap is an application that visually reflects the constantly changing landscape of the Google News news aggregator. A treemap visualization algorithm helps display the enormous amount of information gathered by the aggregator. Treemaps are traditionally space-constrained visualizations of information. Newsmap's objective takes that goal a step further and provides a tool to divide information into quickly recognizable bands which, when presented together, reveal underlying patterns in news reporting across cultures and within news segments in constant change around the globe.

   Newsmap does not pretend to replace the googlenews aggregator. It's objective is to simply demonstrate visually the relationships between data and the unseen patterns in news media. It is not thought to display an unbiased view of the news, on the contrary it is thought to ironically accentuate the bias of it." From www.marumushi .com/apps/newsmap/index.cfm retrieved on July 14, 2004.
3. "A Web Hub for Developing Administrative Metadata for Electronic Resource Management," www.library.cornell.edu/cts/elicensestudy/home.html.

Part III
How Do Libraries Build Local E-Metrics?

Overview

A significant portion of this book has so far been dedicated to the evolution of various e-metrics standards and their respective relevance to a number of important decisions made at both the administrative and service levels of library operations. It is now hopefully clear as to why libraries must monitor the amount of activity on their Web site, Web OPAC, and other networked resources in order to supplement other traditional library use studies, such as gate counts and circulation volume. Information available from the E-Metrics Instructional System (EMIS)[1] by the Information Institute substantiates this need for libraries to produce usage statistics on e-resources and e-services. But what was also revealed in the chapters from Part II was how real-world applications of vendor and local e-metrics should account for measurement variability due to technical, human, and financial resources within any given library environment.

After understanding the application of e-metrics to the management of modern libraries, it is only logical for a reader to begin asking questions about the actual methods and technologies required to acquire and process e-metrics data prior to presenting such data in a comprehensible format with pertinence to library service assurance. The answers to such questions appear in this third and final section of our book. The next three chapters will address the actual technological implementation of e-metrics data capture and processing, in addition to the variety and complexities of project planning considerations in conjunction with both the computing infrastructure and staffing expertise available both inside and outside any given library. In a sense, one may consider this the "how-to" portion of our e-metrics book. By following a format similar to that of the previous section, we will show the degrees to which the three types of library environments defined in Chapter 3 can successfully incorporate combinations of e-metrics solutions according to various criteria and resource parameters.

Chapter 7: E-Metrics and E-Resources: Designing Solutions to Capture Usage Statistics on E-Journals, Databases, E-Books and Digital Documents: This chapter will focus on how to technically acquire and process actionable e-metrics starting from vendor statistics to the development of a multi-level local e-metrics solution. As vendor and local statistics on e-resources have been found to reveal very similar usage patterns, it seems that an integrative view of vendor-produced data and local data represents a positive step towards more actionable e-metrics.[2] The discussion presents in detail the components and reporting options of four different technical e-metrics solutions, from minimal to increasing complexity. We will in turn investigate the technical issues associated with the justification, implementation, and benefits of each solution, all of which can assist a library in achieving greater consistency and comparisons across both vendor-supplied and locally-acquired e-metrics. Additional consideration will be given to other data sources that can provide greater context to usage trends when incorporated with local library e-metrics acquisition.

Chapter 8: E-metrics and Infrastructure: Assessing Servers, Workstations, and Other Technical Considerations: Following the technical steps and details of what is required of a library e-metrics project, this chapter will focus on other important technical requirements and considerations that directly impact the success of each of the four aforementioned e-metrics solutions. In this review of the broader considerations associated with e-metrics technical aspects, we uncover e-metrics data issues common to vendor-supplied and local library capturing methods, such as the storage of generated reports. Still there are some problems specifically associated with homegrown e-metrics solutions, such as the multiplicity of possible server log sources, the dilemma of "whether to build or buy" the transaction log analysis (TLA) portion of the project, as well as what to invest in data processing units. Beyond the inevitable obstacles, we discover in this chapter how the integration of external data can ultimately enhance the context of any e-metrics data source. By incorporating additional data such as impact factor, number of available articles, or date of availability, we show how to create deeper e-metrics on title use, thus avoiding oversimplified reporting interpretations. We also demonstrate how to enrich the reporting granularity of local e-metrics beyond that of vendor statistics by incorporating network address mapping and user demographics. The chapter offers insight into the open possibilities in e-metrics, allowing one to fully grasp the level of e-metrics sophistication achievable in the best equipped libraries.

Chapter 9: E-Metrics and Staffing: Creating Teams and Defining the Project: With an understanding of the technical implementation and possibilities associated with library e-metrics initiatives, we detail the administrative guidelines and staffing needs required for developing an overall e-metrics strategy. Whether the e-metrics data were internally or externally generated, their collection, processing, and interpretation can still be very problematic, creating issues related to methodology, definitions, technology, application, data collection, implementation, leadership, and education. Because positive e-metrics outcomes are truly viable if built on shared vision and collaborative work, in this chapter we explain the role of library administration in the success of an e-metrics project.[3] The discussion will cover topics ranging from the creation of an e-metrics team, the empowerment of librarians, the collaboration with IT personnel, to the creation of sound e-metrics policies. Essentially, a successful e-metrics project should be viewed as a constructive contribution to a library's Electronic Resources Management (ERM) processes.

Notes

1. www.ii.fsu.edu/emis/.
2. Duy and Vaughan 2003.
3. McClure 1999.

7

E-Metrics and E-Resources: Designing Solutions to Capture Usage Statistics on E-Journals, Databases, E-Books, and Digital Documents

With this chapter, we begin a series of rather technical explanations and investigations that cover potential methods for capturing the data that was used to generate the various reports examined in the previous section of the book. The goal of these next two chapters is to detail the planning, technical justifications, and steps that comprise e-metrics data capture and processing. While the focus of these chapters will be technical in nature and probably of greater interest to individuals responsible at systems librarian, programmer, or network administrator levels, efforts are made to make concepts understandable for others interested and impacted by the use and application of e-metrics.

Earlier chapters examined how the recent shift emphasizing digital library collections and services requires new metrics and methods in order to capture the usage of networked resources.[1] In addition to the library performance measures reviewed in Chapter 2, the E-Metrics Instructional System (EMIS) Web site[2] suggests that libraries now consider quantitative surveys, sampling, qualitative methods, transaction log analysis (TLA) or innovative data collection software for improved performance reporting. The administrative and operational applications of such performance measures have already been demonstrated through further analysis of numerous scenarios and examples examined in the previous chapters. But the question still remains: How does one actually go about acquiring and processing the raw data needed to generate meaningful reports applicable to various aspects of library management?

This book began with a quick overview and definition of transaction log analysis associated with data mining of Web server logs. In Chapter 3 we examined some of the reporting mechanisms associated with some vendor-supplied e-metrics reports, showing how information producers, vendors, and publishers process data from TLA, including data definitions and counting parameters.

Yet, even within the brief evolution of the e-metrics field, actions have been taken by information consumers who have opted to mine their own Web server logs through TLA in order to generate supplementary statistical use data. It is important to note that current methods associated with e-metrics data capture and processing, regardless of whether vendor- or locally-generated, are not without shortcomings, for the importance and failings of the TLA technique have been widely detailed in both the e-commerce and library literature.

Therefore, the following technical discussions and explanations will detail the elements, options, and considerations important to libraries in their quest for more informative and reliable e-metrics through the development of library-centric e-metrics projects for e-resources. We will only consider measuring the use and value of e-resources consisting mainly of e-journals, databases, e-books, and other digital documents. After analyzing the possibility of basic Web metrics in libraries, there follows a discussion of the strengths and weaknesses of the vendor-supplied statistics. Finally, we explore the different levels of solutions for locally-collected e-metrics and their potential implementation within the three library environment categories described in Chapter 3, reiterated in Tables 3–12, 3–13 and 3–14 on pages 47 and 48.

Even though the more elaborate local solutions detailed may only be feasible in the most advanced libraries akin to the Library C environment, we believe that even entities similar to that of Libraries A and B should nevertheless consider reading through the entire chapter in order to better gauge the viability of future initiatives and outcomes. Ultimately, one should consider how even local e-metrics efforts supported by a limited number of libraries could assist in improving the understanding of the new digital library environment through constructive debates and eventually lead to fruitful collaborations by sharing ideas and resources.

Analyze Basic Web Metrics in Libraries— Local Solution Level 1

It is at this point that we now explore how the data capture process of e-metrics actually begins. Recalling that the evolution of e-metrics began with the analysis of Web site traffic, and considering that the primary online entry point for library users requesting e-resources and e-services is the library's Web site, we can then say that library e-metrics, taken in a broad sense, really starts with the Web traffic analysis on the library's Web site. And although our performance and usage focus will be confined to virtual visits to the pages of the e-resources section of a library Web site, even such limited basic Web metrics, described in Table 7–1, offers libraries the chance to:

- experience firsthand the promises and the pitfalls of Web analytics, and
- help them formulate reasonable expectations for e-metrics on e-resources

Table 7–1 Characteristics of a Local Solution (Level 1) for Basic Web Metrics

	Basic Solution (Level 1)		
Method/Feasibility by Library Category	Main Objectives	Possible Solutions	Infrastructure Involved
Basic Web statistics / A, B, C	General Web metrics, no custom development	Web analytics software: freeware, shareware, commercial	Library Web server, Web OPAC server, Other local servers, Workstation

Library Web Site Analysis: General Statistics

Although current technologies make it possible for most libraries to at least generate basic Web statistics, initial requirements for gathering the raw statistical data must include:

- The access to the library's Web server logs.
- The installation of some Web traffic analysis software.

Libraries that do not host their Web site on a local server, such as those of Library A's category, should ask to obtain these Web statistics directly from their external network service and Internet Web server provider. For other libraries with environments perhaps more like those of Libraries B and C, such Web server logs are probably readily available for processing through one or more Web analytics applications. Having received the server logs, libraries then can choose from a variety of available Web analytics programs, ranging from open-source freeware to high-end commercial applications.

Typically the process of generating the Web statistics through Web analytics applications is carried out by a Web master, a systems librarian or by other IT personnel working with or for the library. We will not endorse any particular Web analytics application, but rather provide examples of how a few of these solutions operate and compare their respective reporting outputs. The actual steps required of the Web analytics process consist of the following tasks:

1. Install the selected Web analytics application, according to the setup instructions, on a workstation or on a server if authorizations are granted.
2. Prepare the log file. The server log(s) can be downloaded on the workstation or left on the server depending on the application's capabilities.
3. Run the Web analytics program with the transaction log filename as the input parameter. Some of these applications can be launched from the operating system command line, while others have more user-friendly graphic interfaces for application management.

4. Retrieve the generated usage statistics reports. Most Web analytics programs display the reports in a Web browser, while the professional Web analytics applications offer many other alternate formats for the report output.

The actual details of Web site analytics have already been covered in other publications,[3] so we will instead continue to focus on the capture of e-metrics for e-resources. Nevertheless, it is important to remember that in order to use any Web traffic analysis software, one needs to provide a server log with a standardized format known as Common Log Format (CLF) or Extended Common Log Format (ECLF). We have already examined an example of a typical log in CLF (see Chapter 1, Table 1–2), and it is fairly typical for today's Web servers to be configured to generate (E)CLF access log files by default. More detailed descriptions of various transaction log formats can be found at the World Wide Web Consortium (W3C) Web site.[4]

Figure 7–1 shows how two different Web analytics applications process and analyze the same server log, providing a comparison of page view, visit/session and unique visitor counts for a month of activity on a library Web site. The log analysis shown in Figure 7–1 was conducted with Wusage 8.0 by Boutell Inc., which is a multi-platform Web analytics application that can be acquired with a 30–day free trial period; and WebTrends Enterprise Suite by NetIQ, one of the leaders in the Web metrics market at a price (January 2005) ranging from $495 for small businesses to $9,995 for Fortune 2000 enterprises. When deciding which Web analytics application most benefits your library, one should thoroughly consider both implementation requirements and reporting outputs through potential analytics tests. Before investing in more expensive analytics solutions, a library may prefer to start its investigation with a trial of free Web

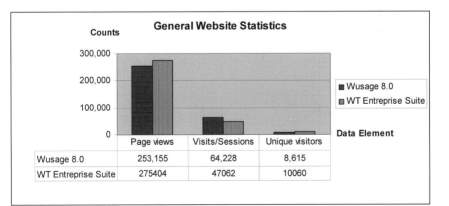

	Page views	Visits/Sessions	Unique visitors
Wusage 8.0	253,155	64,228	8,615
WT Entreprise Suite	275404	47062	10060

Figure 7-1 Comparison between the General Web Statistics from Two Web Analytics Applications

analytics programs such as Analog. The commercially-available analytics packages vary greatly in both pricing and capabilities as recently published by Network Computing.[5]

In reviewing Figure 7–1, it becomes clear how different analytics solutions show:

- Discrepancies between numbers generated by each program, which is in turn due to
- Differences in e-metrics data element terminology

Since Figure 7–1 illustrates a variation in relatively general Web site usage reporting between two different analytics applications, one can begin to understand the potential for analogous deviations in vendor-supplied e-metrics reports and the need for e-metrics standards. But even with such apparent reporting deviation, we can clearly identify similarities in the global e-metrics picture as reported by both software solutions. Yet, the remaining primary problem is that both analyses are too general to inform us about the exact use of our e-resources. Although the general performance measures seen in Figure 7–1 can prove somewhat useful, greater benefits can be found in additional information present in the server logs that has yet remained uncharted.

Library Web Site Analysis: Most Accessed Pages

To further understand the shortcomings inherent in the use of basic e-metrics, we turn to a study realized at the Norris Medical Library University of Southern California Los Angeles, California and published in 2001 by Benjes and Brown.[6] The study details how the number of Web site "hits" to this library's Web site increased dramatically after the site was restructured from static Web pages to include a more interactive database-driven presentation for e-resources. The results of this study underscore two important points. First, it can be clearly demonstrated that changes of the Web site correlates with changes in usage patterns, so that while the number of available titles grew from 300 to 1,500, fivefold increase, the hit counts went from 2,000–3,000 to more than 125,000, or forty times more. And even though both the librarians and library users obviously benefited from a more flexible technological Web site design, ultimately the high hit count was attributed not only to the greater number of available e-resources over time, but also to Web usability and Web design enhancements[7] geared towards the end-users needs. The study's second point highlights the manner in which Web traffic analysis was applied to measuring the amount of activity generated on the library Web site with an emphasis on electronic resources. In early 2001, the measure of use by "hit counts" was the best quantitative method available to libraries willing to venture into the emerging field of e-metrics. But as we will see in our next example,

Table 7–2 Summarized Report Comparison between Wusage 8.0 and WebTrends Entreprise Suite™ for the Most Accessed Pages on a Library's Web Site

Pages	Wusage 8.0 (WU_8.0)			WebTrends Enterprise Suite (WTE)		
	Rank	Entry Count	%	Rank	% of Total	Visitor Sessions
E-journals	4	1,475	2.7	4	9.50%	3799
Databases	6	853	1.56	6	2.27%	910
E-books	10	115	0.21	7	0.90%	360
Catalog	12	107	0.2	10	0.36%	145

the progress since then in e-metrics and in Web traffic analysis applications have given us the opportunity to perform measurements that are more elaborate than simple hit counts.

In Table 7–2 we continue with a summarized comparison between the output from Wusage 8.0 and WebTrends Enterprise Suite™, this time viewing another portion of a Web metrics report so that it focuses on the most accessed pages, or entry pages for the same log and the same month sampled before. A more detailed report from these two applications can be found in Appendix 1 for those interested in expanded analysis and comparisons.

As in Figure 7–1, Table 7–2 underscores the differences of the two applications in terms of both the report presentation and terminology. Yet, both reports help one to see that visits to Web pages related to e-resources are highly ranked by both programs. A comparison between the access numbers for e-resource pages are presented in Figure 7–2.

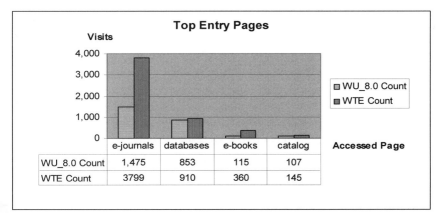

Figure 7-2 Comparison between the Most Accessed Pages from Two Web Analytics Applications

Even with the clear discrepancies between counts reported by the two applications, both analytics programs capture consistent global trends. These results show that Web pages containing links to subscribed e-journals and databases are the most requested by the library users accessing this library Web site. In addition, the Web pages that present links to e-books and the catalog, although exhibiting much lower counts, are nevertheless among the top list of most accessed Web pages and thus certainly merit further study for future enhancements.

One could ask: what is the interest of the basic Web metrics that we have just reviewed if they cannot tell us anything really valuable about the use of our e-resources? The answer is that such studies help us:

- Learn more about the type of traffic and activity on the library's Web site through statistics about the most active days, hours, downloaded documents, active IPs, most popular pages, etc.
- Detect fundamental usage and popularity trends while also pointing out exceptions and anomalies in usage expectations
- Understand the limitations of e-metrics and set realistic expectations for the quality and applicability of such performance measures
- Realize that vendors, publishers, aggregators alike are confronted with the very same issues when trying to collect use statistics from their own servers

Because the general library Web analytics reviewed so far cannot reveal usage trends for particular subscriptions to digital titles, it would seem reasonable then for libraries to depend upon subscription vendors and publishers for vendor-supplied reports, such as those seen in our investigation of COUNTER standards in Chapter 3. But even though vendors of e-resources are the ones who own the server logs that can record the specific e-resource title requests from library users, libraries must still remain concerned with issues that have always been in the center of the e-metrics debate: accessibility, inconsistency, and reliability of vendors' reports.[8]

Evaluate Vendor-Supplied Statistics

The importance of e-metrics to the information community was covered in Chapter 2 in a review of the e-metrics initiatives started by the ICOLC, followed by other e-metrics projects such as COUNTER, ARL E-metrics, and NISO Z39.7. And at this point in time, COUNTER (Counting Online Usage of Networked Electronic Resources) stands as the best e-metrics standard resulting from the international support from librarians, publishers, vendors, and intermediaries, all agreeing upon the urgent need for better standardization of online usage statistics. The current reporting standards still, however, focus on e-metrics for e-journals and databases, reflecting both the historical and economical importance of those two e-resource types. At the same time, one must be aware that despite substantial standardization progress, a study of the recent trends in usage reports found eighteen vendor reports to be COUNTER-ready in August 2003, yet also revealed many persistent unresolved issues such as non-standardized report formats, data reliability, disparity of delivery and accessibility methods, lack of documentation, increased amount of data leading to complex interface, and new trends towards the creation of access fees and e-metrics out-sourcing by vendors.[9] Even though COUNTER is the *de facto* standard for e-resources e-metrics, now is the time for the library community to shape the future standards in this area.

The various reporting examples and administrative analyzes in Part II of the book demonstrated how any library concerned with the world of e-metrics for digital collections must begin by taking advantage of the standardized data available from vendors, even if a library can capture its own local digital collection usage data. So how is a library supposed to manage, process, and ultimately utilize the vendor-supplied reports? Any approach taken with vendor-supplied data should include realistic expectations and proceed with caution, patience, and well-defined methods. A good educational and investigative starting point for such an approach can be found at the E-metrics Instructional System (EMIS), developed by the Information Institute and funded by the U.S. Institute of Museum and Library Services. Based on the NISO 39.7 library statistics standard on e-resources and e-services, and targeted towards public librarians, state library agency staff and library consortia staff. The EMIS covers a much larger scope of e-metrics than those addressed by COUNTER, including an introduction to e-metrics, training modules, and recommendations. Both EMIS and COUNTER initiatives provide excellent basic e-metrics platforms for libraries and further enrich the maturing field of e-metrics for the information community. Through the combined review of EMIS information and application of lessons learned from a thorough examination of vendor-supplied e-metrics reports, libraries can eventually better assess the local e-metrics projects needs in terms of staffing, procedures, policies, technology, and instruction.

Data Collection

Now we should review the requirements for a library depending upon vendor-supplied e-metrics in order to have usage information with detail greater than that found in basic local Web metrics on e-resources, like those seen in Figure 7–1 and Table 7–1. Of course the first task is to collect the e-metrics reports from each vendor. But in the process of obtaining such reports, a library must account for the following constraints:

- *Accessibility issues*: the reports must be "harvested" from multiple sources, most certainly using different interfaces, and requiring individual id and password report access authentication.

- *Multiple delivery methods*: the reports can be emailed, printed, displayed, or downloaded from the vendors' site.
- *Report format disparities*: the reports can be retrieved in text, Excel, HTML or PDF format.

Obviously, the procedures associated with report acquisition and retrieval raise many questions about the staff time involved in the necessary local manipulations of these various vendor reports. Thus handling vendor reports requires a set of standard procedures, documented task assignments, and established assignment deadlines. Additionally, the variety of report information sources and formats must be corrected systematically to facilitate the future exploitation of this acquired e-metrics data. Assuming that this retrieval phase has been completed for the vendor reports that are the most critical for the library, we then move to the data collation phase.

Data Collation

Collating a number of various e-metrics reports and sources requires the library to set rules and policies for handling the amassed data. These reports must ultimately be easily accessed by authorized library staff members. The analysis output must be organized in a logical way that is known to every member of the e-metrics task force. The major considerations for this stage of e-metrics initiatives are:

- A need for some form of a data repository: libraries with limited resources akin to Library A environments typically store their reports on shared network drives within a centralized location. Others, analogous to Libraries B and C, can set up a common database of vendor reports that can be easily queried (PALINET, NFAIS 2004). Many libraries tend to convert the reports in spreadsheets with applications such as Excel, in order to manipulate the data more easily. As reports vary in formats, staff time must again be devoted to this cumbersome task.
- Information overload: the amount of reporting data available from vendors has significantly increased in the recent years not only because of vendor advancements but also as a result of the vague specifications for the key e-metrics data elements expected by libraries. Over time, the cumulative effect of this situation leads to an unmanageable volume of information. As stated by the Information Institute on its EMIS Web site: "There are a large number of e-metrics available for public libraries to collect. Clearly, it is not feasible for libraries to collect and report data for all of these services and resources."

One way that some libraries manage to deal with this report collation step is to focus on reports for a defined scope consisting of a limited number of vendors and titles.

Data Analysis

As extensively demonstrated in Chapters 5 and 6, e-metrics data are crucial for collection management and library administration. Once the vendors' reports and data are locally organized, librarians and library administrators still have to make sense of the compiled data in order to reach consensus on various library management decisions. Unfortunately, the interpretation and administrative application of typical e-metrics reports is far from obvious. Consider the following non-exhaustive list of e-metrics obstacles reported in past and recent publications:[10]

- Lack of reliability: for example only some reports provide the number of turnaways (rejected sessions) for e-resources, even if the access license associated with the subscription does not include limits to the number of concurrent accesses.
- Report unavailability due to technical problems.
- Data mix-up between libraries: reports for one library being exchanged for the report for another.
- Lack of standard definitions, methods, and practices across vendors. For example, in 2002 Elsevier released a white paper detailing the filters used for the Science Direct log data. It is still unclear as to whether such documented TLA practices are the industry norm because publishers seldom disclose, even though such their approaches even though it could also lead to better report standardization.
- Reporting standards non-compliance observed with some vendors' e-metrics. As in any given evolving technical field, we naturally cannot expect every single vendor to be immediately compliant with the evolving standards. In practical terms, however, this is a major hindrance to data comparison across vendor-supplied reports.
- Lack of usage and reporting comparability across e-resource types. Obviously the next step for COUNTER is to consider the data elements for other e-resources such as e-books or other digital documents. But even with the currently available data and usage definitions, would it really make sense to compare e-journals and databases, under the same subject area for example, based on the number of searches from JR4 and DB3?

After considering the various limitations of both standard Web analytics applications and vendor-supplied e-metrics reports, we can see that libraries have become motivated to begin producing their own local e-metrics because of:

- A need for e-metrics terminology and output consistency and comparability across vendors and subscription resource types.
- A requirement for a centralized e-metrics source of data.

- A hope for greater control over the e-metrics data production process.
- Some method of verification and comparison with vendors' usage patterns.
- An interest in higher resolution usage data, including statistics with user demographics and network location distribution.
- A desire to further identify specific sites, links, and e-resource subscriptions requested from the library networked resources.

We have already concluded that the basic Web metrics offered by most Web analytics solutions could not specify which e-resource links were directly accessed by library users from the library pages. So in order to move beyond the types of general assessments and trends seen in Figure 7–1 and Table 7–2, it becomes important to determine which actual e-journals and databases at the title level were requested and, eventually with more detailed examination, by whom. Such augmentation of the general Web analytics requires a mechanism that:

1. captures the visit to the library's e-resources,
2. associates that visit to the selected e-resource title,
3. somehow stores that visit to an identified title before the request is sent to the e-resource provider.

The desired mechanism meeting these three criteria can only be achieved within the technical infrastructure at the local library level.

Explore Local E-Metrics Initiatives

It is at this point that we turn our focus towards a variety of library-developed solutions, which will be examined in order of their increased sophistication, designed to supplement the vendors' data with locally-collected data. These in-house solutions are probably most feasible for implementation within B- and C-type library scenarios. Unfortunately, the infrastructure of libraries like Library A offers little chance to deploy any of the developments to be presented here as the demands associated with these solutions require some system programming and authorization to install the click-through or redirection script on the library Web server.

Quick Review of Some Local E-Metrics Solutions

Table 7–3 illustrates the local e-metrics data collection approaches taken by a variety of library types. Our table shows that the most popular library method for locally capturing online usage statistics combines the creation of a "click-through/redirection" script with transaction log analysis (TLA) through home-grown programming solutions or Web analytics software.

Although a lot more informative than the basic local e-metrics (Level 1: Basic

Table 7-3 Non-Exhaustive List of Local E-Metrics Initiatives in Libraries

Library	Type	Solution	Reference	Comments
Arlington Heights Memorial	Public	click-through / redirection script+custom log post-processing (spreadsheet)+database (Access)	Bill Pardue (2001)	US
Purdue University	Academic	click-through / redirection script+Web analytics freeware (Analog)	Amy S. Van Epps (2001)	US
Vanderbilt University	Academic	click-through / redirection script+custom log post-processing+spreadsheet/database	Marshall Breeding (2002)	US
London Business School	Academic	click-through / redirection script+Relational Database (PostGreSQL)	Jonathan Eaton (2002)	UK
University of Queensland	Academic	Vendor utility+data formatting script+Relational database (MySQL)	Heather Todd, Lisa Kruesi (2002)	Australia
North Carolina State University	Academic	Electronic counter (details not specified)	Joanna Duy, Liwen Vaughan (2003)	US
Pennsylvania University	Academic	click-through / redirection page+Data extraction script (Perl)+Relational database with SQL	Joe Zucca (2002)	US
State University of New York College at Cortland	Academic	Ezproxy+Data extraction script+Access and SQL databases	Karen Coombs, Bob Edgecomb (2003)	US
University of Montana-Missoula	Academic	Click-through method+EzProxy+Data formatting script+Web analytics freeware (Webalizer)	Sue Samson, Sebastian Derry, Holly Eggleston (2004)	US

Web traffic analysis), this intermediate solution (Level 2) for local e-metrics does not answer these questions:

Q1. How could we allow remote access to the e-resources knowing that users are greatly in favor of that type of visit?
Q2. How could we get a more accurate count of unique visitors?
Q3. How could we capture bookmarked direct accesses to the vendors' Web site?

In order to deal with those concerns, we need to go to the next level of a local e-metrics solution.

Intermediate Local E-Metrics—Local Solution Level 2

In addition to the basic Web metrics seen in Figures 7–1, 7–2, and Table 7–1 (solution Level 1), an intermediate library similar to Library B could implement the following solution described in Table 7–4:

- Click-through method + TLA with off-the-shelf Web analytics or home-grown application.

Click-Through Script

There are two main objectives in implementing a click-through method:

1. capturing the external resource accessed by the user and record accessed information in a log, then
2. redirecting the user to the requested resource

After capturing the user's URL request, the redirection script seamlessly redirects the user to the target resource. Even with the addition of this script, the entire hyperlink and redirection operation is totally transparent to the user and gives the library additional raw e-metrics data can be mined and analyzed further.

Some examples of redirection scripts, mostly written in Perl programming

Table 7–4 Characteristics of an Intermediate Solution (Level 2) for Local E-Metrics

Intermediate Solution (Level 2)			
Method/Feasibility by Library category	Main Objectives	Possible Solutions	Infrastructure Involved
Click-through/redirection script/B, C	Capture accessed titles	Same as Level 1 Some degree of custom programming	Same as Level 1 + Possibly a logging database server

language, can easily be found on the Web[11] or in peer-reviewed literature.[12] The internal process of such scripts transparently

a. intercepts the hyperlink clicked by the user
b. records the "clicked hyperlink" transaction and add useful information—in Common Log Format or very similar to it—into an alternate log file different from the access log generated by the Web server
c. sends the user to the intended requested URL

One variation of the click-through script, written in PHP, is found in Appendix 2. It differs slightly from the scripts previously cited above in that it enriches the typical Web server access log rather than creating an alternate log file. Using such a script increases TLA simplicity when combined with the development of custom log parsing rather than depending on the use of Web traffic analysis software.

When using a click-through script, one must also modify every URL that the library would like to monitor for access. Fortunately, this is not an onerous task as modern Web design editors and other powerful text editors, such as VI, make it possible to globally add the click-through script name to every URL link. Mass modification of URLs in the 856 field of the MARC records of the OPAC is, however, less straightforward and should be done with caution. A cost/benefit analysis is highly recommended before proceeding with such an editing project of MARC catalog records.

To better demonstrate the nature of the URL modification associated with click-through implementations, the typical non-redirected link in HTML on a Web page is:

```
<a href="http://www.somesite.net">Some site</a>
```

The non-redirected link directly sends the user to the target URL and bypasses the library's servers. The addition of a click-through script alters the hyperlink format to include the redirection, now appearing as:

```
<a href=http://"www.library.org"/click-through.php?url=http://www.some
site.net>Some site</a>
```

The functionality derived with new formatting of the altered redirected link causes the user transaction to first be sent to the library's Web site and recorded in the Web server log before being transparently redirected to the vendor's Web site. Figure 7–3 demonstrates the sequence of events with the click-through technique.

A key point in this progression of network transactions is that the access to the "modified" link in itself constitutes one visit associated to the selected online title. And more importantly, the combination of the click-through script and the modified URL allow the whole transaction to be stored in the transaction

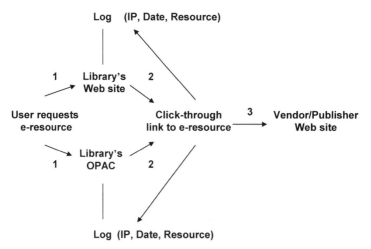

Log (IP, Date, Resource)

Figure 7-3 Schematic Access Sequence to an E-Resource Using a "Click-Through" Script

log of the Web server, whether it be that of the library's main Web server or the Web OPAC server. Table 7–5 illustrates the sequence of events and the potential transaction data that could be collected thanks to the "click-through" method. Now that the purpose of the click-through technique has been clarified, we need to understand how we apply it to capturing the use of e-resources.

What Identifiers Do We Need for Local E-Metrics?

Three major identifiers form the basis of local e-metrics data collection: the e-resource title, the e-resource provider, and the e-resource user. Collecting such data elements enables one to answer the deceptively simple question: "What title is used and by whom?"

Title

Library patrons typically search for an online resource first by title, accessing the main library's Web site, then looking for the desired title by the available locating options (alphabetical listing, organization by format type, by subject, etc.) or searching the library's online catalog. It follows then that a system must be created so that the various server logs can track the selected title access, thereby establishing e-metrics reports that ultimately retrieve the very same title with the correct usage counts. If a library implements a database-driven Web site, then the typically static link to a digital title can be replaced by a unique title identifier, or "title_ID". The use of unique title identifiers can also further reduce text string manipulations during the log parsing portion of TLA. In addition, the coding of the title, full title string or title_ID, ought to be transparent to the

Table 7–5 Potential E-Metrics Data Captured when Using the "Click-Through" Method

Steps	End-User/Patron Level	Library Systems Level	Potential E-Metrics Captured by the Library
Step 1	Access to the list of available e-resources through the library's Web site	Web page with links using "click-through" technique is loaded	
Step 2	Request for a specific title	The "get" transaction associated to the title is recorded in the Web log	– Virtual visit count for the selected title – Visitor identified by his/her IP address
Step 3		Virtual visitor forwarded to the e-resource Web site of its provider	

user on the Web site with the hypertext link including the full title string as in the examples below:

> Full title string = E-metrics%20Online%20Journal (%20 stands for blank space): <a href="http://www.libraryweb.org/click_through.php?title_id= E-metrics%20Online%20Journal&provider_id=DigitalPublisherInc&url =http:// www.DigitalPublisherInc.com/EOJ.html">**E-metrics Online Journal**</a>

and with Title_ID = 5:

> <a href="http://www.libraryweb.org/click_through.php?**title_id=5& provider_id=10**&url=http://www.DigitalPublisherInc.com/EOJ.html"> **E-metrics Online Journal**</a>

Another way to uniquely identify an e-resource, instead of a randomly generated unique title identifier, is to use the title's ISSN/ISBN. Unfortunately, this option would be limited only to serials titles and e-books, whereas other e-resources such as databases and other digital documents would require an alternate solution. Another issue associated with the ISSN/ISBN is the emergence of the electronic ISSN/ISBN or e-ISSN/ISBN[13] which is not yet widely utilized by many e-resource providers. Perhaps in the near future, adoption of the Digital Object Identifier (DOI)[14] will become universal, allowing for a unique identification system applicable to all e-resources types. But for the sake of simplifying our discussion, we will consider in our subsequent examples the locally generated title_ID.

Source

The log file should provide some way to identify the subscription title source in order to get distinct statistics for a title provided by multiple sources. For example, we must discriminate the usage numbers for a title like "American Heart Journal" that can be accessed through "MDConsult" or through "ScienceDirect." For the purposes of local e-metrics, we define a source as the provider of any given title. A provider can typically be a vendor or a publisher or a consortium. Parallel to methods for identifying the e-resource title, we identify a provider or source with its "provider_ID" in our custom click-through hyperlink solution. By combining the click-through hyperlink modification with a customized TLA technique, libraries can thereby optimize the accuracy of their electronic access counts through a higher degree of data resolution. This level of detail is not only useful in viewing the access trends for a single title made available through multiple providers, but also allows for the collection of statistical data on the various providers of e-resources. Although not as critical as the statistics on title use, observing the number of title visits by vendor or supplier can be informative for acquisitions and collection development purposes.

User

In order to gather high resolution e-metrics, one should also identify each user with a unique ID. The only way to truly answer the question: "Who uses our titles?" is to require all patrons to identify themselves when requesting an online title. In the case of e-resource access, that requirement is not only beneficial for e-metrics studies but also guarantees full compliance with licensing agreements. The latter cannot be precisely determined unless each patron has a unique identifier that can be verified against a list of authorized users. Finally, from the programming point of view, user authentication also provides a significant advantage in allowing for faster parsing of the logs by analyzing only those lines containing a valid ID field. A user ID can be, for example, a reader's barcode for a public library or a university ID in an academic setting. The main technical challenge for using a user ID is certainly the maintenance of an up-to-date patron database, for the level of accuracy and resolution of the e-metrics on users can only be as good as the quality of the patron database.

We should note at this point that unfortunately some libraries cannot opt for this user authentication solution enhancement; for them, e-metrics could instead track the user's machine IP address as a representation of the virtual visitor's ID. Although such a solution is undoubtedly inadequate for in-depth and high resolution e-metrics, it could still be used to reveal basic usage trends, similar to those seen in Figure 7–1. Due to the difficult setup and management of a patron database for e-metrics, genuine user authentication methods would be more likely implemented by Library C with local e-metrics solutions analogous to the Level 3, Advanced, and Level 4, Highly Advanced, options described later in this chapter.

Transaction Log Analysis (TLA)

So long as the click-through script seen above can generate a log in CLF (Common Log Format), the log analysis with redirection can be performed analogous to a basic Web metrics solution (Level 1) with Web analytics software. Like basic Web metrics analysis, redirected hyperlinks can still offer transaction statistics showing the most active IPs, referring Web pages, or browser versions. But the additional redirection incorporated into the modified hyperlink helps to establish additional data necessary for improved e-metrics reports that give the number of access counts per monitored link. To go beyond the capabilities of commercial Web analytics solutions, to increase data manipulation of the log file, and to account for customized transaction log formats, some libraries prefer to develop their own log parsing programs or import the raw data into a database for further processing as indicated in Table 7–4. Regardless of preferred approach, the core of any TLA procedure includes text parsing within the server log.

The general definition of the word "parsing" is the process of making sense of a sentence by breaking it down into words. Similarly, we parse the server log in order to extract every part of the entry that could give us some basic information related to any of the e-metrics data elements of particular interest. Given that every entry in the log is based on the same structure, whether in CLF or ECLF, and that the log could be of considerable size, the only reasonable option is to automate the TLA portion of the data mining process.

Whether we use an off-the-shelf log analyzer application or a tool designed in-house, the logic used to parse the log is fundamentally identical. The programming language may differ but they basically have the following pseudo-code:

```
/* Program local TLA */
Begin Program
     Open (Log file)
     Load_External_Data ()
     While not (<end of log file> or <condition met>) do
     | Begin
     |       If is_valid(line) then
     |       Begin
     |             (a) Clean_Up(line)
     |             (b) Break each line into its (E)CLF elements =
     |                 {IP,ID,Date,Request,Status,BytesSent} /*
     |                   CLF */
     |                    Or
     |                 {IP,ID,Date,Request,Status,BytesSent,
     |                   Referrer,Browser} /* ECLF */
```

```
|                  (c)  Build_Stats(element)
|         EndIf
|  EndWhile
   Close  (Log file)
   (d)  Integrate_External_Data(element)
   (e)  Present_Results  (element)

End  Program
```

We should first examine the *While* loop and leave the functions related to external data integration and analysis for later. The program is designed to read every single line of the log until the end of file is reached—that is until there is no more line to be read from the log file in input—or a given condition is met, for example end date parameter. A valid line is a log entry that has an (E)CLF structure with a HTTP status code 200 (OK) or 3xx (example 302=Redirected, 304=cached). The first function Clean_Up(line) gets rid of any unnecessary characters or irregularities. The cornerstone of the whole process is the second step (b) that extracts the basic elements that may be usable for e-metrics reporting purposes. The automation of that step is only possible if patterns or specific markers are identified within the log and if they are consistently and systematically marked as such throughout the entire log. The Build_Stats(element) stores the counts for each selected data element, for example IPs, dates, requests, status and so on. This function processes the raw information in the log with the hope of unveiling hidden trends. Report creation is achieved through the function Present_Results(element), generating outputs usually in some standard formats such as tab or comma delimited text or directly in HTML. The intention is to have report outputs that can eventually be imported into another application, like a spreadsheet or database, for further manipulation.

We should also note that the "click-through" technique allows one to trim down the log to a volume that is truly necessary for our e-metrics purposes. As we explained earlier, an access to the "click-through" link constitutes a virtual visit. For the purposes of future data-mining, log file reduction offers the option of **not** keeping all the other inconsequential hits appearing in the log. In the following example, only the first line (Line 1) in the server access log is relevant to e-metrics data mining. This line contains all the information about the title, in this case a fictitious title "E-metrics Online Journal" (EOJ) published by Digital Publisher Inc.

(Line 1) 127.0.0.1 - - [13/Feb/2004:06:20:49 -0500] "GET
/click_through.php?title_id=5&provider_id=10&url=http://www.DigitalPublisherInc.com/EOJ.html HTTP/1.1" 200 290
(Line 2) 127.0.0.1 - - [13/Feb/2004:06:21:36 -0500] "GET /new HTTP/1.0" 200 15372

(Line 3) 127.0.0.1 - - [13/Feb/2004:06:21:36 -0500] "GET /images/banner.gif HTTP/1.0" 304 -
(Line 4) 127.0.0.1 - - [13/Feb/2004:06:21:36 -0500] "GET /images/btn_hom .gif HTTP/1.0" 304 -

Lines 2 to 4 only tell us that the user's browser loaded two images in GIF format and therefore do not contain any useful e-metrics information about any e-resource whatsoever. Because these lines are of little interest, they will not be retained in our final log processes. After extracting only the meaningful lines from the log file, we will end up with a cleaner log file of reasonable size that can ultimately simplify the log parsing process.

Sample Results

As demonstrated in the library-generated reports analyzed in Chapters 5 and 6, the click-through+TLA technique is a particularly helpful tool for generating in-depth usage reports that ultimately aid in the selection and purchasing process of e-resources. These earlier chapters illustrated how such data is of particular importance for large academic and research libraries who tend to be both volume purchasers and users of digital subscriptions. A concrete administrative argument for using the click-through+TLA technique in public libraries could be the need to track the most accessed links for a regular update or reorganization of the Web site pages (www.infotoday.com/i/2001.). But drawing fast conclusions from the raw numbers is often a common mistake with any statistical data review. Regardless of the information source, interpretation without context is always a perilous exercise suggesting that the same careful analysis of vendor-produced statistics is equally valid for locally-gathered statistics.

We can now view step-by-step the application of the click-through technique combined with custom log parsing for the generation of local e-metric reports. The various elements of the project are the following:

a.   a test Web page on the library's Web site with links to e-resource titles,
b.   the HTML code for the Web page with the click-through technique,
c.   a sample of the ECLF log generated on the server hosting library's Web site,
d.   examples of local e-metric reports after a custom TLA

The e-resource titles and URLs have been simplified for greater readability. The list of titles, their providers and point of access selected for the test are on the following page.

It is worth mentioning at this stage that by creating the title list and the provider list, we have just started to incorporate external data into the data mining process. This part of the TLA operation is taken care of in the processing

Title_ID	Title	Provider_ID	Provider Name	URL
5	JAMA	45	AMA	jama.ama-assn.org
		46	Galegroup	http://infotrac.galegroup.com
25	Nature	5	Nature	www.nature.com
27	Lancet	6	Elsevier	www.thelancet.com

script by the "Load_External_Data()" function prior to the log parsing WHILE loop in our pseudo-code. Possible external data could include:

- additional title information such as the ISXN, ISI factor, e-resource type
- IP mapping with geographic location, department or building information

In this respect, the "build rather than buy" approach to TLA offers a library greater flexibility in both raw log data analysis and external data integration.

    a.   A test Web page with hyperlinks to commercial e-resources on the library's Web site

The Web page presented to the library users would look like:

This is a test for a Click-through page to e-resources:
Go to redirected JAMA from AMA
Go to redirected JAMA from Galegroup
Go to redirected Nature from Nature
Go to redirected Lancet from Elsevier

---

    b.   HTML code with **click-through script+Title_ID+Provider_ID** for the test page

```
<html>
<title>Test Click-through</title>
<body>
<b>This is a test for a Click-through page to e-
resources</b><br>
<p>
```

```
Go to redirected <a
href="http://www.library.org/test/click_through.php?title_id=5&pr
ovider_id=45&url=http://jama.ama-assn.org/">JAMA from AMA</a>
<p>
Go to redirected <a
href="http://www.library.org/test/click_through.php?title_id=5&pr
ovider_id=46&url=http://infotrac.galegroup.com/">JAMA from
Galegroup</a>
<p>
Go to redirected <a
href="http://www.hsclib.sunysb.edu/test/click_through.php?title_i
d=25&provider_id=5&url=http://www.nature.com/">Nature from
Nature</a>
<p>
Go to redirected <a
href="http://www.library.org/test/click_through.php?title_id=27&p
rovider_id=6&url=http://www.thelancet.com/">Lancet from
Elsevier</a>
<p>
</body>
</html>
```

c. Sample of resulting ECLF log entries when users access the titles

The Web server log shows for each accessed title the associated key data elements: requesting IP address, access timestamp, title_ID and provider_ID.

```
[. . .]
192.168.175.217 - - [27/Dec/2004:17:13:21 -0500] "GET
/test/click_through.php?title_id=25&provider_id=5&url=http://www.na
ture.com/ HTTP/1.1" 302 - "http://www.library.org/test/cap-
ture.html" "Mozilla/4.0 (compatible; MSIE 6.0; Windows NT
5.1; SV1)"
192.168.175.217 - - [27/Dec/2004:17:13:29 -0500] "GET
/test/capture.html HTTP/1.1" 200 748 "-" "Mozilla/4.0
(compatible; MSIE 6.0; Windows NT 5.1; SV1)" 427 988
192.168.175.217 - - [27/Dec/2004:17:13:30 -0500] "GET /test/
click_through.php?title_id=5&provider_id=45&url=http://jama.ama-
assn.org/ HTTP/1.1" 302 - "http://www.library.org/test/cap-
ture.html" "Mozilla/4.0 (compatible; MSIE 6.0; Windows NT
5.1; SV1)" 540 247
192.168.175.217 - - [27/Dec/2004:17:13:37 -0500] "GET
```

```
/test/capture.html HTTP/1.1" 200 748 "-" "Mozilla/
4.0 (compatible; MSIE 6.0; Windows NT 5.1; SV1)"
427 988
192.168.175.217 - - [27/Dec/2004:17:13:39 -0500] "GET
/test/click_through.php?title_id=25&provider_id=5&url=http://www.na
ture.com/ HTTP/1.1" 302 - "http://www.library.org/test/
capture.html" "Mozilla/4.0 (compatible; MSIE 6.0; Windows
NT 5.1; SV1)" 542 249
172.31.108.4 - - [27/Dec/2004:17:41:06 -0500] "GET /test/
capture.html HTTP/1.1" 200 748 "-" "Mozilla/4.0
(compatible; MSIE 6.0; Windows NT 5.1; Deepnet Explorer;
SV1)" 405 989
172.31.108.4 - - [27/Dec/2004:17:41:08 -0500] "GET /test/
click_through.php?title_id=5&provider_id=46&url=http://infotrac.
galegroup.com/ HTTP/1.1" 302 - "http://www.library.org/
test/capture.html" "Mozilla/4.0 (compatible; MSIE 6.0;
Windows NT 5.1; Deepnet Explorer; SV1)" 518 247
172.31.108.4 - - [27/Dec/2004:17:41:24 -0500] "GET /test/
capture.html HTTP/1.1" 200 748 "-" "Mozilla/4.0
(compatible; MSIE 6.0; Windows NT 5.1; Deepnet Explorer;
SV1)" 405 989
172.31.108.4 - - [27/Dec/2004:17:41:27 -0500] "GET
/test/click_through.php?title_id=27&provider_id=6&url=http://www.th
elancet.com/ HTTP/1.1" 302 - "http://www.library.org/
test/capture.html" "Mozilla/4.0 (compatible; MSIE 6.0;
Windows NT 5.1; Deepnet Explorer; SV1)" 519 248
192.168.175.99 - - [27/Dec/2004:17:47:13 -0500] "GET
/test/click_through.php?title_id=5&provider_id=45&url=http://jama.a
ma-assn.org/ HTTP/1.1" 302 - "http://www.library.org/
test/capture.html" "Mozilla/4.0 (compatible; MSIE 6.0;
Windows NT 5.2; .NET CLR 1.1.4322)" 514 248
192.168.175.99 - - [27/Dec/2004:17:57:01 -0500] "GET /test/
click_through.php?title_id=5&provider_id=46&url=http://infotrac.
galegroup.com/ HTTP/1.1" 302 - "http://www.library.org/
test/capture.html" "Mozilla/4.0 (compatible; MSIE 6.0;
Windows NT 5.2; .NET CLR 1.1.4322)" 514 248
192.168.156.102 - - [27/Dec/2004:21:38:37 -0500] "GET
/test/click_through.php?title_id=27&provider_id=6&url=http://www.th
elancet.com/
HTTP/1.1" 302 - "http://www.library.org/test/capture.html"
"Mozilla/4.0 (compatible; MSIE 6.0; Windows NT 5.1; Deepnet
Explorer; SV1)" 531 261
[. . .]
```

Table 7-6 Title Usage Statistics

Date: 1-6-2005
Log name:/home/httpd/html/test/test_capture.log
Report: VISITS PER ACCESSED TITLE

Title	Provider	Visits	Visitors
JAMA	AMA	4	3
Nature	Nature	2	2
JAMA	Galegroup	1	1
Lancet	Elsevier	1	1

Total visits: 8
Total visitors/Unique IP: 4

d.   Examples of local e-metric reports generated by custom TLA

After **custom** log parsing using Perl—code provided in Appendix 3—we get the following outputs:

One could legitimately wonder if the counted visits appearing in Table 7–6 can be attributed to actual people or to robots, spiders, crawlers and the likes. Robots are usually small applications designed to gather data for search engine indexes.[15] Unfortunately, the record of a virtual visit by a robot, spider or crawler looks no different in a Web server transaction log than that of a visit by an actual person. Robot visits may be traceable through name identifiers (i.e., Googlebot[16]), or by a high volume of pages accessed in a very small timeframe, or by their requests for a file on the Web site called 'robots.txt.' The latter normally describes what may or may not be indexed from a given Web site by search engines. Nevertheless, if found, visits by robots must be systematically filtered and separately counted or just ignored when assessing the real usage impact of a Web site. Because e-resources are usually commercial products and are password protected, the user authentication process addressed earlier is not only necessary for licensing and copyright compliance, but also prevents search engine robots from artificially inflating the number of actual visits to electronic titles.

The results seen in Table 7–6, a report on the title usage that was generated from Web server log data that captured information from redirected click-through hyperlinks, underscores some important local library e-metrics implementation and solution issues:

1.   By redirecting each and every e-resource link, we have a consistent unit of use (number of access or visit) across titles. This means that:
    a.   even if a vendor does not supply any statistics, we still have an idea of the importance of each title to the library's customer base

    b. we are able to estimate the use of e-books even though measurement standards for this e-resource type are yet to be defined

    c. we can compare the locally-acquired usage patterns with analogous statistics provided by vendors[17]

2. We are also able to evaluate the title usage according to the number of visitors per title and gauge the users' activity for each title by the number of visits per visitor. Because visitors are identified in our example by the machine IP address, the exact number of unique users is only an approximation

3. By adding the provider's reference in the modified URL, titles with multiple providers can be differentiated from one another. We can, therefore:

    a. measure usage across vendors as in Chapter 5, Figure 5–2. In this example, we can break down the use for JAMA for each source (AMA and Galegroup). This reporting possibility gives selection criteria in cases of duplicate title subscriptions, it can be particularly useful when applied to the selection process for collection management.

    b. group titles by vendors and compare packages across vendors as shown in Chapter 6, Figure 6–1

    c. estimate the importance of each title within a bundle as exemplified in Chapter 5, Figure 5–1

4. If, in the example, we substitute Nature with a database offering and Lancet with an e-book title, then we could compare access/visit counts across resource type because we have a consistent unit of use

5. The control over the entire data capture and TLA process allows the library to centralize the data sources, to choose a uniform report format, and to request an on-demand production of e-metrics data

As seen in Table 7–7, usage statistics tracked at the visitors level, each identified by their IP addresses, informs the library about:

Table 7–7 IP/Visitor Usage Statistics

Date: 1-6-2005
Log name: /home/httpd/html/test/test_capture.log
Report: VISITS PER IP

IP/Visitors	Visits
192.168.175.217	3
172.31.108.4	2
192.168.175.99	2
192.168.156.102	1

Total visits: 8
Total visitors/Unique IP: 4

Table 7-8 Provider Usage Statistics

Date: 1-6-2005
Log name: /home/httpd/html/test/test_capture.log
Report: VISITS PER PROVIDER

Provider	Visits
AMA	4
Galegroup	2
Nature	2
Elsevier	1

Total visits: 9
Total visitors/Unique IP: 4

1. the origin of the information access requests
2. the overall activity of the library users with the average number of visits per visitor identified by their IP address

The activity report from an academic medical library, presented in Table 7-8, shows a sample of visit counts by e-resource provider. We could use these numbers for a rough "return on investment" analysis. Once a library can calculate the total amount of paid subscription(s) to each individual provider, it becomes possible to calculate a cost per visit evaluation across all subscription vendors. Such information is undeniably useful during the collection management process of title selection as well as for subscription and budget management purposes. Such a report could also help determine the strategic importance of each of the library's information providers.

Advanced Local E-Metrics—Local Solution Level 3

The Advanced solution, which will be designated as Level 3, is a level more applicable to a Library C infrastructure because it requires the introduction of a new element in the library's technical computing environment: a proxy server. A more detailed description of a proxy server is given in the next chapter, but within the context of our current solution examination we just need to know that a proxy server is commonly used to:

1. optimize the user access to external resources;
2. protect the internal network of an organization from external computer and network security attacks;
3. authenticate remote users before they can access the organization's restricted resources; and
4. request an external resource on behalf of a remote user

In other words, a proxy server is a gateway to the Internet for both on-site and off-site users. Because a proxy server is typically part of the library's network, it can possess an IP address normally authorized for subscription access by vendors. This property allows remote users to be filtered through a proxy server in order to access external resources that are normally restricted to IP addresses from the library's network. The proxy server therefore offers a solution to the aforementioned question Q1 about giving remote users access to the restricted e-resources.

Proxy servers can also help simplify the raw data collection for library e-metrics. By channeling every user's information or subscription title request to the proxy server, we are able to centralize processes for recording users' activities regardless of their title searching origin (main Web site, Web OPAC, e-resource finder). In order to make this solution operational, we must proxy the "modified" or "new" link that we previously used in redirection. Here is our previously "modified" link: <a href="http://**www.library.org**"/click-through.php?url=http://www.somesite.net>Some site</a>

When proxied on the library's Web site page in HTML, it becomes:

<a href= "**http://proxy.library.org**":80/login?url="http://**www.library.org/**"
click_through.php?url="http://www.somesite.net">Some site</a>

In the 856 field of a MARC record in the catalog, we would just have:

---

856 4# $u
http://proxy.library.org:80/login?url=http://www.library.org/**click_thro**
ugh.php?url=http://www.somesite.net

Figure 7–4 depicts our new environment with a proxy server in the equation. In this configuration, we exclusively work with the proxy server's transaction log file instead of getting the raw data from the library's Web server or from the Web OPAC server or somewhere else.

An ECLF proxy entry log would look like:

```
192.168.174.162 - 1234567890 [04/Nov/2003:17:39:43 -0500]
"GET http://proxy.library.org:80/login?url=http://www.library
.org/click_through.php?title_id=25&provider_id=6&url=http://
www.google.fr/ HTTP/1.1" 302 - "http://www.library.org/
test/capture.html" "Mozilla/4.0 (compatible; MSIE 6.0;
Windows NT 5.1; SV1)" 541 248
```

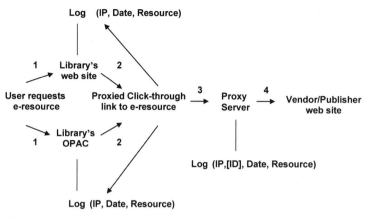

Log   (IP, Date, Resource)

Figure 7-4   Sequence of Events When Accessing a Proxied Online Title

Given the complexity of the newly-generated log entry accounting for authenticated proxy access, the TLA part of the e-metrics solution can now only be done with customized TLA programming developments. As a consequence, only a very small number of Library B-type environments would be able to accomplish e-metrics at this level. But as summarized in Table 7–9, we now know that a proxy server is the advanced response to the question of remote users (Q1).

Highly Advanced Local E-Metrics—Local Solution Level 4

At this point in our discussion, two questions remain unanswered:

Q2. How could we get a more accurate count of unique visitors?
Q3. How could we capture bookmarked direct accesses to the vendors' Web site?

As described earlier, a proxy server is usually set up to filter the remote users' requests for e-resources. But how do we make sure that the person issuing the request is an authorized user? Such assurance only comes via user authentication prior to allowing access to the requested e-resource. Therefore, a maintained list of authorized users must exist for proper proxy server authentication. Typically, the list of users, uniquely identified, can come from the patron database of the library management system or some other existing services within the library. We will examine the importance of this user list issue in the next chapter when we discuss the technical requirements for local e-metrics.

Table 7-9 Characteristics of an Advanced Solution (Level 3) for Local E-Metrics

	Advanced Solution (Level 3)		
Method/Feasibility by Library Category	Main Objectives	Possible Solutions	Infrastructure Involved
Level 2 and Title proxying off-site access+B, C	Centralize data source Allow remote access	Same as Level 2+ custom log parsing	Same as Level 2+Proxy server

Here is a closer look at the proxied URL incorporating a "login" component:

> http://proxy.library.org:80/**login**?url=http://www.library.org/click_t hrough.php?url=http://www.somesite.net

We have now answered question Q2 by uniquely identifying users as part of the information access process. Now, instead of assuming that one IP address represents one user, we are able to get more accurate counts of unique visitors through unique user identification. One flaw needs to be accounted for, as we cannot guarantee that a user has not given his or her ID to another person or has switched seats in front of a given network device with another one during the particular virtual session! Thus a true one-to-one relationship between authentication and individual human being is still not fully measurable.

Nonetheless, it is important to examine one example of a library proxy server solution available in the application EZproxy.[18] This application is widely used in U.S. academic libraries for the authentication of remote users and redirection to restricted e-resources. EZproxy also has an interesting feature that requires "remote users to undergo one validation per browser session to verify their right to access a restricted resource." The key concept here is "one validation per browser session." This means that a user needs only to authenticate once and perform as many requests to multiple e-resources as needed within the same browser session. If the browser is closed thus ending the session, the user must re-authenticate before accessing other titles that are passed through EZproxy. In more technical terms, the EZproxy authentication and session management for virtual visits requires a per-session cookie left in the Web browser. We could exploit this feature to answer question Q3 and overcome the inability of previously addressed solutions to capture direct access to the vendors' Web sites through bookmarks. Thus with EZproxy, even if a remote user bookmarks a Web site that requires proxy authentication, the next time he or she wants to go to that same site through the bookmark, they would have to re-authenticate because the per-session cookie would have expired. While verifying the privileges of the user, the proxy records the new request and therefore the authenticated access would be in the proxy server log.

Now, if we generalize this approach to on-site users as well, then the use of bookmarks and their potential to bypass the use capturing mechanism will be solved for e-metrics purposes, whether users are accessing information from devices and networks inside or outside the library premises. Of course there is potential that use of the proxy server to authenticate all users regardless of network location will create to some degree an access barrier and may be considered at best by the users as an inconvenience or at worst an infringement to the notion of "free" access with a legitimate worry for privacy protection.

In order to address question Q3 and unaccounted bookmarked accesses, the library would have to inform the public that the required authentication is consistent with:

1. the need for systematic authentication as part of its access policies and licensing agreements
2. the necessity of more accurate and comprehensive e-metrics for better use of library budgets and improved collection development

A more thorough discussion of these points appears in Chapter 9 as part of an examination of the administrative ramifications of local e-metrics initiatives and implementations.

As a final note about proxy server logins, the authentication of users clearly offers libraries an opportunity to enrich the resolution of local e-metrics. Because the library already has some information on its users in the library management system, it is not unrealistic to think that data from the users' profile could be used to obtain more meaningful and granular e-metrics. As demonstrated in Chapter 5, Figures 5–3 and 5–4, the objective is not to track the activities of individual users but to detect usage trends by user profile, category, home library, or company department. In other words, by integrating external data on library users with the Load_external portion of TLA scripts, local e-metrics can produce usage statistics with information about user demographics. Thus we see the characteristics and benefits of a highly advanced solution for e-metrics, as shown in Table 7–10. It should now be clear that the complexity of this e-metrics solution level, which consists of the production of local e-metrics further integrated with external data, which we be addressed in more detail in the technical considerations of the next chapter, can only be realized by custom programming.

Mini How-to

Now that we have examined the possibilities offered by four types of local e-metrics solutions established at the library level, we can put together a

Table 7–10 Characteristics of a Highly Advanced Solution (Level 4) for Local E-Metrics

Highly Advanced Solution (Level 4)			
Method/Feasibility by Library Category	Main Objectives	Possible Solutions	Infrastructure Involved
Level 3 and proxy both on- and off-site accesses + Authentication / C	Capture bookmarked accesses Enable total access control External data intergration User demographics	Same as Level 3 Custom programming	Same as Level 3 + Patron database

brief "How-to" for local TLA. In a nutshell, the project consists of four major steps:

1. Create the click-through script (Table 7–11)
2. Modify the HTML links for your e-resources (Table 7–12)
3. Install your Transaction Log Analysis application (Table 7–13)
4. Analyze your server log file (Table 7–14)

Overview of the Local E-Metrics Project

In view of the general and practical evaluation of local e-metrics implementations, we can consider this endeavor from a project management perspective. Without our focus on local e-metrics, we have been defining a virtual visit as a successful request of an online subscription title. The intent is to count a virtual visit regardless of its origin, be it within the library or from outside of the library premises. This all inclusive approach to data collection facilitates the creation of more informative and granular outcomes at a later project stages. By ultimately acquiring their e-metrics data locally, not only do libraries take advantage of their existing infrastructure but they also gain total control over their e-metrics statistics.

With this potential in mind, we divide the complete local e-metrics project, outlined in Figure 7–5, into four major phases: (1) preparation, (2) log analysis, (3) metrics production and (4) administrative analysis. The first phase, which can be considered data collection, selectively gathers information and tracks online accesses to available electronic resources by utilizing a creative solution combining a "click-through script" and modified URLs. The second phase, which is comprised of transaction log analysis (TLA), extracts the usable and relevant data elements from the raw data recorded in the transaction logs stored on the library's servers. The direct output could be called "core e-metrics" consisting of

Table 7–11 Creating the Click-Through Script

1- Creating the Click-Through Script		
Step	Operation	Comments
1.	Create the click-through script in a text editor and save it with the chosen name and suffix	Write your own code or get one from published work. A PHP example is in Appendix 2.
2.	Place the script on the web server where the pages to access the e-resources are located. Most of the time it is the server hosting the library's web site.	For our example in PHP (installed beforehand by your web server system administrator*), the script is placed in the directory: /home/httpd/html/test. For a Perl script, you would have to install it, or have it installed, in the location devoted for CGI (Common Gateway Interface)** scripts directory (usually cgi-bin) on the Web server.
3.	Make the script executable with the right permissions, owner and group authorizations	

*us3.php.net/install
**www.comptechdoc.org/independent/web/cgi; perl.about.com/library/weekly/aa060101b.htm

Table 7–12 Modifying the HTML Links For Your E-Resources

2- Modifying the HTML links for your e-resources		
Step	Operation	Comments
1.	Back up your current Web pages	
2.	Modify the web pages on your web server by adding the "click-through" script in the link	"**OLD**" link on the HTML page is: <a href="http://www.somesite.net"> Some site</a> "**NEW**" link: <a href=http://**www.library.org/click-through.php**?url=http://www.somesite.net>Some site</a>
		If you **PROXY** the link: <a href= **http://proxy.library.org:80/login**? url=http://**www.library.org/click-through.php**? url=http://www.somesite.net>Some site</a>
3.	Repeat the operation for every link you would like to monitor	

Table 7-13 Installing Your Transaction Log Analysis Application (TLA)

3- Installing Your Transaction Log Analysis (TLA) Application		
Step	Operation	Comments
1.	If you use an off-the-shelf solution, then refer to the first section of this chapter on "general Web metrics"	
2.	If you use a homegrown solution, in the simplest case you would have to install the program on a server or a workstation. In our case, our program is written in Perl (in Appendix 3)	There is a great chance that Perl has already been installed on your server by your system administrator. You can freely install ActivePerl by ActiveState on your Windows workstation.*
3.	Make the script executable with the right permissions, owner and group authorizations	

*www.wdvl.com/Authorizing/Languages/Perl/Windows.

visit and unique visitor counts. As we will see in the next chapter, the second phase can also integrate external data into the process whenever possible to produce "deep e-metrics." The third phase, or metrics production, generates structured and constructive e-metrics reports. The last phase of administrative analysis strives accumulate actionable e-metrics data from the reports in order to benefit library strategic planning as covered in Part II.

We have demonstrated that the primary sources of e-metrics data for libraries are the providers of e-resources: the vendors, the publishers and the intermediaries. Even with locally-acquired library e-metrics, only vendor-supplied statistics can record, identify, and measure:

- The result of requests made by library users when they access a specific e-resource title. The outputs for these are the statistical reports on searches, sessions, downloads and turnaways.
- The details sought by library users at the articles level. The outputs for these are the statistical reports on the number of retrieved abstract, TOC, Full-Text HTML or PDF.

The development of tools such as COUNTER has greatly facilitated the adoption of a Code of Practice supported by both producers and purchasers of information. Although the library e-metrics field is far from maturity, it seems that a strategy

Table 7-14 Analyzing the Server Log File

	4- Analyzing the Server Log File	
Step	Operation	Comments
1.	If you use an off-the-shelf solution, then refer to the first section of this chapter on "general Web metrics"	
2.	If you use a homegrown solution: – put the external data files in the designated directory – get the log file from the web server – place it in the designated directory – run the TLA application	In our example, the external data files are the "title_list" and the "provider_list". They are placed in the same directory as the TLA script for simplicity. They are tab-delimited text files. The same operation would be performed for additional data (ISI, IP map, etc.) In Library C, your Systems staff will probably perform the task for you
3.	Get the generated reports and evaluate the results	

that confronts the issues of consistency, comparability and reliability of vendor-produced statistics should:

• Encourage vendors' compliance to COUNTER.
• Formulate better specifications of the libraries' expectations on specific e-metrics standards for e-resources.
• Develop locally-collected e-metrics with an open-source approach and through collaborative work.

Even with the availability of vendor-supplied usage reports, it is remarkable to see that many libraries have developed homegrown solutions for locally-collected e-metrics used to cross-check and supplement vendors' statistics. With varying degrees of sophistication, many libraries have opted to implement customized click-through scripts and transaction log analysis (TLA) for their own eventual e-metrics data production. For expediency, some libraries chose to complete their respective TLA with off-the-shelf applications. Still others have tried to acquire a high level of details after determining a need for greater data processing flexibility or additional external data integration with their e-metrics. The success

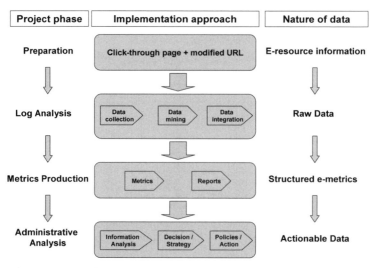

Figure 7-5 Overview of the Local E-Metrics Project

of such elaborate e-metrics endeavors will vary depending on the technical, financial resources and skilled staff at their respective library's disposal.

Because it is possible within locally-collected e-metrics data to establish the number of accesses or visits as the unit of use across titles, vendors and e-resource types, this measurement allows for the production of consistent and comparable statistics with on-demand availability. The caveat, however, is that no local solutions will ever be able to directly capture users' activities occurring once those activities include interaction with Web elements controlled strictly on the vendors' Web site. Similarly, local e-metrics cannot record any virtual requests that bypass the library's infrastructure or queries not originating from library-controlled access such as with a "link-out" from other e-resources. The "Linkout" feature of Pubmed,[19] for example, enables users to link directly from a Pubmed citation to the full-text articles or related resources made available by the publisher. The library can capture the visit to Pubmed but would be unable to account for the visit originating from Pubmed to another publisher's Web site. In order to gather statistics on linked-out titles, a library could rely on e-resource providers[20] or communicate with users through surveys and feedback requests. Both solutions have their limitations but could at least help a library discern basic usage trends. Table 7–15 summarizes the main problems and solutions encountered in developing local e-metrics. It also ranks the feasibility of each solution by library category A, B, and/or C.

Reported comparable usage patterns between vendor-supplied and locally-produced e-metrics[21] are a confirmation that achieving comprehensive accountability and measure of e-resources use in libraries is not an impossible task.

Table 7-15 Local E-Metrics Solutions and Feasibility by Library Category

Problem	Possible Solution	Feasibility by Library Category
1. How to identify most requested e-resource pages	Local TLA on Web site server's regular access logs with Web analytics software	A, B, C
2. How to get most accessed e-resource links	Click-through / redirection + Local TLA on alternate log with Web analytics software homegrown or not	Possibly A B, C
3. How to get most accessed titles with distinct provider	Click-through / redirection + Local TLA on alternate or regular Web access log with home-grown Web analytics application	B, C
4. How to centralize data source and allow remote access	Solution to problem 3- + Proxy / gateway off-site access with cookie per session enabled + authentication + in-house programming	Possibly B C
5. How to capture bookmarked links and visits with demographics	Solution to problem 4- + on and off-site proxying + authentication + external data integration	C
6. How to capture uses for linked-out titles	No direct solution	

Such projects do necessitate time, money, skills and commitment from all stake-holders. However, one must keep in mind that the production of reports and numbers is only the beginning of e-metrics initiatives. Ultimately it is the usability and reliability of the measures that really count. Still, the combination of information extracted from both vendor reports and locally generated reports, while never revealing the actual intention of the library user, is the best compromise achievable to comprehend the users' behaviors.

In the next two chapters, we will scrutinize how we could, technically and administratively, move beyond the "core" e-metrics to build "deeper" and more actionable e-metrics in modern libraries.

Notes

1. Luther 2000; Shim, McClure, Fraser, and Bertot 2001.
2. http://slis-six.lis.fsu.edu/students/usdevcorps/SunshineLewis/emis/index.cfm.
3. Breeding 2002; Troll Covey 2002.

4. www.w3.org/Daemon/User/Config/Logging.html#common-logfile-format.
5. www.networkcomputing.com/story/singlePageFormat.jhtml?articleID=20003001.
6. www.pubmedcentral.nih.gov/articlerender.fcgi?artid=31730.
7. More on library Web site usability available at www.elsevier.com/framework_products/promis_misc/672915lcpamphlet5.pdf.
8. Davis 2000; Bertot, McClure, and Davis 2002.
9. Shim 2004.
10. Duy and Vaughan 2003; Samson, Derry, and Eggleston 2004.
11. Schwartz 1998; Pardue 2001.
12. Van Epps 2001; Breeding 2002.
13. See for example www.blackwellpublishing.com/xml/dtds/4-0/help/journalcodes.htm.
14. See www.doi.org/; See NISO Z39.84.
15. www.ranks.nl/resources/robots_white_paper.pdf.
16. More on robots at www.webyield.net/directory/searchengine/robots.html.
17. Duy and Vaughan, 2003.
18. www.usefulutilities.com/.
19. www.nlm.nih.gov/bsd/pubmed_tutorial/glossary.html#1.
20. www.ncbi.nlm.nih.gov/entrez/linkout/doc/2004TipsMLA.ppt#302,22,LinkOut Enhancements; www.nfais.org/Usage_Stats_Pesch.ppt#313,34,Link-out activity.
21. Duy and Vaughan, 2003.

E-Metrics and Infrastructure: Assessing Servers, Workstations, and Other Technical Considerations

We turn our attention in this chapter to the technical ramifications of an e-metrics implementation, defining the e-metrics infrastructure as the basic technological equipment managed by the library that is deemed necessary for successful completion of e-metrics projects. We will exclude, however, the overall networking components of this infrastructure—such as routers, hubs, and wires alike—because such large Internet elements are not usually supervised by libraries and without such technological givens, there would not be adequate available network connections with enough bandwidth for library users to access the library's online resources in the first place. The discussion of infrastructure in this chapter will focus only on the combination of servers and workstations which are seen as vital throughout all stages of the e-metrics project.

The architectural analysis will first present the technical issues related to any e-metrics project, regardless of whether the final statistical reports are acquired from e-resource vendors, publishers, intermediaries or produced as part of homegrown library applications. For example, it seems most probable that every library will somehow confront the problem of report storage and the necessity of importing external data for enhanced title usage studies. The second part of the discussion will center on the technical constraints and possibilities associated with the development of a local e-metrics enterprise. This portion will examine how to handle multiple server logs as possible raw data sources for a local data collection, the requirements for data processing, and finally the demanding but beneficial integration of external data with information about IP addresses and user demographics.

Consider Common Issues for Vendor and Local E-Metrics

As soon as a library commits itself to exploring the universe of e-metrics, it invariably faces two pressing questions:

1. How to store and manage the increasing volume of usage reports produced either locally or from vendors
2. How to integrate external data on titles to obtain more enlightening e-metric reports

Statistical Report Storage

Certainly as the collection and analysis of e-metrics become part of standard performance measurement practices in libraries, the number of library statistical reports will grow exponentially over time. What can a library do with all of this usage data? The answer depends on the IT infrastructure, technical support, and financial assets available to the library. Libraries of types A and B, without many resources or with limited ones, could solve the data storage issue for the short term by investing in one of the many light technologies available for data storage. A quick and affordable storage solution could be found by storing the various files on one or multiple networked server(s) with significant shared disk space. Another solution that could be combined with the previous one is to archive the data directly on some high-capacity storage devices such as digital tapes, DVDs, and the like. Although still considered a very basic storage alternative, this option will usually satisfy short term library data archiving needs. Such storage devices make it easier to deploy a data storage environment within a reasonable period of time. But it is also foreseeable that, in the long-run, the increasing complexity of the library's world in the digital era will lead to more voluminous in-depth e-metrics. Libraries will then have no choice but to put the adequate tools and technologies in place in order to effectively and profitably manage the collected statistical information.

More advanced libraries, like Library C, will require a sophisticated e-metrics archiving method that extends beyond the traditional static data repository. Modern libraries could integrate their e-metrics as part of a data warehouse.[1] Such a data warehouse would consist of a large centralized database holding the e-metrics data along with other library data from various sources and in different formats. The library staff and managers would then query the database for archived e-metrics and generate *ad hoc* reports for future use in their decision-making process. Building a data warehouse from scratch is a large and costly project, but if a library is willing to consider in-depth e-metrics as a top operational priority, then a server tailored for e-metrics development with an on-demand reporting function is an ideal choice. We could imagine such a server installed:

- with various programming tools for custom-designed applications,
- with a database for reporting and statistics storage, and
- with a web server to handle requests and queries for e-metrics reports through a Web-based interface.

A server dedicated to data warehousing should be capable of handling multiple terabytes of data and processing huge transaction loads. The cost associated with the Web analytics software component can be minimized by using open-source technologies available for free or for minimal fees. Because the setup of such a data management system can be rather involved, the major constraint with this type of solution is the library's initial investment in both the infrastructure and skilled staff.

External Data Integration Related to Title Usage Studies

Although crucial indicators, the in-depth analysis limitations inherent in search, session, virtual visit and unique visitor counts will often necessitate the integration of external data into e-metrics title usage studies. Even though this additional step in the e-metrics project undeniably widens the e-metrics project scope and increases its complexity, including external data offers libraries new ways of assessing the use of their online resources. Because each additional data element automatically introduces associated specific constraints, the e-metrics project team must expect challenges related to external data availability, accuracy, consistency, compatibility, storage, and maintenance, regardless of the type of external information that is being integrated. Table 8-1 presents some data options to consider as part of enhanced reporting and collection management processes.

Once the necessary external data are identified and correctly formatted, they are usually combined with the core e-metrics. The data combination phase can be performed with different degrees of automation depending upon the source and the nature of the external data. When working with vendor-supplied reports, the external data integration will almost certainly be a manual process whereas this operation applied to locally-generated e-metrics can be automated

Table 8-1 External Data on Title Information and Possible Use

E-Metric Data Element	Possible External Data	Possible Use
Title	– ISXN/e-ISXN – Impact factor – Number of articles – Date of first access – Subscription price	– Identification of the e-resource – Selection process – Collection management – Cost/use analysis

once the data files are created and correctly formatted. In our pseudo-code example in the previous chapter, the Load_External_Data(element) and Integrate_External_Data (element) functions in our application would take care of this external data integration step before and after the log analysis.

ISXN, Impact Factors, Number of Articles

The data associated with ISSN, impact factor, and number of articles are additional e-metrics criteria relevant only to e-journals. Such data are produced annually in the summer following a year of coverage of e-journals in "science" and "social science" editions. This annual data can be obtained from the Thomson ISI (Institute for Scientific Information) Journal Citation Reports (JCR) database. Although the appropriate use of these evaluative indicators has generated much controversy in the research community, they have been long used as part of bibliometrics to help librarians in journal selection and collection development.

Unfortunately, the process of acquiring these numbers for reporting purposes is totally manual. It is almost impossible to automate their acquisition because there is no option to directly download the data over a network from the JCR Web site. One must instead choose and mark a selection of data to be saved as a text file with semi-colon delimited fields (for example: Abbreviated Journal Title; ISSN; 2003 Total Cites; Impact Factor; Immediacy Index; 2003 Articles; Cited Half-Life). Probably the best way to address this process is to assign a member of the library e-metrics team this manual task and perform data updates once a year. The resulting saved text file of ISI data can be easily manipulated and imported in various ways for different purposes for later e-metrics report use. But in order to avoid duplication of retrieval efforts between libraries, it would be convenient to create a centralized data repository containing simple export functions. However, for this solution to work, libraries would have to be members of a consortium that shared the subscription costs to access JCR and complied with the licensing agreement required by the vendor.

Date of First Access

Unlike the JCR data, the date of actual first access and/or the date of first public availability to a subscription title must be provided as part of the library's internal record-keeping procedures. The choice between the use of one or the other date is mostly dictated by the feasibility of the necessary operations to account for the date information. But it is unquestionably important to include this type of information in order to avoid a misinterpretation of low access counts for newly available titles. A title could indeed be made available online but not accessed by users. Among the most plausible explanations for such a situation is that either the title is too new or it is really of low interest to the library's public base.

With a local e-metrics solution, the precise date of first access for every title can only be obtained by data extraction from a "master" server log. In Library B and C, for instance, a master server log would be a cumulative server log from the library Web server or proxy server since the library made the e-resource first available to its users. The exact date of first access to every title, past and present, would be recorded by retaining the first occurrence of the valid access for each title after a parsing of the master log. The obvious drawback of working with such a history log to acquire the first access for every title is the generation of a gigantic log file that has grown over time.

The use of the first date of access being impractical, a more realistic solution is for the cataloging department to record, in a spreadsheet or a database table, the date of online availability every time a library subscribes to a new title. This method simplifies established-date management although it offers less accurate data when compared to an actual virtual visit extracted from a server access log. Ideally, in a library such as Library C, which could set up a database-driven library Web site, the internal database could be easily updated by the cataloging department with the availability date for each e-resource.

Once the statistical reports from TLA are made generated, then the additional access or availability date information can be incorporated to a given title's e-metrics. This type of data integration will almost certainly be a manual process when applied to vendor-supplied reporting solutions. Recalling the pseudo-code for local TLA detailed in the previous chapter, the Load_External_Data(element) function will automatically load the correctly formatted information, for example in a tab or comma-delimited file or directly queried from the internal e-resource database in the case of Library C, before the actual log parsing. Further on in the pseudo-code, the Integrate_External_Data(element) function enriches the final reports once it appends the additional information for each data element after the log analysis.

Example of an E-Metrics Report with Title External Data

Table 8–2 presents an example of a locally-produced e-metrics report that was generated with integrated external data. A vendor report, such as JR1 with the Number of Successful Full-Text Article Requests by Month and Journal or JR4 with the number of Total Searches Run by Month and Service, would look very similar once the external data have been manually added, unless a programmer found in a library like Library C can create a smart way to automate the process. Such an automated solution would be possible if the vendors' reports and the external data are stored in database tables. Then the process would require that the journal ISSN be used as the matching point between the title statistics and the associated external data so that an enhanced report could be generated with a query that joins the two data tables.

Table 8-2 Locally Generated E-Metric Report for E-Journals with Integrated External Data

Report date: 03/22/2004 10:30:27
Statistics for E-JOURNALS only
Log from 01/Nov/2003:00:11:41 to 30/Nov/2003:23:59:30

Rank	Title	Source	ISSN	Impact Factor 2002	Articles 2002	Date First Accessed	Total Visits	Unique IPs
1	Nature	Nature	0028-0836	30.432	889	1-May-02	952	251
2	New England Journal of Medicine	MMS	0028-4793	31.736	378	8-May-02	886	227
3	The Journal of Biological Chemistry	ASBMB	0021-9258	6.696	6444	1-May-02	671	156
4	Cell	Cell Press	0092-8674	27.254	350	1-May-02	579	172
5	Science	HighWire	0036-8075	26.682	987	1-May-02	555	167
6	JAMA	AMA	0098-7484	16.586	383	1-Jun-03	518	147
7	Proceedings of the National Academy of Sciences of the United States of America	NAS	0027-8424	10.7	2911	12-Jun-02	487	126
8	Lancet	Science direct	N/A	N/A	N/A	1-May-02	311	92
9	Journal of Immunology	AAI	0022-1767	7.014	1666	13-Jun-02	308	65
10	JAMA	Galegroup	0098-7484	16.586	383	1-May-02	291	88

To understand the depth of the e-metrics data in this report, consider how the third title, "Journal of Biological chemistry," has a low impact factor according to international measurements but is heavily accessed according to local library usage trends. By considering the impact factor as the sole determinate of title value without the virtual visits count, this title would have been probably considered to be a low priority title based due to its low impact factor. The foreseeable consequence of inadequate data comparisons could be an inappropriate subscription cancellation during a period of library budget cuts. But as we explored in Chapter 5, we could use a general rule for title cancellation based on low access counts rather than only on low impact factors. The potential oversight issue for this rule, however, is that recently acquired resources cannot possibly have a high number of visits and would be mistakenly eliminated from the collection. But by including the date of online availability of every title in the e-metrics report, we avoid such usage misinterpretations. Still, in the case of a very strategic title used by a small pool of highly specialized users, the visit count could also be very low. In such a case, only a contextual interpretation of the numbers by an experienced analyst could prevent an erroneous title subscription cancellation based on low use.

Title Price

Many questions arise when it comes time to determine the individual title price as part of a reliable and accurate cost-per-use study. This endeavor becomes especially challenging when the title is part of a bundled package subscription. Would an arithmetic mean price (title price = cost of the bundle/number of titles in the bundle) "fairly" differentiate a highly authoritative, and therefore theoretically more expensive publication, from a more obscure title? Should we consider the price of each individual title as if it were not part of a bundled package? Which title is fairly priced and should we keep when there is complex pricing with print and online titles?

Due to the difficulties of associating a title with the right price, the process of subscription cost data integration is often performed outside of any automated e-metrics procedure. This means that an independent cost study conducted by other departments in the library can be done later, but only once the final vendors or locally-produced e-metrics reports are made available. Afterwards, such costs analysis would be carried out on a case by case basis and would inevitably involve manually processing of the data.

Incorporate Technical Issues Specific to Local E-Metrics

When a library decides to tackle the local collection of e-metrics data, it must put together the road map (a plan of action) and the actors (a project team), both detailed in Table 8–3.

Table 8–3 Road Map and Actors

PHASE I: PROJECT MANAGEMENT	
Road map	Actors
– Analysis and planning – Development and implementation – Testing and optimization – Production and monitoring – Use and preservation	– Library administrators – Library public relations – Technical services – IT department – Electronic resources manager

The analysis and planning step in the Road Map is crucial to the project and should include a complete inventory of the library's technical assets. The inventory should account for the involved actors with clues to the feasibility of the project, as well as to potential actor roles and contributions. At this stage it should be clear to everyone that the e-metrics project requires mobilizing the library's technical and human resources. These planning steps should also help the project team set realistic expectations based on the technical limitations of the library.

Once the project road map is agreed upon, the library must take advantage of the specific elements of its infrastructure, as summarized in Table 8–4, in order to achieve its goals. The data collection and the data processing phases make the most extensive and intensive use of the infrastructure to ultimately generate the necessary outputs leading to the e-metrics reports. During the data collection phase, the technical infrastructure produces the various logs considered as the raw data. These logs then become the input material for the different Web analytics

Table 8–4 Elements of Infrastructure Data Collection and Data Processing

PHASE II: DATA COLLECTION	
Elements of infrastructure	Outputs
– OPAC server – Main Web site server – Proxy server(s) – Printing server(s)	– (E)CLF logs – Print logs
PHASE III: DATA PROCESSING	
Elements of infrastructure	Outputs
– Transaction Log Analyzer – External data integrator – Report generator – Patron database server – Printing server	– Core e-metrics – Deep e-metrics – Printing reports

Table 8–5 Identifiers and Generated E-Metrics Reports

PHASE IV: REPORTING	
Identifiers	Type of E-Metrics
– Title	– Title use by sessions, visits
– Provider	– Provider statistics
– IP	– Statistics by domains, subnets
– User ID	– Unique visitors counts and demographics

applications—commercial or custom-built—during the data processing phase. The outputs of this phase are then made as datasets of e-metrics measurements.

We should note here the reference to "core" and "deep" e-metrics. NISO Z39.7 defines 4 core datasets for services:[2]

Number of sessions;
Number of searches (queries);
Number of units or descriptive records examined (including downloads); and
Number of virtual visits.

As part of our focus on local e-metrics, we consider the number of virtual visits and the number of unique visitors as "core" datasets. "Deep" e-metrics, on the other hand, will encompass measurements that require the integration of external data such as demographics, title information, or IP address mapping.

At the final reporting phase, presented in Table 8–5, the datasets are arranged and categorized by selected identifiers—title, provider, IP, user ID—to produce the final e-metrics reports.

A more detailed technical examination of Phases II through IV follows.

Data Sources for Data Collection

We first turn our attention to the most common entry points for library users to access e-resources: the library's Web server and catalog server. It is most likely that these two servers are already part of the standard technical equipment for every modern library. The proxy server, on the other hand, is more commonly installed as an additional solution among larger academic and research libraries. As demonstrated in Chapter 7, a proxy server is an interesting e-metrics solution that can prevent direct access to e-resources through bookmarks.

Library Web Server

If we omit for the moment the direct accesses to vendors' Web sites through bookmarks, the most common public access point to the online library resources is probably the library's main Web site. This type of hyperlink access environment motivates the need for two critical elements in our local e-metrics gathering solution:

1. the modified URLs with "click-through script," and
2. the "access log" and its management.

As explained in Chapter 7, every title on the online resources page should be hyperlinked with the "click-through script" information. Hyperlink modification is a daunting and error-prone task especially when there are thousands of titles that require or already have associated hyperlinks. Despite the possibility of creating a "global change" to URLs through some type of batch processing within available Web design software, the library would be well advised to hire, train, and work directly with a webmaster or a person proficient enough in HTML, who can maintain and troubleshoot the modified links. The ideal technical situation, in an environment like Library C for example, would include the development of a database-driven Web site that offers an interface prompting library staff to input the appropriate data for the resource title, the target URL, and the hyperlink source (publisher, vendor). Such a system would then generate the modified URL to be inserted or updated on the e-resource page. Accuracy in the process is important, since the presence of too many inactive or incorrect hyperlinks will not only reflect poorly on the library's quality of service, but it will also skew the final e-metrics results.

The second most important element for a local e-metrics project is the Web server "access log" that records every visitor's activity. Assuming that the library has been granted privileges to obtain the server log, one unavoidable issue is server log management. These access logs typically grow in size quite quickly, thereby requiring systems administrators to adopt various log management techniques. The most common log management method includes regular "log rotation" perhaps on a daily, weekly, or monthly basis. The rotation system archives the log data accumulated between rotation periods before reinitializing the log to begin storing new data again. Sometimes the archived logs are compressed and backed up for future analysis on some data storage server or on other digital media. But if a log rotation procedure is not implemented, the log will need to be emptied at some point because the file size will reach a critical size limit and prevent the server from working properly. Any downtime of a library's Web server should be averted as much as possible, not only to assure library users' satisfaction but also for optimal e-metrics accuracy.

Library's Catalog Server

Once a user visits a library's Web site, they can also access an online resource, such as an electronic serial title or an e-book, through a record retrieved from the catalog server. A title available in an electronic version can be cataloged with an 856 MARC tag containing the appropriate URL. That URL can be customized to include the "click-through script," as described in the previous chapter, and later be made available through the Web OPAC. In other words, the use of the 856 tag is a way to determine the proportion of online resources requests emanating from the Web OPAC.

Although the Web OPAC, or public interface for the library's catalog, is fully integrated within an ILS (Integrated Library System), it usually has a Web server running behind the scenes, therefore keeping its own transaction logs. Administration issues of the library Web server regarding access permissions and log management are equally relevant to the Web OPAC server. While one could consider parsing the Web OPAC access log to extract some title use data, it would be more pragmatic to first assess if collecting data from the Web OPAC is worth the effort given the possible built-in report capabilities of the ILS. Another item to consider is the strong possibility that more data is present in the library Web server logs instead of the OPAC logs because users show a strong preference for the library's main Web server as a primary point of entry for e-resources.

Proxy Servers

Since the early years of the World Wide Web, proxy servers have been utilized to enable faster Web surfing, to improve bandwidth sharing and conservation, to improve network security, and to filter sensitive content.[3] As far as statistics are concerned, libraries could, as shown in Chapter 4, Table 4–8, proxy the network activity of their public workstations in order to evaluate how those computers are being used. Are they used for surfing, e-mailing, chatting, gaming or anything else? More recently though, there has been a renewed interest in proxying online databases, e-journals, and e-books both for remote access control and for e-metrics.

The first role of a proxy server for e-metrics is to reinforce the accuracy of the click-through solution by preventing the user from bookmarking the title's URL once on the vendor's Web site. In step 3 on Figure 8–1, the user is outside of the library domain and can bookmark the title's URL. For our fictitious title in Chapter 7, the original bookmarked URL would be:

http://www.DigitalPublisherInc.com/EOJ.html

As has been mentioned a few times, it is impossible for the library to capture any activity data once the user is on the vendor's Web site. If a user bookmarks the vendor's URL, the usage statistics become skewed because the library's click-through script is bypassed and the visit is not counted. To account for that potential usage practice in e-metrics, a "URL rewriting" proxy

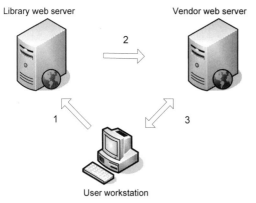

Library web server   Vendor web server

2

1

3

User workstation

1- User requests title with click-through page and modified URL
2- Library web server sends user to vendor web site
3- User workstation exchanges data with vendor web site

Issues:
- Title access not counted if vendor's URL bookmarked by the user
- No possible authentication
- Session duration difficult to determine
- Remote access impossible

Figure 8-1   Traditional Pathway for a Title Request by a User

server[4] could be installed so as to force users to go seamlessly to the library's proxy server before reaching the vendor's Web site as shown in Figure 8–2. In this case, the bookmarked URL for our fictitious title would look like the following:

http://80-www.DigitalPublisherInc.com.**proxy.libraryweb.org**/EOJ.html

When the user tries to access the same title through the bookmarked URL in a new session, the request will always first go to the proxy server before reaching the vendor's Web site. The proxy server will, therefore, record the request to the bookmarked URL in its access log file. We should note that proxy servers are, in the majority of cases, configured to create (E)CLF access logs.

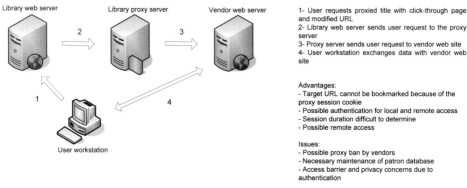

Library web server   Library proxy server   Vendor web server

2   3

1   4

User workstation

1- User requests proxied title with click-through page and modified URL
2- Library web server sends user request to the proxy server
3- Proxy server sends user request to vendor web site
4- User workstation exchanges data with vendor web site

Advantages:
- Target URL cannot be bookmarked because of the proxy session cookie
- Possible authentication for local and remote access
- Session duration difficult to determine
- Possible remote access

Issues:
- Possible proxy ban by vendors
- Necessary maintenance of patron database
- Access barrier and privacy concerns due to authentication

Figure 8-2   User's Request Interception by a URL Rewriting Proxy Server

The second role of a proxy server in e-metrics lies in its ability to request information on behalf of users' workstations by substituting its own IP address for those of the users' networked computer devices. Such capability is particularly useful because more and more vendors/publishers restrict the availability of their online resources to only the library's IP ranges or buildings. A user working from home, for example, would normally be denied access by the publisher's server because their IP address is not part of the authorized IP address range of the library. But if a proxied title is requested by a remote user with a non-library IP, the access to the title would be granted because only the proxy server's IP address is visible to the targeted Web server on the vendors/publishers' end. However, when enabling remote access to restricted online titles, an additional authentication mechanism becomes a necessary technical requirement.[5]

Verifying remote user identities is a necessary step in providing electronic access to digital collections because a library must ensure that only authorized users are granted permission to the restricted online resources. Non-verification of users would violate the licensing agreements with vendors and publishers. In addition, as we detailed in the previous chapter, the authentication of virtual users is a key factor for high-resolution e-metrics.

As a result of the data pathway created for a proxied online title discussed earlier in Chapter 7, Figure 7–4, any access to a proxied URL will be logged by the proxy server whether it comes from the library's online resources page or from the library's Web OPAC. Table 8–6 gives a glimpse at the HTML required of a typical proxy server implementation and result of this new access centralization.

Table 8–6 Proxying of a Modified Hyperlink and the Resulting Entry in the Server Log

HTML Link Format and Sample Log Entry	Result
PROXIED LINK	
<a href="//proxy.library_site/login?	Proxies modified link
url=http://library_site/click_through.php?	Captures base link
Title_id=tid&provider_id=pid&	Uniquely identifies title
url=http://proxy.library_site/login?url=//	Sends to vendor's site
vendor_site/title_page	
=> Resulting Log entry	
127.0.0.1 - - [13/May/2004:18:42:20 -0500] "GET	Gets IP and timestamp
http://proxy.library_site/login?url=//library_	Captures base link
site/click_through.php?	
Title_id=tid&provider_id=pid&	Uniquely identifies title
url=http://proxy.library_site/login?url=//vendor_	
site/title_page	Sends to vendor's site
HTTP/1.1" 200 3083	

Needless to say that from the data extraction standpoint, a unique data source provides the most advantageous environment for limiting margins of error by dramatically reducing repetitive intermediary log analysis steps and offering a consolidated log source.

The ideal situation for the local e-metrics project therefore combines a proxied network environment that uses the "click-through" technique associated with the modified URL containing the "title" and "provider" information. Such a setting

1. greatly facilitates the data collection from the proxy server as the unique access log provider,
2. as described in the preceding chapter, increases the accuracy of the final e-metrics data because the proxy server configured for a per-session cookie would prevent vendors' Web site bookmarking, and
3. offers the choice for an interested library to authenticate its remote users in order to generate high-resolution e-metrics. The overall result would help address one fundamental question of the project: who uses what and from where?

Print Servers

Although not considered a typical e-metrics data source, statistics provided by print servers can also give interesting indications of e-resource use by capturing the volume of articles printed out from online titles. A typical report of printing activity is exemplified in Chapter 4, Table 4–9. In order to capture such data, a library traditionally sets up a print server over a computer network for better control and management of multiple network printers. Many libraries have been investigating or have installed a "pay-for-print" system in an effort to limit wasteful printing and to cut the cost of supporting printing services. A review of the print records stored by the "pay-for-print" software can give us an idea on the volume of printout from online PDF or downloaded articles and on the printing of full-text or abstracts. Sometimes the number of prints and downloads are also included in the vendors' or publishers' statistics as can be seen in some of the COUNTER reports. But the problem with printing statistics is their integration, as external data, with the other e-metrics data acquired from the TLA and from the vendors. The data format of print statistics, usually from "pay-for-print" software, cannot be easily imported into the other e-metrics data. Still, the current lack of focus on printing statistics may simply be that efforts have been devoted to core and deep e-metrics from networked Web server transactions.

Open URL Servers

In conjunction with e-metrics data capture methods, further consideration needs to be given to the emerging technologies of context-sensitive or open link technology[6] using the draft OpenURL standard protocol. The key element of this technological architecture is the OpenURL server that acts as a "link resolver." This server contains a knowledge base of the library's available resources, including a list of possible targets offering the appropriate services to the user. An OpenURL resolver can be hosted on a stand-alone server managed by the library, within an Integrated Library System (ILS), or on a third-party proprietary server.

Because the OpenURL server captures the users' title information requests, it is also capable of gathering usage statistics. The data captured with an OpenURL solution can definitely supplement core e-metrics data by showing multiple levels of detail about user searches (title, article, table of contents, abstract, full-text, citations, author, etc.) and services (document delivery, catalog searches, etc.). Unfortunately, the collection of such usage statistics from OpenURL solutions is greatly complicated by multiple factors:

1. the open link technology is currently still evolving quickly with draft standards for the protocol and usage metrics. Even at the end of the year 2004, the convergence between e-metrics standards and OpenURL metrics specifications remained very marginal to say the least,
2. the functionality of OpenURL is mostly focused for the time being on hyperlinks for serials articles,
3. not every vendor/publisher offers linking that is OpenURL-compliant,
4. not every ILS offers linking that is OpenURL-compliant,
5. some OpenURL software solutions offer pre-defined usage reports, while others require additional in-house development for report creation

Data Processing Requirements

The various transaction logs that have been mentioned so far were initially created for systems administrators to assist in troubleshooting the administration of Web sites and other servers. Over time a secondary use for these logs was identified as increased scrutiny in the e-business world revealed a new data source for CRM (Customer Relationship Management explained in Chapter 1). Earlier we defined transaction log analysis or TLA as the technique used to generate e-metrics data with a computerized log parser. Thus, any library interested in e-metrics should evaluate commercial, open source or custom designed applications capable of performing TLA.

Using Off-the-Shelf Software

In response to the high demand in the business world for Web analytics, many affordable TLA programs became commercially available. These offerings are usually easily deployed, provide a fairly good graphic interface to their operation, and produce user-friendly reports in various file formats. Despite the improved flexibility that has been added to these software solutions over time, these programs are designed with a "one-size-fits-all" approach in order to meet the needs of e-commerce. But are such commercial programs adaptable for library e-metrics use?

The often proprietary format of logs from online library catalogs cannot always be deciphered by off-the-shelf Web analytics software, therefore resulting in the creation of unusable reports. On the other hand, if the library's main Web server logs are created in a (E)CLF-compliant format, the library can still obtain interesting usage reports using commercial TLA programs. Most commercial ILS offerings that include the standard Web servers like Apache and Microsoft IIS can typically be configured to create (E)CLF logs. But these same TLA programs are of little use against log files that have been altered to measure e-resource usage captured from clicks of customized URLs similar to those seen in the examples of proxied titles with click-through techniques.

Using Open Source Software

The growing interest in open source technologies has also had an impact on the field of e-metrics. The attraction of open source software solutions is their ability to be acquired at no purchase cost but usually under some type of licenses like GPL (General Public License).[7] In addition, the source codes for open source applications are publicly available and can be improved, tweaked, and customized. But under such licensing agreements and publicly open technical specifications, one essentially uses open source programs without many of the guarantees of off-the-shelf software packages. Are these solutions adaptable to the library e-metrics environment?

Even though open source software can be freely downloaded, its hidden costs may be found in the complexities and problems associated with its deployment. Some open source programs lack documentation and most require some level of administration and programming by individuals possessing fine knowledge in open source operating systems. Other implementation difficulties may arise when centralized support for such software is minimal or unavailable, although one can always subscribe to some listserv and converse with the global open source community of software and solutions contributors. But much like commercial solutions and their inherent TLA limitations, even open source solutions may still have difficulty in analyzing transaction logs of modified e-resource URLs. As with commercial software, open source TLA still needs to address these specialized URLs without any guarantee of success. For these reasons, some libraries prefer to develop homegrown TLA applications.

Using Custom Designed Tools: Homegrown or Outsourced

So far, our review of e-metrics project considerations has shown that getting quality library e-metrics requires a high degree of customization. Achieving this may lead a library with a Library B-type environment, for example, to out-source the development of TLA applications. Environments more closely akin to that of Library C with their own IT support/specialists already in place could decide to develop all aspects of the TLA solution in-house. This approach is certainly the best option if the programming skill set is available internally because a library's developers are more likely to be familiar with the library's environment and needs. Another justification for internal TLA software development is the concern of privacy protection from third party actors, especially if additional user authentication information is included in the e-metrics solution. But would these customized TLA options solve the inherent problems associated with e-resources usage statistics?

Whether a library chooses to outsource or develop in-house TLA applications for e-metrics, both choices offer a better chance of creating programs that take into account the very specific data capturing adaptations required and made by a library. Still, the major technical difficulties of these options are:

1. writing codes[8] to parse the server logs with the modified URLs similar to:

(Line 1) 127.0.0.1 - - [13/Feb/2004:06:20:49 -0500] "GET
http://www.library.org/click_through.php?title_id=5&provider_id=10&
url=http://www.DigitalPublisherInc.com/EOJ.html HTTP/1.1" 200 290

---

2. integrating external data related to the titles, the IP addresses, and the users if they are being authenticated
3. generating reports in some standardized format, i.e., text with tab delimiters easily imported in applications like Excel

Needless to say that customized TLA programs would probably require many test and correction cycles before reaching a satisfactory compromise between reporting expectations and technical constraints. There is also a very high probability that using an in-house developed e-metrics solution will increase the complexity of the project with each new question and request that arises after each series of steps required for output verification and interpretation.

Necessary Development Units

Depending on the type of e-metrics solution selected by an individual library, e-metrics data processing can be accomplished on hardware ranging from standard desktop personal computers (PCs) to powerful servers.

If the library chooses to use commercial or open-source applications for e-metrics, the TLA and report data processing could be easily accomplished using a regular PC, on workstations, or on servers with a Unix-type operating system such as Linux. While both application types are designed for TLA that benefits the business world, neither type requires too much technical investment although they are typically limited to recording core e-metrics, such as visits and unique visitors. Thus neither type is truly capable of or suited to the integration of external data for deep e-metrics.

Data processing hardware choices for TLA solutions based on home-grown applications can vary from standard PCs to small workstations or servers with an open source environment necessary for programming and data processing. One incentive for using Unix-flavored operating systems for TLA and e-metrics is their built-in scripting capability which can be utilized to perform flexible log manipulation. For example, when performing log analysis, we may only be interested in lines containing the "click-through" script in the log. With a Unix command like "grep" that enables one to find a specific text string in a file, we can considerably reduce the log size by retaining only the relevant lines before parsing the log. Such Unix commands allow for the creation of a smaller log file with the most relevant data that ultimately results in faster data processing.

If we want to obtain more in-depth e-metrics from our log analysis, then it becomes mandatory to utilize a more powerful and stable system because the amount of data manipulation dictates the need for considerable disk space. Perhaps the most demanding log data processing configuration is called for when reports generation dictates that e-metrics data processing be carried out in combination with a database management system.[9] In this case, the log is parsed and stored in a database from which usage reports are generated with some database query language. This particular solution requires the presence of one or multiple servers with powerful processor(s), considerable memory, and a large amount of disk space.

Predictable data overload and the need for processing flexibility should be taken into account regardless of the preferred data processing choice. In light of such considerations, the implied technological requirements therefore include both massive computing power for rapid data processing and high storage capacity for the potentially voluminous output.

External Data Related to IP Addresses and User Demographics

If we want to enrich e-metrics reports with data that are not directly extracted from the logs, then we need to use additional customized applications to incorporate "external data" that are typically loaded before the actual TLA starts. Nevertheless, the integration of external data still takes place after the log parsing process in order to create more meaningful, contextual, and in-depth e-metric reports. Such data integration applies to three critical data identifiers: title, IP and user. Regardless of which particular identifier we are interested in tracking, we must know beforehand (1) the external data source, (2) the data format, (3) the quality of the data, (4) the periodic data update frequency, (5) the

Table 8–7 External Data on IP and User Information and Possible Use

E-Metric Data Element	Possible External Data	Possible Use
IP	– Map of domains and subnets	– On and off-site visit count – Geographic distribution of recorded accesses
User	– Affiliation – Status – Category	– More accurate unique visitor count – Demographics – Access control for licensing compliance

possibility of automation for the data import, and finally (6) the estimated volume of information to be dealt with. This external data integration phase always necessitates additional program developments to streamline operations as much as possible. Table 8–7 details the possible use, in a deep e-metrics report, of external data related to the IP and User data elements.

IP: Address Mapping and Subnets

Whenever a user requests access to an online title, the network IP address of his/her machine is recorded in one of the access logs of the library's servers. Every library normally knows the range of its network IP addresses, not only for the purposes of network administration but also in response to vendors' licensing restrictions to on-site access. The IP address field can be very informative for the library because one can easily determine volume of internal library network versus external network virtual visits. In other words, we can determine if the user is using the library on-site or off-site, from the library computers or not. A quick analysis of each requesting IP address can be performed during the log parsing process so as to gauge the proportion of remote versus on-site access connections. The resulting report, similar to one presented in Table 8–8, would inform us about the delineation of on-site and off-site virtual library visits.

As demonstrated in the Part II chapters, the application of such statistics can be important to online resources access management while providing close monitoring of possible licensing contract requirements and constraints. From another perspective, such measurements help us appreciate how important the loss of library service is for every online title when its access is restricted to only on-site or in-building connections.

The domain name of the library user's networked computer device can also be determined from the IP address field in the log. This information could be of some interest for libraries interested in identifying the broad "geographic" locations of their users. But it is even more informative to use this information to

Table 8-8 On-Site and Off-Site Access Report

Report date: 03/22/2004 10:30:27
Statistics for E-JOURNALS only

Rank	Title	Source	Total Visits	Visits From *On* Site IPs	% of Total Visits	Visits From *Off* Site IPs	% of Total Visits
1	Nature	Nature	952	440	46.22%	512	53.78%
2	New England Journal of Medicine	MMS	886	378	42.66%	508	57.34%
3	The Journal of Biological Chemistry	ASBMB	671	327	48.73%	344	51.27%
4	Cell	cell Press	579	279	48.19%	300	51.81%
5	Science	HighWire	555	257	46.31%	298	53.69%
6	JAMA	AMA	518	206	39.77%	312	60.23%
7	Proceedings of the National Academy of Sciences of the United States of America	NAS	487	258	52.98%	229	47.02%
8	Lancet	Science Direct	311	163	52.41%	148	47.59%
9	Journal of Immunology	AAI	308	190	61.69%	118	38.31%
10	JAMA	Galegroup	291	106	36.43%	185	63.57%

Table 8–9 Access Report with Network Subnet Mapping

Report date: 03/22/2004 10:30:31
Counts of Unique IP from each subnet

Rank	Subnet	Unique IP Counts	% of Total IPs
1	Off-campus	2497	58.4641
2	West Campus	622	14.5633
3	Academic VLAN	299	7.0007
4	Clinical VLAN	233	5.4554
5	Computer Science	170	3.9803
6	Research Thicknet Network	125	2.9267
7	Library	109	2.5521
8	South Campus	77	1.8029
9	Hospital	38	0.8897
10	AppleTalk VLAN	21	0.4917

obtain activity statistics by IP subnets within the library or host organization. For example, a library could ask the networking department or an equivalent IT service responsible for network administration to outline the subnet distribution for each department, section, building, or branch of the library. Then when performing log parsing, the IP address of each request is mapped and statistics would be gathered by subnet. From this information, a library could observe comparative use between library branches or sections. The only external data necessary to complete this analysis then is the map of subnets. Again, the difficulty in this reporting process comes not from the integration of the specific network data but rather from the acquisition of the IP subnet mapping. But for libraries that have a map of their IP address attributions, their resulting e-metrics can offer further usage details. In Table 8–9, we see how an academic library can identify the geographic distribution of the workstations used by its patrons.

In the absence of a user authentication process, the statistics showing the geographical distribution of online requests gives some low resolution insights into the most active patron access points. Generating statistics that show network sessions by active IP subnets is not technically complex and a very achievable goal once the library receives additional help from a networking department or an Internet Service Provider (ISP).

User: Affiliation, Status, Category

One of the most sought after use statistics are those related to virtual users. If users are indeed authenticated when accessing an online title, a library would be able to generate a more detailed report with user demographics. Demographics reports are achievable because the user's ID is used for accurate counts of unique users for a given title. This scenario is akin to the assignment of the user's ID as the primary key to a user database built on the model of any customer database in the business world. Each user would have specific attributes determined and assigned by the library and statistics would be generated based on those very same attributes. Some typical user attributes are the affiliation (township, branch library, campus department etc.), status (active, blocked, terminated etc.), and category (student, professional, young adult, senior citizen, etc.).

When generating deep e-metrics, it can be difficult to use the borrower list from the library's management system as the source for user information, primarily because it is usually in a proprietary format, designed for a very different use, and difficult if not impossible to export for e-metrics use. It is also highly unlikely that a library would decide to build a user database just for the purposes of e-metrics; chances are that there is already an existing user database used for other administrative reasons.[10] The technical challenge to integrating user-specific data is to find a way to integrate the relevant and approved user's information into the e-metrics data processing stage. One possible solution is to first export the user database into a flat text file as a user list with the various fields and a standard delimiter (tab, comma, or semicolon). Then, when a user ID is read from the server log, the user-related statistics—like affiliation or category—are updated based upon the user's attributes retrieved from the user list.

There are several variables associated with the user database that can affect the quality and the accuracy of deep e-metrics. For many libraries, the user database undergoes data changes over time, creating issues of how and when to use such external data in the e-metrics project. If we want to rerun e-metrics reports to measure activity of a past time period, our statistics should be based on the user list that reflects the status of the library population that existed during that same time frame, not the user data as it exists today. One possible solution to this problem is to keep data snapshots of the user database at predefined periods of the year, for example every quarter, every six months, at the end of year, and so on. While this snapshot solution ultimately increases the number of user database copies in the data repository, this method offers greater potential for creating more accurate e-metrics reports. In the end, the application of a user database is worth the investment for in-depth statistics but still requires careful planning, technical adjustments, and on-going maintenance.

Server for Library User Database

It is particularly difficult in e-metrics to measure user demographics and detect user behavior patterns. But by implementing a user authentication process it becomes possible to collect e-metrics that includes demographics data. After instituting user authentication, it becomes necessary to compare the user ID against a database of authorized users and to associate more specific information to the user.

For example, in an academic environment, the statistics showing the affiliation of the library user requesting e-resources can be vital for identifying cost centers and population service points. The accuracy and the granularity of this type of collected information ultimately rely heavily on the quality of the patron database queried for user authentication. Table 8–10 details the ranking of users' departments by number of visits to a particular title.

By having a user authentication system in place, we could analyze through e-metrics the sample title usage by the number of visits received, by the number of unique users who requested the title, and by the number of visits per unique user. Each analysis approach complements the other one and minimizes possible restrictive interpretations that may not reflect the complexity of real world user information access trends. For example, a low title visit count could be due

Table 8–10 Specific Title Use by Department

Report date: 03/22/2004 10:30:31
Log from 01/Nov/2003:00:11:41 to 30/Nov/2003:23:59:30
Use by DEPARTMENT for NATURE through NATURE

Rank	DEPARTMENT	Visits	% Total Visits	Unique Visitors	% Total Unique Visitors	Visits Per User
1	Biochemistry	157	0.2856	25	0.173	6.28
2	SSW	74	0.1346	12	0.0831	6.17
3	Alumni Unknown Department	70	0.1274	7	0.0485	10.00
4	Microbiology	60	0.1092	11	0.0761	5.45
5	Undergraduate Student Unknown Department	54	0.0982	8	0.0554	6.75
6	Unknown Department Research Foundation	51	0.0928	11	0.0761	4.64
7	NOT registered Unknown Department	44	0.0801	7	0.0485	6.29
8	Graduate Student Unknown Department	42	0.0764	7	0.0485	6.00
9	Pharmacology	33	0.0600	10	0.0692	3.30
10	Neurobiology and Behavior	31	0.0564	8	0.0554	3.88

to a small pool of users, and as a consequence the count of visits per user would give a fairer picture of the most active department.

After integrating the external data of the patron database, it becomes possible to perform a title usage study by user's affiliation. The in-depth output of user analysis could be then be separated by department in an academic environment or by local library in a non-academic setting.

A report similar to the one in Table 8–11 gives libraries a tangible way to identify which online titles their patrons favor most. Because the measurements of visit counts and unique visitor counts are repeatable and consistent across titles and patrons' affiliation, they can be used to optimize the title selection process. Not only are such measurements crucial for collection management but they also provide more data to better support and leverage library's funding requests. As with any statistical report, one must keep in mind that the quality of the gathered information is always subject to the reliability of the back-end patron database.

Understandably, user authentication may not be widely used in libraries for multiple reasons such as concerns of privacy protection, the access barrier effect, or the burden of maintaining an up-to-date user database. Any library wishing to uniquely identify their users must first invest in one or more servers that can host a database management system. Then, the library should define clear policies regarding data protection and usage. In any case, a minimal rule is that there must be a total disconnect between user IDs and personal data in the final reporting analysis. Once such a system is set up and secured, the database must be created, populated with the necessary data, and made available for queries. Since user demographics and affiliations will be queried from the user database as part of the log analysis, the data entry quality and data maintenance of the database are absolutely crucial for accurate e-metrics analysis. If the information retrieved from the user database is erroneous or incomplete, then it is of negligible value for e-metrics. In other words, the quality of in-depth e-metrics with demographics is only as good as the quality of the user database.

We conclude this chapter with a synthetic view of the possible and non-restrictive architectural elements that could be involved in an e-metrics project, as shown in Figure 8–3. Both mandatory and optional servers/workstations, according to our classification, have been represented for the different stages of the project implementation.

Our review of the technical considerations for vendor-produced and locally-acquired e-metrics has demonstrated that realistic objectives and expectations, combined with a correct assessment of technical, financial and staffing resources, are instrumental in the success of this endeavor. Of course a cost/benefit analysis must be carried out prior to any implementation of e-metrics initiatives. It should also be noted that it is not possible to plan everything in advance and that optimizations are achieved only by trials and errors. Nevertheless,

Table 8-11 Most Accessed Titles by Department

Report date: 03/29/2004 16:48:06
Log from 01/Nov/2003:00:11:41 to 30/Nov/2003:23:59:30
Use by TITLE for BIOCHEMISTRY department

Rank	TITLE	Provider	Visits	% Total Visits	Unique Visitors	% Total Unique Visitors
1	Biochemistry	American Chemical Society	242	0.4403	62	0.4292
2	Nature	Nature	157	0.2856	25	0.173
3	Cell	cell Press	149	0.2711	22	0.1523
4	PubMed+Full-Text LINKOUT	NLM	125	0.2274	11	0.0761
5	Science	HighWire	89	0.1619	19	0.1315
6	Annual Review of Biochemistry	AR	79	0.1437	20	0.1384
7	The Journal of Biological Chemistry	ASBMB	60	0.1092	14	0.0969
8	Journal of Cellular Biochemistry	Wiley	57	0.1037	14	0.0969
9	Trends in Biochemical Sciences	Science Direct	51	0.0928	9	0.0623
10	Proceedings of the National Academy of Sciences of the United States of America	NAS	49	0.0892	14	0.0969

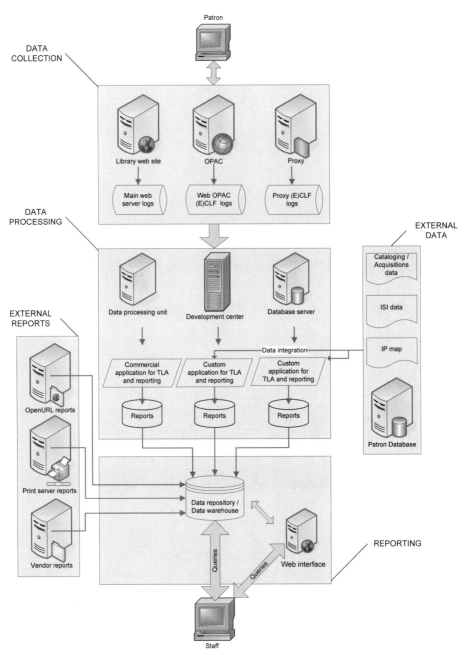

Figure 8-3 Synthetic View of Possible Elements of Infrastructure for an E-Metrics Project

successful outcomes will be based on flexibility, insightfulness and above all creative use of the e-metrics infrastructure. But as we will explore in the next chapter, the catalyst for a really profitable e-metrics project exists in the definition of sound and clear library administrative policies.

Notes

1. See the original definition at www.intranetjournal.com/features/datawarehousing .html.
2. www.niso.org/emetrics/current/appendixA.html.
3. More detailed explanations about proxy servers and techniques are available at www.pandc.org/proxy/slides-recent/index.htm and libmain.stfx.ca/gbertran/ welcome.htm. A 2000 survey gives a glimpse on the use of proxy servers in public and academic libraries at www.pandc.org/proxy/survey/report.html.
4. A good technical explanation is available at www.usefulutilities.com/support/ technical.html.
5. A good explanation for this solution can be found at www.usefulutilities.com/ ezproxy/userauth.shtml.
6. More on the framework at www.niso.org/committees/committee_ax.html.
7. A detailed description of the "open source" movement is available at www.open source.org.
8. It is up to the developer(s) to choose his (their) tools, preferably open source, but it is very likely to be some kind of scripting languages like Perl for the log parsing with regular expressions (some examples of regular expressions are at http://en .wikipedia.org/wiki/Regular_expression and some definitions at http://computing dictionary.thefreedictionary.com/Regular%20expression). Another alternative also exists with PHP/MySQL for Web-oriented development.
9. An example of such intense e-metrics processing was demonstrated by Joe Zucca University of Pennsylvania at www.arl.org/stats/newmeas/emetrics/arljune2003 .ppt.
10. See also at www.usefulutilities.com/support/usr/.

9

E-Metrics and Staffing: Creating the Team and Defining the Project

After examining the various technical details associated with e-metrics project implementation, it becomes important to understand the larger view of an e-metrics project, thus focusing on the ways in which the e-metrics data collection enterprise must be supported and initiated by the library's administration as part of a global vision for collection development and Electronic Resource Management (ERM) as covered in Chapter 6. The main objective of this chapter is to examine the organizational and staffing components of an e-metrics project. In contrast with the preceding chapter on the technical implications of e-metrics, this section will be more inclusive. Thus the three classes of libraries A, B, and C, as categorized in the second part of this book, should find most of the topics treated here relevant to their respective situations. In order to gather e-metrics data, the administration of almost any type of library needs to define its course of action according to a decision tree illustrated in Figure 9–1.

The chapters in Part II of the book provided numerous examples of how e-metrics data can, indeed, provide measurements of title use needed by library administrators to support informed management decisions on digital library collections. Library administrators must advocate e-metrics projects knowing that e-metrics can supplement ERM strategies by affording the best methods for producing performance indicators for e-resources. Through a focused examination of the strategic approach and mindset expected from the library administrators and librarians in their quest for better e-metrics, we will try to answer the following questions:

- Can using e-metrics help in adjusting library staff to the shift to digital collections and environments?

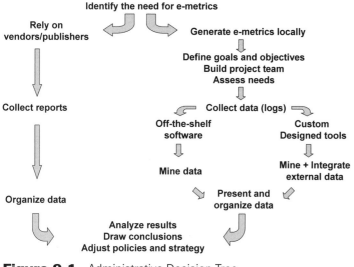

Figure 9-1 Administrative Decision Tree

- What is expected from the librarians and the systems personnel in order to facilitate the implementation of an e-metrics project?
- What are the library' e-metrics management policies regarding the definition of title use, patron authentication, report processing, title persistence over time?

Set Up the E-Metrics Team within Library Organization

The switch from print to digital is irreversibly redefining the role of libraries. Now that the public is accustomed to accessing e-resources over computer networks, the efforts necessary for a library and its staff to keep those online resources available all the time unfortunately remain less obvious to the outside world. The workload within libraries has progressively shifted from the physical handling of physical materials to the management of electronic data by using new technologies to deliver services and information over computer networks. In other words, a modern library in the digital age must fully recognize and embrace the growing importance of its IT component to better serve its constituency.

The proper assessment of overall library staffing requirements is critical to the e-metrics project. The first organizational reform must take place within the library itself; otherwise a simple installation of an enhanced library technology infrastructure would soon become inoperable if it is not supported by adequate and knowledgeable personnel. Establishing an e-metrics project can help library administrators assess the strengths and weaknesses of the library organization, specifically with regards to the ERM workflow. In addition, the integration of e-metrics into library operations can provide a real opportunity to evaluate the potential internal "digital divide" affecting some departments and library staff members. Such information can then be used to address staffing skill levels by focusing training on emerging technologies that have already altered the processes and workflows of any digital or "hybrid" library.

During the e-metrics planning phase it is important to identify a project team. In order to foster a team approach and a collective awareness needed to overcome e-metrics challenges, the project team should include people from different departments and with various professional backgrounds. A diverse staff perspective will ultimately facilitate establishing the best e-metrics solution while keeping every actor informed of the limitations that the library will certainly encounter throughout the project. The project team should include representatives concerned with library administration, public access and reference services, technical services, IS (Information Systems), and electronic resources management.

Library Management

For some years now library administrators have been confronted with the lack of e-metrics that would help them make cost-effective decisions for the management of their e-resources. The chapters in Part II demonstrated how increased budgetary constraints make the collection of consistent, standardized, and systematic e-metrics a pressing administrative matter. And a significant portion of this book has illustrated how despite some progress made in the last two to three years, vendor-supplied data, when available, are seldom tailored to all of the various library reporting needs.

Initiating an e-metrics project in a library is a political decision that should be made by the library's top-level management. The decision should be seen as a proactive action that has multiple strategic ramifications for current and future library activities. External pressures, like the revolution in the online publishing environment and the volatile economic models of e-commerce, are forcing libraries to justify their existence as well as to review their relationship with the information stakeholders: the vendors, the financiers, and the users. The combination of vendor-supplied and locally-acquired e-metrics constitute a major opportunity for libraries to (1) review their negotiation power with vendors, (2) quantify the return on investment in their subscriptions for online resources, and (3) support educated decisions made during the title selection process. But even if the project objectives are clear, only a strong leadership can successfully mobilize all the resources necessary to tackle the project issues.

Finally, library managers should be involved in the e-metrics project assessment because they have the authority to make the project a high priority both locally and within the library community. Their awareness of the administrative problems and commitment to resolving them could improve efforts to bring the most needed personnel, budget, and technical infrastructure resources to the project implementation. Projects such as these can potentially hasten the development of library-oriented e-metrics software and the standardization of e-metrics in libraries. The possibilities for e-metrics advancement may increase if several library leaders can produce some concrete and applied e-metrics, perhaps motivating further networking and collaborative work between libraries. But as shown in earlier chapters, as long as libraries cannot get reliable and consistent usage statistics, they will mainly rely on various assumptions and unsubstantiated observations to make critical management decisions. With insufficient performance data, libraries may not only mismanage their fiscal resources, but also create dissatisfaction among users who might ultimately never get the adequate services they desire and need. In addition to their application to ERM endeavors, e-metrics fit well into the Evidence-Based Librarianship[1] (EBL) approach. E-metrics can definitely contribute to the continuous improvement of libraries in the six EBL domains: "reference/inquiries, education, collection, management, information access and retrieval, and marketing/promotion".[2]

Access Services and Reference Departments

The access services and reference staff, acting as frontline interfaces between the public outside world and the daily library activities, provide important feedback on user needs and remarks. This staff's input could reveal some systemic problems or suggest improvements in the library information delivery system. Such staff frequently addresses accessibility issues as users interact with the variety and complexities of a library's technology implementation. Issues with broken URLs, unreachable vendors' Web sites, network glitches, rejected authentications, missing titles, expired subscriptions, complex navigation, concurrent user limitations, and ADA (Americans with Disabilities Act of 1990) non-compliance are all examples of concerns reported by users. Apart from poor service quality, such potential access inhibitors could cause missed virtual visits and lower e-metrics if they persist for too long. Needless to say that alerts from the public access and reference staff or directly from users become crucial clues for library systems troubleshooting. Depending on the nature and description of the access issue, the technical support staff can quickly diagnose the problem and hopefully fix it within a reasonable timeframe. Library staff members directly in contact with the public must therefore be included in the e-metrics project team in order to report incidents and to assist users in their use of the library's electronic services.

Technical Services Department

We next need to consider the project role of library technical services staff, typically consisting of individuals responsible for managing the acquisition, cataloging, authority control, and physical processing of library materials. Technical services staff, including serials librarians, are true producers and consumers of e-metrics. On the one hand, they help gather e-resources statistics locally by, for example, correctly cataloging titles with electronic access. They can also contribute to the production of in-depth e-metrics by providing external information such as ISBN/ISSN/e-ISSN, date of availability of a title, date of subscription cancellation, title price and ISI impact factors. On the other hand, technical services are the prime beneficiary of e-metrics data in their resources management activities. Usage statistics, even during the print era, have always been one of the most sought-after data that can assist in collection management. It is therefore fundamental that the locally-generated e-metrics reports fulfill at least the collection development and management needs of these staff by providing in-depth resource asset and usage datasets whenever possible.

Finally, for title selection and collection development purposes, the technical services staff is expected to store, organize, and analyze the usage reports from various vendors, whether or not the library is able to collect its own local e-metrics. Because the members of this department confront the complexity of manipulating e-metrics data firsthand, they can therefore provide constructive feedback on both the limitations and optimizations of local e-metrics production if such a project is launched within the library.

Electronic Resources Manager

If the IT department is responsible for the technical accessibility of the digital resources, the electronic resources manager must guarantee that those resources are duly licensed for ongoing availability.

The job duties of an electronic resources manager are increasingly complex because of the ever-changing environment in the electronic publishing world. Every modification in contractual agreements translates into potential changes in user access and must be promptly reflected on the library's Web site and OPAC. As a result, the accuracy of e-metrics counts, generated from both the vendors' end and from the library's side, depends upon the availability of the e-resources to the public. It is critical that the person in charge of the e-resources have a highly dynamic interaction with the rest of the library because any problem with these e-resources is often immediately noticed and reported by users. Updating URLs and troubleshooting remote access issues are tasks that the electronic resources manager needs to perform sometimes independently or sometimes in collaboration with the other actors in the e-metrics project.

As a liaison between the library and the digital resource distributors as well as between the library and the users, the electronic resources manager therefore has a strategic role in the success of the e-metrics project. He or she must have a good understanding of Web technologies (browsers, hosts, proxy, authentication, URLs), networking terminology (IP ranges, subnets, remote access, firewalls), and a constant interest in observing the developing parameters in the vendors' digital publishing and electronic access environment (market consolidation, pricing models, compliance with industry standards).

IT Department

The Internet revolution in the 1990s brought the online delivery of information to a new level so that libraries could no longer ignore nor avoid the importance and increased role of IT in modern libraries. As libraries and their processes initially became more computerized over time, many curious, courageous, and technically savvy librarians became "systems" librarians by choice or by necessity. But the complexity of the technologies behind the Web eventually led most libraries to invest more in their IT or Systems department for technical infrastructure setup, programming, and troubleshooting.

As a gateway to e-resources, the library must confront the technical and staffing complexity of a Web-driven environment. The apparent simplicity of browser-based access to online resources obfuscates the complexity of managing heterogeneous applications, technologies, and infrastructure. Equally challenging is the need to devise new effective ways to aggregate and make sense of disparate data generated and transmitted over the Web. Based upon our prior study of the infrastructure, libraries obviously need to be supported by systems administrators, by Web masters, by analysts programmers, and by database administrators. Systems administrators ensure that library servers are up and running for digital collections to be accessible. Web masters are responsible for the library's public Web site(s) as well as other possible internal Web sites used for in-house library communication. Analyst programmers are those who can develop customized applications for the library. And finally database administrators set up, manage, and maintain the various databases fundamental to many library services and operations. But we cannot realistically expect to find a sizable IT department in every library. Based on its resources and list of projects, it is up to the individual library to determine what type of IS team adequately fits the needs to achieve its respective library mission.

The gradual evolution of e-metrics data collection over time proves that libraries and vendors are trying to cope with a technological revolution that holds much promise yet is difficult to keep pace with. Therefore, e-metrics stakeholders need to collaborate with IT specialists who can help them achieve their respective goals in the field. This coordination is necessary because systems staff can assist in obtaining the highest return on investment from the different technologies that disseminate information and offer the best services to all users of online resources.

Determine Librarians' Skill Set Expansion and Coordination

Recalling some of the performance reports viewed in the Part II chapters, the high volume of e-metrics data measuring online activities may give some people the impression that there can be a significant reduction in the amount of library staff assistance provided to users in their quest for information. Nothing could be farther from the truth; in fact, librarians continue to provide both online help and one-on-one support to the public whenever necessary. Users, like customers in the business domain, are not often aware of the totality of the information supply chain. However, putting online resources at the users' fingertips requires an increase in staff information literacy—from the reference and circulation staff, to the catalogers and the librarians in technical services. So as technology advances in this Information Age, library administrators will need to continue to advocate for staff skill enhancements.

Public Relations for Reference and Circulation

How can reference and circulation librarians possibly affect the collection of e-metrics data? The answer to that question lies in two service aspects of libraries: public relations and "information relay."

When serving as the primary "human" interfaces for the library to the outside world, the reference and circulation departments are in a strategic position to promote the library's online services and resources. Proactive public relations strategies including development of information literacy classes, user guides, helpdesk, online chats, and "ask-a-librarian" services can directly or indirectly translate into better e-metrics.

As "information relays," reference and circulation librarians are part of the library "alert system." When users cannot access the library's online resources, user complaints, suggestions, and questions are usually received by e-mail, direct phone calls, or in-person visits to the circulation or reference desk. The staff of the circulation and reference departments can improve the library's reaction time to user needs by performing first level library user support and by alerting the other appropriate library services involved in data and systems management. It is important to note that staff response to user needs should not be filtered and prioritized according to staff perceptions: the goals of these frontline public service units should be to decrease library system downtime and provide increased information access to the public, thereby increasing the chances for the library to acquire better e-metrics data. It is in the library administration's best interest to keep the relevant personnel up-to-date about the access policies for the Web services and online resources available to the public.

Cataloging E-Resources

The shift from print to digital has created a whole new set of problems for collection catalogers. Take for example a title that is available in both print and online format. In order to accommodate this "in-between" or "two-in-one" situation, the 856 MARC field has become the primary tag for delineating electronic location, mostly for URLs, and access information to an electronic resource.[3] But the cataloging of electronic resources has so many intricacies; even the Anglo-American Cataloging Rules (AACR2) devotes a whole chapter to it, known as the "revised Chapter 9 for cataloging electronic resources."

In our discussion of local e-metrics initiatives, we essentially focused on modifications to the 856 field that enable the capture of requests for online titles through the library Web OPAC. But even this solution accomplishes our main objective of collecting "core" e-metrics, if there still remains some unformulated standards in e-resources data that can eventually impact potential external e-metrics data integration. A perfect example of such additional bibliographic information is the "e-ISXN" which is not yet a commonly used standard for books or serials. Also, it is difficult to predict the impact of future cataloging guidelines on fixed and variable MARC fields for electronic resources. The only thing that we can be sure of is the ongoing task for the library community to revise and standardize existing documentation on electronic resources cataloging, as seen in the "OCLC-MARC coding guidelines for electronic resources."[4] As a logical administrative consequence of our e-metrics project analysis, the cataloging department staff should maintain up-to-date knowledge on the evolution in cataloging standards and its importance to e-metrics for modern libraries.

ERM Team

As we progress in the digital era, the management of electronic resources will become one of the highest priorities for many libraries. Because e-metrics currently provide the only rational means to measure the return on e-resources investments, they should then be seen as one of the most anticipated ERM tools. However, we should not forget that even the most well-conceived tool or technology will never produce the best expected results with poorly organized and untrained operators. It is crucial that library administration takes the necessary strategic planning steps that include a careful analysis of staffing knowledge and needs.

Regardless of whether e-metrics come from vendors or are locally acquired, library administration can better prepare its organizational issues by answering the following set of questions:

Present organization:
- What policies, structure, and procedures are already in place for capturing and measuring print collection statistics?
- What policies, structure, and procedures are already in place for ERM?
- How can we integrate e-metrics into the ERM work flows and processes?
- How many people are or will be part of the ERM team?

Personnel:
- What will be the impact of e-metrics on the existing job description of each staff member?
- How will we train the staff in e-metrics use?
- What additional skills are needed in IT, in terms of statistical analysis, and in terms of applying national and eventually international standards to data gathering and information access?

Data collection strategy:
- How will the e-metrics data be collected and managed by the ERM team?
- How will the team handle the diversity of reports?
- What would be the criteria for determining e-metrics data validity?

Frequency:
- How often will e-metrics data collection and analysis take place?
- Is there a plan to address the data analysis over time?

Communication:
- How will the ERM team report its findings internally and externally?
- How will the ERM team coordinate its operations with the other departments of the library?

Monitoring:
- How will the ERM team evaluate its activities and review its procedures?

Viewed from a different angle, every library that plans to implement an e-metrics project would need to reorganize staffing and processes according to the nature of its specific situation. In other words, a library must assess its own goals, resources, strategies, actions, and feedback mechanisms for a positive e-metrics project outcome.

Consider Additional "Systems" Personnel

Our present time has been frequently referred to as the "Information Age" and so libraries must keep up with information technologies to fulfill their mission and continuing role as gateways to information. The shift from print to digital is another event in the IT revolution that ultimately pressures modern libraries to augment their investments in IT. The previous chapter gave us an idea of the possible technical infrastructure elements that a library could consider for an e-metrics project. But one must also evaluate the technology needs in terms of systems personnel for user support, in-house development, and data repository management. In keeping with our three generic library environment categories, a 1999 survey[5] offers a good indication of the disparity between academic, public, school and special libraries and their respective available technical support resources. As the number of e-resources and e-services has increased dramatically since the completion of this study, so has the need for IT support in libraries. Although Library B and C environments would really be the only ones inclined to invest more in IT infrastructure and support, the pivotal role of systems for e-metrics can not be ignored by Library A.

User Access Management

Use counts and usage patterns for online resources can be immediately affected by a variety of technical difficulties. As a consequence, the library must have solid technical support available to diagnose, troubleshoot, and inform users about incident resolutions. As we said earlier, the reference librarians and the electronic resource manager can provide first level user support in times of denied information access to digital content. But if these individuals identify or suspect the issue to be a local problem, then they need to contact the systems librarian or the IT help desk. This troubleshooting scenario implies that one way or another the library needs to train some staff members or hire new staff with IT skills to ensure continuity of information services.

In response to the ongoing expansion of the Web and other network services, libraries are required to invest, maintain, update, and upgrade their IT infrastructure and applications on a regular basis. Unfortunately, not every library can afford to have local IT support on-hand because of the costs incurred against potentially flat or reduced library budgets. But not having IT assistance readily available could cause increased computer and software downtime which ultimately leads to a reduced quality of user service and a lower return on library technological investments. Such a lack of support can ultimately frustrate the library's users and prevent librarians from fulfilling their responsibilities to the best of their abilities.

The technical implications of using an authentication system of library users as part of e-metrics data integration offers additional justification for increased or improved local library IT support. If a library decides to institute a user authentication process for improved compliance with licensing agreements and more informative e-metrics, then it must take into account the constraints inherent in the maintenance of an authorized users database. With the inclusion of the user authentication processes, one can anticipate that any unsuccessful authentication could result in communication with the library's helpdesk. Once again, the first level support staff could find the solution for trivial cases, but anything that involves the data validity and integrity of the user database will naturally require more experienced IT professionals. Depending upon available staffing resources, libraries could choose to assign such troubleshooting responsibilities to entities outside the library's organizational units. Ultimately, the obligation for libraries to protect the privacy of their users should dictate a decision not to outsource the management of their user database. As a consequence, a reliable and responsible user authentication system demands an administrative library commitment to establishing strong internal IT support.

In-House Programming

Of the multiple services offered by a library, access to online resources is probably the most Web-oriented. The library's Web site design and availability are therefore crucial for the collection of informative e-metrics data. It is possible that for some libraries, the maintenance of the library's Web site is partially or totally outsourced. Yet, a general practice within many libraries has been since the early days of the Web to hire or train a local Web master. The maintenance of the library's main Web site and the public catalog or Web OPAC has become a priority not only because these interfaces offer the public image of the library but also because they are the primary access points to digital information and services. We also know that the ease of Web site use is fundamental to obtaining the best e-metrics results, further justifying the need for library IT staff with skills in Web technologies.

But apart from the strategic role of IT in every library activity, a more compelling reason for hiring a local systems team is the dramatic need for "collateral" or "add-on" applications to fulfill the new and specific operations in information and data management. In an increasingly complex environment that poses potential information and data overload, modern libraries cannot always find the tools they need to accomplish some of their tasks more efficiently. If we just consider the possible types and sources of performance and measurement statistics that a library could, should, or has to produce for its core activities and applications, we realize that not every available pre-packaged software application has a well developed statistical reporting component. The immediate consequence of using such software is seen in time-consuming data processing that is required to take place behind the scenes. In some instances, such software requires the staff to manually collect and enter the data, typically in a spreadsheet, and then compute the numbers in order to obtain some statistical data. It is possible that some of the routine staff data management operations could be automated or that data be extracted from some applications and then processed with home-grown programs. But without reasonable IT staffing within the library, many statistical efforts may be duplicated leading to poor utilization of human resources assigned to manual data processing across the different departments of every library.

In the case of e-metrics and ERM in general, the demand for local library IT skill sets is more predicated on the absence of adapted tools, the rapid evolution of Web technologies, and the impossibility of manual data processing to evaluate online resource use. But by investing more in systems librarians and IT specialists, a library can improve its management of issues posed by ERM and design whenever possible through various in-house solutions developed in conjunction with other IT-related library activities. Therefore, these e-metrics and ERM initiatives can easily dictate a considerable shift in a library's IT priorities. Library administrators should consequently re-evaluate the size and expertise of library IT departments based on the short-, medium-, and long-term plans that they envision for the library.

Library Systems Administration

In order to deliver digital content and online services to users, every library must ensure that its network, servers, workstations, and printers are fully operational at all times. The library, therefore, needs skilled staff to manage its IT resources. Depending upon a library's size, financial assets, and organizational structure, IT personnel could consist of a combination of a systems librarian(s) and systems administrator(s) with backgrounds and training exclusively in IT.

If we reflect on the evolution of Integrated Library Systems (ILS) over the years, both the software and the hardware necessary for those ILS have become increasingly complex as they incorporate cutting-edge technologies. Most recent ILS offerings, if not all, use a client/server approach built on a relational database foundation with a Web-based content delivery system for the public catalog interface. There are considerable support, maintenance, and upgrades implications related to ILS use which lead to significant library resource investments. In addition, it is possible that the more complex ILS management processes involve not only external IT support from the vendor but also internal IT staff for the day-to-day operations, customizations, and enhancements.

Looking beyond the administrative and support requirements associated with a library's ILS, libraries also need to account for other online services that are offered to the public through portals, link resolvers, and federated search engines alike. These new search and retrieval options are logically supported by emerging technologies which, in turn, raise questions about the staffing and skill sets needed in libraries looking to implement and maintain such access alternatives. Based on the technical layout presented for innovative operations like the e-metrics data collection, a library would at least need people proficient in application and software programming, server administration, Web management, and database administration.

In summary, libraries can only deliver online services and resources to the public if they are equipped with an up-to-date IT infrastructure that is supported by competent personnel. For this reason, any library evaluating its information systems organization needs to review its recruitment policies and consider training possibilities for IT skilled personnel whether they are systems librarians or pure IT specialists. We should also note that among the type of support listed in the SLS 1999 survey, some libraries "shared their technical support with other libraries, schools or agencies." There may be future options for pooling the IT resources amongst libraries for specific and strategic IT-related projects or perhaps an "open source" approach is adopted where "leader" libraries would share their IT solutions with less technology-savvy libraries.

Establish E-Metrics Management Policies

Consider the answer to the following simple hypothetical question: "How many times was this title used in the past three months?" One would expect to get an answer that offered a solid figure, but would the person posing this question ponder the methods for gathering this information in the first place? Unless the criteria determining the "use" portion of this question is clearly defined, the lack of standard definitions in e-metrics, the dynamic nature of online publishing, the divergent interests of the different stakeholders, and various technical constraints can make the measurement of title use a particularly sensitive topic.

Multiple Ways to Count a Title Use

Therefore, we must first define what constitutes a title use in e-metrics. A survey of various e-metrics reports shows that some limit the criteria of title use to some combination of the number of visits and sessions, others identify it by the number of unique visitors based on IP addresses, while others yet on the appearance of unique user IDs. Because it is so difficult to uniquely identify a user without authentication, the common title use standard currently focuses on visits and sessions. The number of unique visitors can certainly be an excellent indicator of the title coverage and cannot be compared to the number of visits. But if the number of unique visitors is all that the log file provides, then we have no choice but to use that number for title use e-metrics.

By Visit

We have seen that whenever a user connects through the main library Web site or through its OPAC to one of the e-resources offered by a virtual library collection, an e-metrics virtual visit is counted. Once a user clicks on an online title hyperlink, the request is directly sent to the vendor or publisher's Web server. But unless a library uses a redirection solution with a "click-through" script, that library will be dependent upon vendor-supplied reports that only gather the number of visits to their particular site. Unfortunately, as mentioned in Chapter 7, such information is not always available from all vendors or publishers.

By creating a local e-metrics solution, a library can at least count outgoing title requests. Even with local e-metrics mechanisms, a library cannot know if a virtual visit is a "real" visit or not. Furthermore, a local solution cannot measure activity once the user roams through a provider's Web site. The data resolution with a local solution is therefore limited to the title level and will not account for accesses to table of contents (TOC), article abstracts, or specific article level. In other words, the library cannot tell from the library's end if the user really "used" the site to read, download, or print an article, for only the provider can confirm that fact.

By incorporating the redirection solution, a library can still tell if a user accessed a title but will not be able to verify if they succeeded in reaching the desired site or if the request was turned away. So, obviously, portions of a locally-developed e-metrics solution still have some limitations, leaving some measurements to be formulated and interpreted with some assumptions. However, a local library e-metrics solution is really the only way to collect data for every title to which a library virtually subscribes and offers the only opportunity to introduce a certain degree of measurement and data standardization.

By Search and Session

Some e-metrics reports from vendors contain the number of sessions for access to their titles. A session starts when the user connects to an online resource and the session ends when the user disconnects or logs off. A common e-metrics practice is to consider a session to be 30 minutes in length for a unique user. Following such parameters, the definition of a unique user is then based on the fact that access requests will come from the same IP address or domain for 30 minutes or less. We can easily understand that only a log analysis from the provider can give the exact duration of the session. But if the actual session exceeds 30 minutes, then the number of sessions is overestimated because a person who spent 31 minutes would count for two sessions when in reality it was one unique session. However, the compromise over the 30-minute session length is reasonable because the log analysis would become too complex and time consuming if there were no defined fixed-time threshold.

It is also difficult to count sessions on the library's end because users can succeed one another in use of the same workstation in public computing settings. Unless the workstation requires a log in/log out system with some form of authentication, we can only estimate the number and duration of session per virtual visitor from any given public computing device. In light of the fact that libraries do not have access to the vendor or publisher's server logs, it is preferable for the library to rely on the session counts from the providers when they are available. An alternate solution could consider the number of searches as indicator of use; although such criteria cannot report on the success of the search operation nor decipher the real intention of the user, it should reveal fundamental trends with more accuracy than the session counts when used consistently across titles.

By Unique Visitor

Gauging the popularity of a Web site or of a title by the number of unique visitors is another way of measuring use. The major issue with this analysis criterion is the identification of a unique visitor. The only reliable solution to gathering this information is to authenticate every user using a Web site. The most common form of this practice for access to online library resources is to authenticate users through a proxy server. In order to collect an accurate count of total unique users, authentication should be required for both internal and external information access requests. There are, however, some problems connected with this type of authentication policy, but we will address these at a later point. As for those libraries that are completely unable to authenticate users, they must limit themselves to analyzing the counts of unique IP addresses.

The logic in the reports sorted by user analysis presumes that a unique visitor is associated with a unique computer identifiable by its IP address. In fact, we cannot tell for sure if the same machine was used by one or more visitors. Additional consideration must be given to the potential that the same user could connect to the same title from different computers, for example from one at their place of employment and from one at home. Another variable must account for the way that Internet Service Providers (ISP) can assign different IP addresses to the same machine, also known as dynamic IP-addressing. Finally, the use of a proxy a server, that hides the actual IP address of the requester, leads systematically to an underestimate of the unique visitor counts by IP.

Many commercial Web sites try to work around the inaccuracy of the count by IP address with the use of cookies.[6] A cookie is a simple text file sent by a Web server to a user's browser. It identifies a user's machine during the current and subsequent visits to a Web site. A session cookie disappears after the browser is closed whereas a persistent cookie is stored on the user's hard drive until it expires or is deleted by the user. The former cannot personally identify a user but the latter has the ability to collect information such as personal Web surfing habits or personal preferences and profile on a specific Web site. By utilizing cookies, a Web server could generate and keep in a database a unique ID number for each visitor and then store that number in a cookie on the user's hard drive. Unfortunately, users do not always accept cookies or delete them mainly due to privacy concerns.[7] Again, the lack of cookies results in an inaccurate

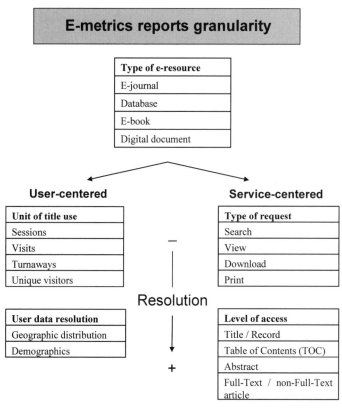

Figure 9-2 Data Resolution for User-Centered and Service-Centered E-Metrics

count of unique users. We now see that if libraries authenticate their user for on-line resources and if they use the "click-through" technique, then they would be able to evaluate with fairly high data resolution the use of their online titles both by visits and by unique visitor counts.

Figure 9–2 sums up the different levels of data resolution achievable by the combination of vendor and local e-metrics. Each library can chose what criteria will determine the unit of use and the depth of usage analysis.

User Authentication

As we have stated all along, the authentication of users requesting e-resources offers the most accurate and in-depth e-metrics data. But we also know that libraries do not always have the personnel or the infrastructure to support this data collection option. Still, when implementing an authentication system, usually through a proxy server, a library would need to address issues of access barriers, privacy protection, and user database management.

Access Barriers

It is a well-known fact that many people are somewhat reluctant to register on-line or provide any form of identification over the Internet for fear of identity theft and for privacy concerns. Those legitimate suspicions can be aggravated by an encounter with various technical computer glitches. Whenever a user needs to authenticate and get access, there is always a possibility that the operation could fail. It is then the role of a library to verify if the problem originates from its technical infrastructure or somewhere else along the network of access connections. Such a scenario offers a glimpse into the responsibility of the library in providing the necessary support to solve the users' access difficulties.

Technical access barriers range from badly formed e-resource Web links, or a malfunctioning Web server or proxy server, to an outdated user database. This brief list of problems outlines the variety of troubleshooting skills that should be part of a library's requirement to provide high quality technical support. Perhaps an electronic resources manager can do a preliminary degree of technical troubleshooting, but in the end the library must work with more specialized systems librarians or purely IT specialists when technical issues end up being more complicated.

Privacy Issues

A whole chapter could be dedicated to examining the issues associated with protection of privacy and confidentiality principles while collecting data for statistical purposes.[8] For the sake of clarity in our practical approach and to keep within the scope of the current discussion, we will only concern ourselves with these issues in relation to user authentication. The authentication of users as part of information access mandates that libraries develop additional security methods for internally collected information. We will only enumerate the critical data security measures that ought to be taken in this area, but not describe them in detail as they fall outside the scope of our study for e-metrics:

1. The first level of security is to make sure that every server is secured according to IT security standards regarding encrypted connections, physical access restrictions, password protections, firewalls, patches and backups.
2. The second level of privacy protection is to safeguard the various transaction logs from the public view. It is indeed possible to trace someone's activities from the logs with the person's ID. Again, the library must take all measures to store the logs in a well-protected location. Once processed, the logs could even be taken off-line completely to minimize the risk of data theft.
3. The third level of security is the protection of personal information and the confidentiality of users' records in any format. The user database must absolutely stay out of reach of any intruder, unauthorized persons

or government or law enforcement authority that may request access on the grounds of some governmental policy, such as stated in sections of the USA PATRIOT Act[9] for example. All staff access to the database must be password-protected, monitored and strictly limited to authentication troubleshooting.

Burden of User Database Management

For the purposes of achieving high-quality e-metrics, one can see how important it is for a library to have a user database for access control and for statistics. However, libraries have really two choices in this implementation: utilize an existing user database or build a new one. Many libraries opt not to build a user database from scratch because of the aforementioned difficulties associated with this process and because such a project is ancillary to the production of core e-metrics. If a library, typically one with resources similar to that of the Library C scenario, decides to proceed in this direction, then it must devote resources for the database design, the server setup and configuration, the data input, and finally the database maintenance. In short, the library must take charge and sponsor the construction of a user database that will meet its needs for the e-metrics project.

If, on the other hand, a library favors utilizing an existing database, there is a high probability that additional necessary tangential micro-projects will arise in order to adapt or adjust the data extracted from the database. Because the user database was not initially built with the e-metrics specifications in mind, some external data input from the database might be off-target, vague, or missing. The existing user database might only provide information of partial relevance to e-metrics, forcing a library to find ways to consolidate various data from multiple sources. This limitation typically necessitates additional custom programming to extract the user data from various sources before reaching a satisfactory compromise of reporting and technical requirements.

No matter which solution is agreed upon, a library must be prepared to make additional investments in time, staff, and funding if it wants a reliable and high quality user database. Again, the e-metrics project team must analyze the scope, objectives, and constraints of the user database within the context of the overall e-metrics project. The team should be able to give precise technical directions that answer an apparently simple question: What do we need to know and what can we know about our users for our e-metrics project?

Report Processing

Information overload has become a major concern for library administrators. It is critical that the right data are efficiently extracted from the innumerable reports that libraries both receive from vendors and generate locally. Thus it becomes important to determine the acceptable criteria of validity for a given report or vendor before attempting to cull through the mass of reporting data. Is the vendor COUNTER compliant? Is the vendor a major provider for the library? After analysis of past statistical trends, is the title in question considered a high priority for the library's constituency? Does the report provide the administration with the necessary elements for decent quantitative analyses on e-resource usage? Would the local collection of e-metrics data bring more standardization and better data resolution? Those questions, while certainly helpful for determining prioritization, should not outweigh the need for rational management of the reporting process.

We have demonstrated that the volume of information and the lack of reporting consistency between vendors necessitate a clear strategy for the report analysis phase. It is obviously impossible to collect, collate and analyze the e-metrics reports for every title from every vendor. The best solution is therefore to select, based on the determined priorities, a limited number of titles and vendors for analysis. Even so, any title selection process based on e-metrics is far from straightforward and completely reliable. It is therefore necessary to set up administrative selection guidelines with the strategic approach of the library in mind. Selection should include a systemic methodology that considers the complexity of the online publishing world while avoiding an oversimplification based on raw numbers interpreted without context. Such analysis would include a systematic use of deep e-metrics, with external data, whenever possible regardless of whether the core data are vendor-supplied or locally-collected.

Report Accessibility Records

The multiplicity of titles and vendors makes it difficult to follow-up with the changes of access to online statistics. As the report delivery method often varies from one vendor to another and over time, it is a good practice to share and centralize some critical information about the report portals in some location known to every member of the e-metrics team. The typical concerns with vendor statistics usually occur with:

- *The delivery method*: knowing how the reports are distributed helps to gauge the work load for their data collection.
- *The report access ID and password*: they can be modified or reinitialized, sometimes without notice, and should be regularly checked and updated.
- *The URL*: reports can be moved to a different Web site because of internal reorganization on the vendor's side or because of market consolidation.
- *The contact information*: customer service reference should be always available for emergency cases or for simple queries.
- *COUNTER compliance*: with evolving standards, knowing if a vendor is compliant[10] could be useful for the selection process.

A very simple way to track various vendor report criteria is to keep track of the updates in a spreadsheet saved in a shared network location.

Frequency and Format Standardization

Whether the reports are delivered or retrieved from vendors, locally created or both, an agreed upon published schedule of e-metrics project processes offers the safest way to limit information overload possible with e-metrics analysis. By collecting the reports on a regular basis, the e-metrics team will not only adjust their processes as needed but also identify the existing and potential problems with the project deployment.

Standardization methods for the various e-metrics report formats need to be addressed early on in the reporting project. How easy is it to work with multiple reports in HTML, text, Excel or PDF? What if we would like to make some comparative statistics reports through charts and graphs? How much processing would be necessary to convert the data files or re-key the numbers from the different reports?

If reports and their analysis are to be effective then the first step should be to choose the most functional format. More than likely, the spreadsheet or Excel format would be the most acceptable report format standard for any type of library because of its popularity and functionality. Excel, however, has limitations within worksheets and workbooks.[11] More elaborate reporting solutions, such as databases, often offer more flexibility for the more technically savvy of library environments. The second reporting project step is to figure out how to convert the existing preformatted report data partially or fully. The last project step is to decide who in the team will be responsible for the report data conversion. Without consistent and comparable data formats, it is very likely that the outcome of the reporting project would be of little interest and administrative value.

Preservation

We alluded to the subject of data storage in the previous chapter but only in terms of its technical implications. However, administrative planning for data preservation should consider both the short and the long term ramifications. In the case of locally-generated reports, the various data storage decisions can be easily put into action. However, for vendor-supplied reports the task is more complicated because of the possible high number of titles and vendors required for comprehensive e-metrics output. As a consequence, the library must prioritize its choices of titles and providers if data storage is to be constrained to some degree.

A specific data storage policy should, nonetheless, address the issue of tracking usage history and cancelled subscriptions. The vendors are supposed to give libraries access to reports of their last three years of subscriptions

(NFAIS—National Federation of Abstracting and Information Services—2004). Thus, in anticipation of e-metrics reporting projects, libraries must decide their administrative and procedural course of action every time a subscription is canceled. Finally, cautious considerations should be given to the interpretation such historical data as the methods for maintaining such information might vary dramatically over time in response to the evolution of standard practices, data definitions, and market consolidation in the publishing sector. The publishing market conditions make it particularly difficult to monitor the modifications of title use, format, and labeling over time.

Title Persistence Over Time

Tracking the access of an online title over time and accounting for other change parameters that affect the title use count add complexity to a local deep e-metrics project. Title use from past reports both from the vendors, as explained earlier, and locally in archived reports should be available to both library staff and administration. However, in order to generate local deep e-metrics over time, we need to account for the multiple events that can affect a title during its subscription lifetime. There are four major events that we should record at the local level: a new title subscription, a title modification, a change of provider and a title cancellation.

New Information on a Title

Establishing new subscriptions to an e-resource and title changes are two events that have a direct impact on use counts. The moment a new title is put online or a title renamed, the captured use data will be logically low because the advertisement of the title's public availability, if any, cannot have an immediate effect. But as was discussed earlier in the previous chapter in conjunction with the e-metrics integration of external data, by recording the date of the title's availability, we can avoid misinterpreting low access counts as an indication of low title use.

Source Change

The third event affecting use measurement is title distribution through a new vendor or a new publisher not previously contracted with the library. Thanks to the structure of our redirected URL, which includes the title_ID and the provider_ID, described in Chapter 7, we can track any change of provider for a given e-resource. Included in the construction of our modified URL for an online resource, we uniquely identify an e-resource by its title and its provider. The provider_ID identifier was designed to generate separate statistics for one title distributed by more than one provider. We can see how the additional criteria for tracking a new provider will result in an initial low title use in the statistics. With this tracking mechanism in place, any given title may automatically start with a zero count use and a new date of availability when the title in question is distributed by a new provider.

Title Subscription Cancellation

The last event that we need to trace for deep e-metrics is a title cancellation. When a title is cancelled, the title disappears publicly from the library's Web site and should also be hidden from public view within the ILS catalog. However, data that has tracked the access to the cancelled title will still appear in the logs up to the date that the title was publicly removed. How would we then distinguish an active title from a cancelled one in the transaction logs? One possible solution is to store the latest timestamp of access in the log for the targeted title. However, this option is not very efficient considering that there could be thousands of titles and possibly voluminous logs. Another option is to note when a title is found in the server logs and then check it against the list of active titles on the library's Web site. If the title is no longer present, then the title found in the log is flagged as cancelled, making it easier to detect cancelled subscriptions from the other current titles in the final e-metrics reports.

As just described, whenever there is a change affecting an online title, the library's Web site must not only reflect the change but also store the nature of the event and its timestamp for future reference when analyzing the collected e-metrics data for the impacted titles. Long-term manual management of the various parameters that can affect title usage numbers is probably rather impracticable, particularly as the number of online title subscriptions increases within libraries. Again, the implementation of a dynamic rather than a static Web site seems to offer the most appropriate data management infrastructure. A logical technological choice, therefore, should include development of a database-driven Web site which can be easily updated and queried for past transactions and changes, thereby accumulating several pieces of historical transaction and management data for the library's Web site. The impact on usage counts due to changes on the Web site could then be more accurately accounted and rigorously quantified to avoid misinterpretations of such usage measurements.

As we conclude this chapter, we must reiterate that the development of e-metrics standards is still a work in progress. We have seen how both libraries and electronic content providers continue to struggle in generating "actionable" e-metrics in some consistent manner. Consequently, library administrators and their respective ERM teams must be fully aware of the imperfections of the current procedures for e-metrics, regardless of whether the data are provided by vendors or locally-produced. A library's administration has to come up with a plan that at the start specifies the level of desired data and report granularity and establishes conditions that can actualize these choices. We must keep in mind that a higher degree of desired e-metrics resolution will require a more ambitious administrative plan.

Administrators will also need to continuously comprehend and embrace the general impact and importance of IT in the modern library environment. First, IT redefines the interactions of the library with the external information stakeholders—the public and the e-resource suppliers. Second, IT modifies the internal workflow of the library. Third, the disposable library resources in terms of time, money, and staff are finite in contrast to the seemingly endless possibilities offered by new technologies. It is only logical, then, that new metrics, methodologies, and organizational structures be devised to monitor the online activities and services of modern libraries. IT will continue to permeate almost every sector of libraries operations, regardless of potential unequal IT proficiencies observed between librarians and staff within the same institution. It is therefore imperative that the two worlds—library and IT—work collaboratively and communicate smoothly without further delay. On a larger scale, a library's e-metrics project and ERM processes offer the best opportunities for the information community to put that collaboration into action. We will see how such opportunities could evolve as the next and final chapter investigates the future of e-metrics and its interaction with emerging standards, technologies, and business models.

Notes

1. www.ucrg.org.uk/events/conference_reports/booth_181104.ppt; www.mcmla.org/meetings/2004/EBL04Keynote.pdf; www.shef.ac.uk/scharr/eblib/webography.html.
2. www.shef.ac.uk/scharr/eblib/ecdk1.ppt#261,7,EBL Domains.
3. www.loc.gov/marc/856guide.html#intro.
4. www.oclc.org/support/documentation/worldcat/cataloging/electronicresources/.
5. www.sls.lib.il.us/infotech/surveys/technical/.
6. See a definition at www.webopedia.com/TERM/c/cookie.html.
7. More details at www.cookiecentral.com/faq/.
8. ICOLC Guidelines (1998), Luther (2000), Breeding (2002).
9. www.ala.org/ala/washoff/WOissues/civilliberties/theusapatriotact/alaresolution.htm.
10. www.projectcounter.org/articles.html.
11. Search for 'specification' using help in the version of Excel you are using.

10

E-Metrics and the Future: Standards, Restrictions, Implementation, and Emerging Technologies

We have demonstrated in the preceding chapters how e-metrics are complex and multidimensional in their relevance, composition, and acquisition. But the e-metrics evolution shows that there is still much work to be done in the area of their development and purpose within libraries. Now that we have covered the history, necessity, application, and implementation of e-metrics for individual libraries, we have a chance to consider what the future of library e-metrics may hold. Looking ahead is always a difficult task, especially with a topic so intimately tied to the unpredictable and exponential growth of information and computer technologies.

We can make some general statements about e-metrics issues that will continue to be intertwined with the developments of libraries and technology. As libraries reconsider the value and application of e-metrics to a wide variety of library operations and policies, additional e-metrics specifications will probably become necessary for better library administration. We should also anticipate a future requirement for both library staff and administrators to obtain greater understanding and skills in the areas of digital technologies. Furthermore, an improved comprehension of the impact computers and networks will continue to have on library collections and services will assist in the growth and utilization of e-metrics within physical and virtual libraries. In addition to these broad predictions, we can attempt to at least outline some of the e-metrics issues that could be looming on the horizon. Such yet-to-be resolved aspects of future e-metrics developments can be delineated according to two major categories: standards and technical considerations.

Review of E-Metric Standards

Perhaps the core issue that needs to be addressed first in the collection and analysis of e-metrics is the establishment of standards. As has been demonstrated in both Chapters 2 and 8, the dramatic shift in collection emphasis and user expectations will further demand that libraries, publishers, vendors, and reporting organizations reach agreement on the definitions, parameters, and techniques that constitute e-metrics. Without such standard measurement and criteria definitions, libraries will experience continued difficulties in acquiring, managing, and supporting virtual collections at their greatest potential. It has also been shown with several examples throughout this book how more detailed e-metrics can be achieved at the local library level. With such knowledge available at each individual library, there could be increased opportunity for greater collaboration between libraries and vendors in uncovering the reporting needs of both entities. Such partnerships could rejuvenate the e-metrics standards and methods discussion with a new underlying perspective of mutual reporting goals.

Open Access Initiatives

There are additional questions in relation to future e-metrics standards that for now appear associated with advances in the publishing sector. At the time of this writing, there is a growing interest in Open Access (OA) initiatives as a viable alternative to the large and expensive subscription contracts currently offered by publishers and content aggregators. The difference is that OA journals primarily use a funding model that does not directly charge readers or their institutions for access. Instead, several OA journals support publishing costs by charging authors for the right to publish in individual OA titles. Since OA does not yet have the established business and marketing infrastructure of those well-funded digital publishing and media outlets, what e-metrics processes will be applied to these types of titles?

We might predict that because the financial obligation of OA publishing is shifted from the library to the author, authors would want e-metrics information that will help them determine the value of a given OA title in which they intend to publish. One e-metrics option available to OA publishers and distributors are those currently implemented by Project COUNTER. COUNTER-compliant e-metrics would give authors of OA articles the ability to see the number of searches and downloads for their respective writings. But while COUNTER e-metrics can provide authors with some idea of title and perhaps even article use, would there come a point where these same authors would like to know if their texts are of interest to a particular reader demographic? For example, one could imagine that a biologist publishing in the OA journal *Public Library of Science Biology* (www.plosbiology.org) would want to know if his published OA articles are being read by others in the biological research field. Title and article use by user demographic would also be helpful in knowing if published articles and OA titles attract readers across multiple disciplines.

E-metrics may also assist in properly assigning fiscal responsibilities as the OA publishing and access model evolves. There may come a time when the library, with its current centralized functions of collection and subscription management, is asked to assume the OA financial responsibility on behalf of several authors from an institutional or special library. Such a request would require the library to evaluate the value of these titles both in terms of volume of use and in relation to the types of users that access such titles. The information that can be reported by combining COUNTER-like e-metrics results with those from the subscribing library may support the position that library budgetary constraints dictate for well-funded institutional departments to absorb the author publishing costs for their researchers.

Publishing Sector Market Consolidation

We have already spent some time reviewing some of the issues connected with the continuing consolidation trends occurring in the publishing and media sectors. In Chapter 5 we examined how such corporate mergers impact both library electronic resource management and collection development options. But what affect will an industry with several very large publishing and distribution players have on the future of e-metrics standards? One possible issue for those libraries dependent upon vendors for e-metrics will be the types use measurements captured and reported over a period of time that includes corporate acquisition. In much the same way that other information outlet measures, like the television Nielsen Ratings, track a variety of historical tendencies, it will become increasingly important for libraries to be able to identify irreversible usage trends for the purposes of collection development and acquisition. The following scenario illustrates the increased the complexity such mergers on digital library collections management.

Suppose that a library has a license for a bundled package of titles from Vendor A and another package from Vendor B. The library has been receiving use data from Vendor A using one set of e-metrics standards and Vendor B who uses COUNTER-compliant e-metrics reports. After two years of library subscriptions to both vendors, Vendor B acquires Vendor A in a corporate merger. Now the reports for both former Vendor A titles and current Vendor B titles are being generated according to COUNTER standards. But how would the library be able to compare the former Vendor A title use over time when in the midst of their subscription and use, the e-metrics report standards for those titles changed? Will there be some kind of definition table provided with the report that indicates how the old Vendor A e-metrics criteria equates to current Vendor B COUNTER parameters?

As the publishing sector undergoes consolidation, there may be additional subscription options that provide only certain types of vendor-supplied e-metrics reports, with more detailed ones available only at an increased service cost. An e-metrics vendor standardization model could even develop in such a way that the e-metrics needs of various library types—such as public, academic, and special—are all forced to accept the same report type, regardless of the different needs of the individual library. Such a development would be akin to the bundled title package option that has increasingly become the *de facto* subscription industry standard. While the focus of the e-metrics investigation in both this book and in the various international initiatives has been on full-text digital journals and databases, one wonders if vendors will at some point expand their e-metrics definitions to include a number of other potential subscription formats, such as e-books and digital image libraries. How will future subscription formats, perhaps sound and video, be accounted for in e-metrics methodologies?

These questions, in anticipation of future e-metrics predictions, underscore the need for some level of coordinated e-metrics efforts between libraries and publishers. While COUNTER illustrates how the definitions and data sets established by library and standards organizations can be incorporated into vendor-supplied offerings, it may become necessary for libraries to have greater input into the future developments of vendor e-metrics. Perhaps there should be an eventual convergence between the types of e-metrics collected and distributed by vendors and those that we have shown can be captured and analyzed individually by local libraries. Without such library input, it could become increasingly difficult for vendors and libraries to capture and analyze e-metrics in order to account for the current and future variety of library types, the variety of virtual library collection formats, variety of subscription models, and variety of access parameters.

Factor in the Technical Considerations

Although this book has detailed one method of capturing and analyzing e-metrics data, one should consider how the rapid pace of technological change will impact the various technical and digital components of e-metrics processes. The evolution of the e-metrics field will continue to be dependent upon new innovations in the IT sector. In view of the pace of modernization in IT, the ever-changing economic model in the publishing industry, and the current state of e-metrics in libraries, we will focus on possible short term e-metrics developments. Potential e-metrics growth may be impacted by changes in information access models, e-metrics data preservation, the anticipated importance of e-metrics for other online services, the consequences of emerging technologies, and the combined library costs and resources needed for the implementation of a local e-metrics project.

Access Restrictions Through Licensing Agreements

As electronic resources have become increasingly popular among the public and within library collections, information access regulations associated with vendor licensing agreements have evolved in multiple directions. Of concern for the future of e-metrics developments are those licensing conditions that have a direct impact on local e-metrics data collection. Of particular interest are licensing policies that cover on-site access only, library proxy server bans, and denied access to backfiles after cancellation of a subscription title.

Some current licensing restrictions on electronic resources tend to limit access to on-site visits taking place within the physical library network. Such access limitations can be dictated by the publishers and vendors according to geographic locations or by IP ranges. However, these practices appear to be in opposition to the very way in which the Internet was designed to allow access to remote electronically-stored resources over various computer networks. Continued acceptance and standardization of this type of access trend would directly affect the organization of distance learning and remote research supported by academic libraries, and would limit the access possibilities for individuals with reduced mobility served by libraries world-wide. In short, such subscription access constraints would significantly inhibit the development of new library and information access services that could predictably take advantage of the Internet's expansion.

In terms of its impact on e-metrics, restricted off-site library access to subscriptions will certainly lead to reduced virtual visits from outside the library premises. But more importantly, because many libraries do not collect any data for in-house use, the possibility of acquiring meager e-metrics information gathered from remote access could essentially disappear, leaving libraries with little or no possibility of capturing local e-metrics data of any significant value. Libraries would then have to choose between collecting in-house use of online titles or revert to some other less accurate means of determining online title use.

In response to these licensed access restrictions, some libraries have installed proxy servers to enable remote access. Unfortunately, some licensing contracts now prohibit the use of such proxy servers because this technological solution prevents vendors from identifying the actual customers' IP addresses used to remotely request an e-resource or an e-service. Although we can understand some of the rationale for preventing the use of library proxy servers, such license agreements also reduce a library's ability to (1) increase the security of their network, (2) grant remote access to those legitimate library users who are external to the physical library and (3) perform patron authentication. In other words, legal controls of contract agreements can be used to restrain the legitimate utilization of a library's own technical infrastructure. And more generally, these types of restrictions can defeat the whole purpose of networking over the Internet for improved information access. No matter how we view these constraints, their blockage of potential users can only translate into the acquisition of low quality local library e-metrics. Worse, under such conditions those libraries that are using proxy servers to authenticate users will lose valuable deep e-metrics that measure remote accesses to the library's resources.

In addition, more subtle and less visible changes are taking place in licensed access restrictions. For example, some licenses make backfiles inaccessible once a library cancels its subscription to some of its digital titles. With print-based title subscriptions, past issues of a title can still be made available to patrons after the subscription is cancelled by the library. In the new digital publishing and access model, the archival article and title information may be totally lost for both the library and the patrons because of a new economic model and not because of a failing technical infrastructure. Cancellation of electronic titles and loss of archival access also raises a fundamental question on the diffusion and exchange of past knowledge in our society for the present and future generations. Viewed from the perspective of library performance measurements, such agreements result in lost access to the information and therefore in lost e-metrics proportional to the number of cancelled subscriptions.

The bottom line is that when information access restrictions become too rigid, they create an under-utilized library technical infrastructure, limit or prevent access to information for patrons, and thereby ultimately reduce the volume of use of vendors' resources. Such restrictions will also hinder the progress in the collection of local deep e-metrics. The combination of all these negative effects will certainly be detrimental to all stakeholders in the information access equation.

Preservation and Value of E-Metrics Over Time

Information preservation has always been part of a library's mission. But how do libraries plan to store and use their e-metrics data over time? Due to the current lack of standard practice in the production of e-metrics, e-metrics preservation is just not yet considered a priority. However, sooner or later libraries will have to address this question.

If the preservation of locally-acquired e-metrics seems straightforward, in part because the library controls their production, the process is far more difficult to address with vendor-supplied e-metrics data. There are a few reasons why libraries cannot afford to leave the preservation of this important statistical subscription use data up to vendors. What would indeed happen to this data when a title subscription is cancelled? As mentioned in Chapter 9, COUNTER expects vendors to keep the last three years of e-metric reports to their customers. But what happens when vendors are not COUNTER-compliant? Chances are good that in addition to title access, the historical use statistics for that title will be lost as well. This scenario would mean that if the historical statistics are not perennially available to the library, then the library has to keep a local copy of all vendor-supplied statistics for as long as it has commercial ties to a vendor. The direct consequence of this storage requirement is an increased amount of work and library resources that must be mobilized for that type of data archiving operation.

The issue of data preservation becomes more complicated when one considers the multiple vendor e-metrics report formats and non-standardized report delivery methods. Libraries must therefore decide what e-metrics data to store and how to store those statistics in a reasonable way. But even if a library managed to set up an e-metrics data repository system that can be queried for past e-metrics reports, the legacy of non-standardized definitions of past reports would still be a problem. How would the library identify usage trends for titles with non-standardized or incompatible standards? Would the statistics from the same vendor be comparable over time? How would the library organize and analyze the use of a title after it was transitioned to a different publisher as a result of market consolidation? In other words, the library must consider the usability of preserved e-metrics before investing time, money, staff, and infrastructure into such a project.

If we suppose that a library ultimately decides to create a data repository for vendor-supplied and local data, what technical solutions would need to be available and at what cost to the library? It seems very likely that the e-metrics data warehouse model will prevail if this is to become a future e-metrics requirement. We can predict that the future information access enterprise will increasingly rely on complex database management systems for administrative library support. The library would also have to decide where the data repository would be hosted and make sure to protect any confidential information. Would the library have in-house the infrastructure and skill set needed for such a system or would it pay some external service provider for its development and support? Once such a system is in place, what sort of services would such a data repository provide? For example, would a library be able to retrieve past e-metrics reports by title, by resource type, or by vendor? Or would a library be able to compile monthly and yearly reports for each subscribed title? Ultimately, the repository system must provide highly scalable features, efficient data retrieval, powerful data processing, and advanced reporting capability.

As we can see, the solution for an e-metrics data repository is yet to be designed for both vendor-supplied and locally-collected e-metrics. In addition to considering the importance of IT in addressing historical e-metrics data needs, libraries and vendors would most likely need to work collaboratively to choose the appropriate data preservation strategies and maybe produce a common architecture and standards.

Applying E-Metrics to E-Resources and E-Services

The on-going efforts in e-metrics are understandably focused on e-resources such as e-journals and databases because they currently dominate the available titles in most library subscription budgets. And as we saw in the previous chapter, e-metrics data resolution could be categorized by either user- or service-centric information. But if we step back from the details of e-metrics, we can observe how the collection of e-metrics data could be relevant to other e-resources and to e-services, as schematized in the non-restrictive multifaceted approach to e-metrics on Figure 1–1 presented in Chapter 1 (page 6).

Currently e-books and other digital documents represent a portion of digital library collections that are typically less monitored for consistent use. And because of the priority given to e-journals and databases, monitoring those other e-resource types is almost non-existent for many libraries. However, it could be informative to track the use by the public of other digital information types not only for cost analysis but also for usage pattern studies. According to eMarketer.com the use of e-books soared about 46 percent in the first quarter of 2004 compared to the first quarter of 2003.[1] But the same article also states that the number of sales of e-books has yet to reach that of traditional books. Regardless, a library collecting e-metrics on e-books and other digital documents would be able to identify some cultural trends and adjust its strategy accordingly.

But should e-metrics be limited to e-resources only? Since acquisition of e-metrics through reporting functions within the Integrated Library System (ILS) is now a common practice in libraries, why not extend that approach to the emerging library e-services? Unfortunately, such a principle is not that easy to put into practice because libraries tend to be more "disintegrated" in their approach to e-services. For example, many ILS vendors now provide modules like e-reserves or ILL/Document Delivery in their products but many libraries typically already implemented third party solutions before those modules were even available as part of the integrated system. It is therefore obvious that, in the immediate future, many of the new e-services offered by libraries will be performed outside the functionality of their ILS. Furthermore, it is inconceivable that an ILS would ever offer e-services that are as heterogeneous as e-learning tools, portals, or digital reference through e-mails, Web forms, Internet relay chat, instant messaging, voice over IP, interactive video, and all the yet-to-come digital communication means (McClure, Lankes, Gross, Choltko-Devlin 2002).

The variety of technologies involved in e-services as of yet does not allow the design of a unified tool for collection of their respective use data. Some current examples of the methods used to collect e-services e-metrics data include Web-based and print-based surveys,[2] transaction log analysis, and software specific statistics. We can immediately see that the collation and consolidation of those data from disparate origins would alone constitute a major challenge. If we then consider the complex interpretation required of the compiled data, we cannot help but ask, as we did for e-resources, what specific standards should be developed for use statistics on e-services. As pointed out by multiple studies on e-resources, Blecic, et al. (2001), Davis and Solla (2003), to cite a few, even with improved data standardization expected to reduce inconsistencies in vendor-supplied statistics, the lack of such consistency in e-services measurements results in low data resolution, and thus can be easily misinterpreted because they cannot reveal the actual user intent or satisfaction. What constitutes a use, what level of data granularity do we want, and how much e-metrics detail can we achieve with e-services? How would such e-services e-metrics standards mesh with the existing ones? A holistic approach towards answering such questions would, in fact, require the combination of e-metrics, collected locally and from vendors, with performance indicators obtained via more traditional methods like circulation studies, ILL and reference statistics, citation reports and user surveys.

Impacts of Emerging Technologies like Federated Search Engines and Deep Linking on E-Metrics

MetaSearch and OpenURL[3] are two emerging technologies in content delivery that belong to e-services. Here we treat them separately from the other e-services because they pose their own e-metrics difficulties. The standardization of both federated-search technologies, with the Metasearch Initiative[4] and Committee AX[5] under the auspices of NISO, is underway. For that very reason, the number of vendors that are metasearch-compatible and/or openURL-aware, and the number of libraries that have actually implemented them, although growing, have not yet reached a critical mass to create a large scale movement in the information community. Besides, as with any cutting-edge technology, the number of organizations willing to experiment is usually limited to those with solid technical and financial assets. It is undeniable, though, that "Google-like" tools for libraries, with metasearching and link resolver capabilities, have a definite appeal in a user-centric information service strategy.

As far as usage statistics from such search technologies are concerned, they are marginally mentioned by the vendors of these search solutions. A glimpse at the reports available as part of SFX™, the leader of the market in OpenURL, shows the following:

Full List of Available Statistical Reports[6]
1. Number of SFX requests and clickthroughs per date.
2. Number of SFX requests and clickthroughs per source.
3. Number of SFX requests and clickthroughs per object type.
4. Number of SFX requests and clickthroughs per service type.
5. Number of SFX requests with/without full-text services.
6. Top target services shown in the SFX menu.
7. Number of clickthroughs per target.
8. Number of clickthroughs per target service.

9. Number of clickthroughs for one particular journal.
10. Most popular journals selected by target.
11. Most popular journals selected by source.
12. Journals requested but have no full-text.
13. Selected document delivery targets by source.
14. Books accessed via SFX ranked by use.
15. Services preferred over full-text.
16. Unused full-text journals.
17. Number of SFX requests which resulted in SFX menu screen without services.
18. Number of SFX requests and clickthroughs by IP address.
19. Most popular journals.

We immediately notice many similarities between the SFX search statistics and those generated by vendors of subscription e-resources. The orientation of the statistics for Metasearch as well seems to parallel the data generated from the COUNTER Project.[7] From the library's standpoint, this movement means that the level of report detail for some of the e-metrics currently provided by vendors could be reached locally and would complement the data directly received from the vendors themselves. But this projection would become common practice in libraries only when Metasearch and OpenURL are stable and well-established standards accepted and implemented by both vendors and libraries.

Cost of Local E-Metrics Implementation

Among the potential concerns of libraries for the implementation of a local e-metrics project is its cost associated with a complex technical infrastructure. However, if we look more closely we see that the major portion of the technical infrastructure needed to implement the local library e-metrics solution underscored in previous chapters is most likely already in place for most libraries. The minimum technical requirements of the local e-metrics solution are, indeed, an operational network, a Web server, a catalog server for the data collection, and a workstation or a low-end server with a lot of disk space for e-metrics data processing. If we want to generate reliable deep e-metrics, then the library additionally needs a proxy server and a server hosting the patron database for the authentication part of the local solution. A proxy server installed for network security and content-filtering could be set up for the library and then configured to control the user authentication and information access. As for the patron database, it could be either exported from the library catalog or created from scratch. A list of authorized users would not have to exist in some sophisticated format for in its simplest form, it can be a regular text file with all the patrons' card reader numbers. The real challenge in the authentication component of the e-metrics solution will be in keeping that list up-to-date.

Once the technical infrastructure has been prepared, the access logs must be collected from either the Web servers or the proxy server. Then the access logs must be run through some type of transaction log analysis software, commercial, open-source or home-grown, to generate the e-metrics reports. One could hope that in the near future, some Open-source solution(s) for local e-metrics in libraries would be developed by and become freely distributed in the library community. Analogous efforts have already been taken for other library-oriented tools like the MARC Perl module[8] or open-source solutions for libraries OSS4lib.[9] Such a proposed e-metrics initiative would certainly be cost-effective for those libraries that are short on financial, technical, and staffing resources. It would also help in designing more professional e-metrics applications with user-friendly interfaces and flexible reporting functions.

Conclusion

We close our chapter and book by looking back on the relationship between the various library management applications of e-metrics and the current competing e-metrics standards and data elements. In summary, the increasing and evolving complexities of digital and networked information access will require more detailed performance measurements for publishers, content distributors, subscription agents, libraries, and their readers. As the future electronic information landscape shifts and turns with the advancement of computer technologies, there will come a time when the e-metrics that can be gathered and analyzed by the various information outlets will need to be commonly understood across the multiple information sectors. The types of e-metrics data acquired by individual local libraries, the COUNTER Project, ARL E-metrics initiatives, federated metasearch services and protocols, and other international information organizations standards will require a level of unification. Perhaps such e-metrics compilations will become the primary responsibility of local libraries in their quests for better administrative and e-resource management tools. As we have seen, the multifaceted aspects of e-metrics can become more appreciated and comprehensive when many types of information professionals participate in the creation of e-metrics infrastructures, whether they be at the beginning, middle, or end of the e-metrics processes and procedures. It seems more likely that the importance already assigned to e-metrics in its brief lifetime foreshadows the need for a greater multidisciplinary approach towards the e-metrics future.

Notes

1. www.emarketer.com/Article.aspx?1002874.
2. See also http://informationr.net/ir/9-4/paper187.html.
3. www.niso.org/news/events_workshops/MS-2003_ppts.html.
4. www.niso.org/committees/MS_initiative.html.
5. www.niso.org/committees/committee_ax.html.
6. www.lib.umn.edu/digilab/sfx/usestats/031113-040212.phtml#reportlist.
7. www.niso.org/committees/MSpapers/MSStatstistics.pdf.
8. http://marcpm.sourceforge.net/.
9. www.oss4lib.org/.

Appendices

Appendix 1

Report Comparison between Two Web Traffic Analysis Software

The two following reports were obtained based on the same Web server log for a month-long worth of data. The line entries directly related to our e-metrics study, measurements for e-resources, are in bold. As noted in Chapter 7, formats, terminology, and access counts can significantly differ from one application to another. Basic trends should, however, be more or less consistent across applications.

1–Wusage 8.0

Rank	Entry Page	Entry Count	%
1	/[Referrers]	42,385	77.59
2	/public	3,927	7.19
3	/navigate.html [Referrers]	1,621	2.97
4	**/resources/e-journals.html [Referrers]**	**1,475**	**2.7**
5	/resources [Referrers]	1,097	2.01
6	**/resources/databases.html [Referrers]**	**853**	**1.56**
7	/push.php [Referrers]	313	0.57
8	/clickgo.php [Referrers]	227	0.42
9	/accounts/lab_account_request.php [Referrers]	217	0.4
10	**/resources/e-books.html [Referrers]**	**115**	**0.21**
11	/services [Referrers]	111	0.2
12	**/catalog.html [Referrers]**	**107**	**0.2**
13	/resources/web-resources.html [Referrers]	78	0.14

2–Webtrends Enterprise Suite

Rank	File	% of Total	Visitor Sessions
1	My Library - www.library.org/	37.09%	14827
2	My Library - www.library.org/welcome.html	23.33%	9328
3	My Library - Navigation Toolbar - www.library.org/navigate.html	12.01%	4802
4	**Electronic Journals - www.library.org/resources/e-journals.html**	**9.50%**	**3799**
5	Resources - www.library.org/resources/	2.39%	959
6	**Research Databases - www.library.org/resources/databases.html**	**2.27%**	**910**
7	**Electronic Books - www.library.org/resources/e-books.html**	**0.90%**	**360**
8	My Library - www.library.org/public/	0.53%	212
9	Account - www.library.org/Accounts/lab_account_request.php	0.36%	147
10	**Online Catalog – www.library.org/catalog.html**	**0.36%**	**145**
11	Map and Transportation - www.library.org/map.html	0.29%	119
12	Job/Employment Opportunities - www.library.org/jobs.html	0.28%	112
13	Information Systems - www.library.org/services/systems/	0.28%	112

Appendix **2**
Click-Through Script

More on PHP and header redirection at http://us3.php.net/header

```php
<?PHP

/*
 * click_through.php
 * Simple PHP Script to demonstrate redirection. Use as you'd
like
 * Syntax: http://server/path/to/script?target=http://www.target
.net
*/

/* header("Location: $_REQUEST[target]"); */
if (IsSet($url))
{
$url2=str_replace("*amp*","&",$url);
$url3=str_replace("*26*","%26",$url2);
/* redirect browser to url */
header("Location: $url3");
exit;
}
else
{
header("Location: http://www.library.org/nourl.html");
exit;
}

?>
```

Appendix 3

Custom Log Parsing Script

More on Web server access log parsing in Perl at www.oreilly.com/catalog/perlwsmng/chapter/ch08.html

```perl
#!/usr/bin/perl
#
# Name: parse.pl
# Function: custom log parsing of web server log in Common Log
Format with click-through script
# Input: web log
# Output: stats for title use in TTL_logname,IP counts in
IP_logname, and visit counts per provider in PROVIDER_logname
#
# Usage: perl parse.pl log_filename
# Working directory /home/httpd/html/test/
#
use strict;

#############
sub load_list
#############
{
  my %hash=();
  ## open file of list passed in parameter to function
  ## load fields in list into hash
  ## list tab delimited text
  my $file=$_[0];
  open(LST, $file) or die "cannot open $file";
  while (<LST>) {
```

```perl
        chomp;
         my ($f1, $f2)=split (/\t/, $_);
         $f1 =~ s/^\s+//;
         $f1 =~ s/\s+$//;
         $f2 =~ s/^\s+//;
         $f2 =~ s/\s+$//;
         $hash{$f1}=$f2;
  }
  close(LST);
  return(%hash);
}


#############
sub print_date
#############
{
 ## Get the all the values for current time from system clock
 my ($Second, $Minute, $Hour, $Day, $Month, $Year, $WeekDay,
$DayOfYear, $IsDST)=localtime(time);
 $Month+=1;
 $Year+=1900;
 return ("Date: $Month-$Day-$Year\n");
}
########################
sub count_unique_visitors
########################
{
 my $ref_hash_visitors_per_title=shift; #hash visitors per title
 my $ref_hash_unique_visitors=shift; # hash unique ips
 my $ttl_indx=shift; # index title src
 my $ttl_src_ip=shift; # index title src and ip
 my $vip=shift; #visitors ip
 if (!(exists($ref_hash_visitors_per_title->{$ttl_src_ip})))
 {
   $ref_hash_unique_visitors->{$ttl_indx}++;
   $ref_hash_visitors_per_title->{$ttl_src_ip}=$vip;
 }
}


###############
sub print_output
###############
{
 my $ref_input_file=shift;
 my $ref_output_file=shift;
 my $ref_rpt_ttl=shift;
 my $ref_array_hdr=shift;
```

```perl
my $ref_hash_visits_per_data_element=shift;
my $ref_hash_unique_visitors_per_ttl=shift;
my $ref_tot_vis=shift;
my $ref_hash_ip=shift;

open (OUT, "> ${$ref_output_file}") or die "Cannot create
${$ref_output_file}";

## print current date MM-DD-YYYY
print OUT &print_date();

## print Log name
print OUT "Log name: ${$ref_input_file}\n";

## print report title
print OUT 'Report: '.uc(${$ref_rpt_ttl})."\n\n";

## print the column headers
foreach (@$ref_array_hdr) {
   print OUT "$_\t";
}
print OUT "\n";

## print visits per data element sorted in descending order
foreach my $k (sort { $ref_hash_visits_per_data_element->{$b} <=>
$ref_hash_visits_per_data_element->{$a} } (keys
%$ref_hash_visits_per_data_element)) {
  print OUT $k."\t".$ref_hash_visits_per_data_element-
>{$k}."\t".$ref_hash_unique_visitors_per_ttl->{$k}."\n";
 }
 print OUT "\n";
 print OUT "Total visits: $ref_tot_vis\n";
 ## print number of unique visitors by IP address
 my $i=0;
 $i += keys %$ref_hash_ip;
 print OUT "Total visitors/Unique IP: $i\n";
 print OUT "\n";

 close (OUT);
 print "Results in ${$ref_output_file}\n";
}
############
```

```
### MAIN ###
############

system "clear"; ## clear screen, use cls for dos

unless ($#ARGV == -1)
{
 my $log_file=shift; ## web server log to analyze passed to the
parser

 my $log_dir='/home/httpd/html/test/'; ## LOG directory
 my $output_dir='/home/httpd/html/test/'; ## Directory for
reports
 my $input_dir='/home/httpd/html/test/'; ## Directory for input
data, external data

 my $ttl_lst=$input_dir.'title_list.txt'; ## external data,
list of title ids
 my $provider_lst=$input_dir.'provider_list.txt'; ## external
data, list of provider ids

 my %tid=&load_list($ttl_lst); ## list of titles and their id
number, text tab delimited
 my %pid=&load_list($provider_lst); ## list of provider and
their id number, text tab delimited

 my %ttl_visits=(); ## hash for accessed titles, hash
key=title+provider, hash value=access count
 my $total_visits=0; ## total count of overall visits
 my %ip_count=();
 my %visitors_per_title=();
 my %unique_visitors=();
 my %visits_per_provider=();

 my $input_file=$log_dir.$log_file;
 print &print_date();
 print "Working on $input_file . . . \n";

 open (F, $input_file) or die "$input_file: $!";

 while (<F>)
 {
  chomp;
  ## extract each data element from each line from log in CLF
  ## \S represents non-white space character
  my ($ip, $rfc, $id, $date, $ttl, $status, $bytesent,
$referrer, $platform) =
```

```
  /^(\S+) (\S+) (\S+) \[(.+)\] \"(.+)\" (\S+) (\S+) \"(.*)\"
\"(.*)\"/o;
  ## Count for each data element only if
  ## accessed through click_through page and valid return
code=200 (successful), 3xx (redirection, cached)
  ## Analyze accessed title and count visits
  if (($ttl =~/click_through\.php/) and ($status =~/200|3??/))
  {
  ## Extract data element title_id, provider_id and url
captured with click_through script
  my ($usedttl, $src, $url) =
/click_through.php.+title_id=(.+)&provider_id=(.+)&url=(.+)[\s]HT
TP.+$/;

  ## Each title is identified by title and provider to
distinguish multiple subscription
  my $accessed_ttl=$tid{$usedttl}."\t".$pid{$src};

  #################### Generate output in CLF format for
WebTrends or other web analytics software
  #################### page accessed=vendors url,
referrer=provider
  #################### comment out line below and redirect
output to a file as a CLF log
  #################### print "$ip $rfc $id \[$date\] \"GET $url
HTTP 1\.1\" $status $bytesent \"$pid{$src}\" \"$platform\"\n";

  ## visit counts
  $ttl_visits{$accessed_ttl}++;
  $total_visits++;

  ## visitor count per title
  my $vpt_index=$accessed_ttl."\t".$ip;
  &count_unique_visitors(\%visitors_per_title,
\%unique_visitors, $accessed_ttl, $vpt_index, $ip);

  ## IP counts
  $ip_count{$ip}++;

  ## visits per provider
  $visits_per_provider{$pid{$src}}++;
  }
}
 close(F);
```

```
#### Print title visit counts in descending order
my $output_file=$output_dir.'TTL_'.$log_file.'.out';
my $rpt_ttl='Visits per accessed title';
my @col_header=qw (Title Provider Visits Visitors);
&print_output(\$input_file, \$output_file, \$rpt_ttl,
\@col_header, \%ttl_visits, \%unique_visitors,
$total_visits,\%ip_count);

#### Print visits per IP in descending order
my $output_file=$output_dir.'IP_'.$log_file.'.out';
my $rpt_ttl='Visits per IP';
my @col_header=qw (IP/Visitors Visits);
&print_output(\$input_file, \$output_file, \$rpt_ttl,
\@col_header, \%ip_count, \%unique_visitors,
$total_visits,\%ip_count);

#### Print visits per provider in descending order
my $output_file=$output_dir.'PROVIDER_'.$log_file.'.out';
my $rpt_ttl='Visits per Provider';
my @col_header=qw (Provider Visits);
&print_output(\$input_file, \$output_file, \$rpt_ttl,
\@col_header, \%visits_per_provider, \%unique_visitors,
$total_visits,\%ip_count);

print "Done.\n";
}
else { print "Usage: perl parse.pl log_filename\n";}

### END ###
```

Bibliography

Alsmeyer, David. 2000. *Economics and Usage of a Digital Corporate Library*. BT Advanced Communications Research. Available at www.si.umich.edu/ PEAK-2000/alsmeyer.pdf.

Amin, Mayur, and Michael Mabe. 2000. "Impact Factors: Use and Abuse." *Perspective in Publishing* 1. Elsevier Science.

Anderson, Caryn. 2004. "National Federation of Abstracting and Information Services (NFAIS) Conference Report 1 October 2004 New York City." Available at http://web.simmons.edu/~andersoc/erus/nfais.html.

Anderson, Ivy. 2004. "Using Library Resources in Course Web Pages: Linking and Permissible Uses." Available at http://hul.harvard.edu/ldi/slides/ Linking_and_Permissible_Use.ppt.

Anglada, Lluís, and Núria Comellas. 2002. "What's fair? Pricing Models in the Electronic Era." *Library Management* 23, nos. 4, 5: 227–233.

Antonucci-Durgan, Dana, and Ugen Gombo. 2004. "Where Did that E-journal Go? E-Journal Changes and Access Problems." North American Serials Interest Group (NASIG) Conference Milwaukee. Available at www.nasig.org.

ARL (Association of Research Libraries). 2001. "Measures and Statistics for Research Library Network Services." *ARL E-Metrics Phase II Report*. Available at www.arl.org.

ARL (Association of Research Libraries). 2003. "Fact and Figures. Holdings of University Research Libraries in U.S. and Canada, 2001–2." *The Chronicle of Higher Education* 49, no. 38.

Bakst, Diane. 2000. "The Mane Event." *School Library Journal* 46, no. 3.

Ball, David. 2002. "Public Libraries and the Consortium Purchase of Electronic Resources." *The Electronic Library* 21, no. 4: 301–309.

Ballard, Aron. 2003. "Berkeley Professor Challenges Publishing Status Quo. The Daily Californian." Available at www.dailycal.org.

BECTA (British Educational Communications and Technology Agency). 2002. "Providíng Rremote Access to School Networks." Available at www.ictadvice.org.uk.

Benjes, Candice M., and Janis F. Brown. 2001. "Database-Generated Web Pages: The Norris Medical Library Experience." *Bull Medical Library Association* 89, no. 2 (April): 222–224.

Bergstrom, Carl T., and Theodore C. Bergstrom. 2003. "The Costs and Benefits of Library Site Licenses to Academic Journals." *PNAS* 101, no. 3: 897–902.

Bertot, John Carlo. 2001. "Library Network Statistics and Performance Measures: Approaches and Issues." *Liber Quarterly* 11: 224–243.

———. 2002. "Measuring Public Library Networked Services: Preparing Your Library to Collect Network Statistics (E-metrics)." Available at www.ii.fsu.edu.

———. 2004. "Libraries and Networked Information Services: Issues and Considerations in Measurement." *Performance Measurement and Metrics* 5, no. 1: 11–19.

Bertot, John Carlo, Charles R. McClure, Denise M. Davis, and Joe Ryan. 2004. "Capture Usage with E-Metrics." Available at www.libraryjournal.com.

Bertot, John Carlo, Manimegalai Subramanian, Charles R. McClure, and Denise M. Davis. 2003. "Librarian Education for the Collection Analysis and Use of Library Networked Services and Resources Statistics, Interim Report II." Available at www.ii.fsu.edu/projects/2005/imls_training/interim.report3.01_30_2004.pdf.

Bishop, Ann Peterson. 2002. "Measuring Access, Use, and Success in Digital Libraries." *Journal of Electronic Publishing* 4, no. 2.

Blake, Julie C., and Susan P. Schleper. 2004. "From Data to Decisions: Using Surveys and Statistics to Make Collection Management Decisions." *Library Collections, Acquisitions & Technical Services* 28, no. 4: 460–464.

Blank-Edelman, David N. 2000. "Chapter 9: Log Files." In *Perl for System Administration*. 1st edition. Sebastopol: O'Reilly & Associates.

Blecic, Deborah D., Joan B. Fiscella, and Stephen E. Wiberley, Jr. 2001. "The Measurement of Use of Web-based Information Resources: An Early Look at Vendor-supplied Data." *College and Research Libraries* 62, no. 5 (September).

Blixrud, Julia C. 2002. "Measures for Electronic Use: the ARL E-Metrics Project. International Federation of Library Associations." Available at www.lboro.ac.uk.

Boardman, Bruce. 2004. "Analyze This: Web Analytics Can Help You Process a Vortex of Raw Site Visitor Data to Reveal Truths About Customer Behavior." Available at www.nwc.com.

Bocher, Bob. 2001. "Issues in Public Access to the Internet in Public Libraries or How to Avoid Becoming Roadkill on the Information Highway." Available at www.dpi.state.wi.us.

Bol, Jennifer, Dean Smith, and Arkady Mak. 1998. "What Are the Models for Licensing, Pricing, and Contracting for Print and Online Subscriptions?" *CBE Views* 21, no. 6: 198.

Booth, Andrew, Jonathan Eldredge, and Anne Brice. 2004. "An ABC of EBL: What is it and Where Has it Come From?" Available at www.shef.ac.uk/scharr/eblib/ABC.ppt.

Borghuis, Marthyn G. M. 2002. "What to Count & What Not? A White Paper on the Filters to Be Applied to Raw Usage Data Before Usage-Analysis Can Start. ScienceDirect." Available at www.info.sciencedirect.com.

Bravy, Gary J., and Feather K. Celeste. 2001. "The Impact of Electronic Access on Basic Library Services: One Academic Law Library's Experience." *Law Library Journal* 93, no. 2.

Breeding, Marshall. 2002. "Strategies for Measuring and Implementing E-use." *Library Technology Reports* 38, no. 3: 68.

Brophy, Peter, and Peter M. Wynne. 1997. "Management Information Systems and Performance. Measurement for the Electronic Library: eLib Supporting Study (MIEL2) Final Report." Available at www.ukoln.ac.uk/dlis/models/studies/mis/mis.rtf.

Buckley, Brad. 2003. "Metasearch Usage Statistics." Thomson/Gale. Available at www.niso.org/standards/resources/buckley.ppt.

Burby, Jason, and Matt Jacobs. 2003. "Mastering the Web Site Optimization Process." In *Keys to Unlocking Your Web Marketing Genius*. NetIQ/WebTrends. Available at www.netiq.com.

———. 2003. "Optimizing Site Performance Using the ZAAZ Analytics Methodology." NetIQ/WebTrends. Available at www.netiq.com.

Buystream. 2001. "Move From Site Metrics to Business Metrics on the Web." Available at http://webdesign.ittoolbox.com.

Callender, John. 2001. "Chapter 8: Parsing Web Access Logs." In *Perl for Web Site Management*. Sebastopol: O'Reilly & Associates.

Calore, Michael. 2001. "Log File Lowdown." Available at http://webmonkey.wired.com/.

Chen, Ya-Ning. 1998. "The Internet's Effect on Libraries: Some Personal Observations." *Library and Information Science Research* 8, no. 1 (March 31).

Christie, Anne, and Laurel Kristick. 2001. "Developing an Online Science Journal Collection: A Quick Tool for Assigning Priorities." Issues in Science and Technology Librarianship. Available at www.library.ucsb.edu.

Chudnov, Dan. 1999. "Open Source Systems for Libraries (oss4lib)." Available at www.oss4lib.org/about.php.

Clinton, Peter. 2003. "The Print to Digital Transition: Recent Developments and

Future Directions." Available at www.library.utoronto.ca/its/
presentations/peterclinton/update-29May03.pdf.
Coleman, Anita, and Chris Neuhaus. 2004. "Bibliography of Webmetrics."
Available at http://webmetrics.comm.nsdl.org.
Cooke, Helen, Eric Hornsby, and Heather Todd. 2002. "The Cybrary—
Seamless for the Customer, Fine Needlework for the Staff." Available at
http://www.vala.org.au/vala2002/2002pdf/36CoHoTo.pdf.
COUNTER (Counting Online Usage of NeTwork Electronic Resources). 2004.
"The COUNTER Code of Practice Release 2. COUNTER (Counting
Online Usage of NeTwork Electronic Resources)." Available at www
.projectcounter.org.
Cowhig, Jerry. 2001. "Electronic Article and Journal Usage Statistics (EAJUS):
Proposal for an Industry-wide Standard." *Learned Publishing* 14, no. 3
(July).
Crane, Allen S. 2003. "Actionable E-Metrics." Available at www
.intelligententerprise.com.
Cremer, Monika. 1998. "The Image of Libraries in the Internet." Available at
www.ifla.org.
Cutler, Matt, and Jim Sterne. 2000. "E-metrics: Business Metrics for the New
Economy." SPSS. Available at www.spss.com.
Davis, Denise M. 2000. "Electronic Access and Use Related Measures:
Summary of Findings." U.S. National Commission on Libraries and
Information Science (NCLIS). Available at www.nclis.gov.
———. 2001. "E-Metric Initiatives in the United States." U.S. National
Commission on Libraries and Information Science (NCLIS). Available at
www.nclis.gov.
———. 2001. "Middle Ground: Reaching Agreement on Vendor-supplied
Database Use Statistics." U.S. National Commission on Libraries and
Information Science (NCLIS). Available at www.nclis.gov/statsurv/
presentations/use_stats_ASIST_11_05_01.pdf.
———. 2002. "E-Metrics: What You Need to Know to Get Started." U.S.
National Commission on Libraries and Information Science (NCLIS).
Available at www.nclis.gov.
———. 2002. "Where to Spend Our E-Journal Money? Defining a University
Library's Core Collection through Citation Analysis." *Portal: Libraries and
the Academy* 2, no. 1: 155–166.
———. 2003. "Effect of the Web on Undergraduate Citation Behavior: Guiding
Student Scholarship in a Networked Age." *Portal: Libraries and the Academy*
3, no. 1: 41–51.
———. 2003. "Why Usage Statistics Cannot Tell Us Everything, and Why We
Shouldn't Dare to Ask." *Against the Grain* 15, no. 6: 24–25.
———. 2004. "For Electronic Journals, Total Downloads Can Predict Number
of Users." Available at http://muse.jhu.edu.

Davis, Philip M. 2004. "Letter To the Editor." *Journal of the American Society for Information Science and Technology* 55, no. 4: 369–371.

Davis, Denise M., John Carlo Bertot, and Charles R. McClure. 2001. "Network Performance Measures Focus Group: Group Discussion #3 Summary Notes." U.S. National Commission on Libraries and Information Science (NCLIS). Available at www.nclis.gov.

Davis, Philip M., and Leah R. Solla. 2003. "An IP-level Analysis of Usage Statistics for Electronic Journals in Chemistry: Making Inferences About User Behavior." *Journal of The American Society For Information Science and Technology* 54: 1062–1068.

De Groote, Sandra L., and Josephine L. Dorsch. 2003. "Measuring Use Patterns of Online Journals and Databases." *Journal of Medical Library Association* 91, no. 2 (April).

Dole, Wanda V. 2001. "Annual Report 2001, Section on Statistics." International Federation of Library Associations (IFLA). Available at www.ifla.org.

———. 2003. "The Role of National Library Associations in Developing Tools for Statistics and Assessments." Available at www.gpntb.ru/win/inter-events/crimea2003/eng/confer.htm.

Dowling, Thomas. 2001. "Lies, Damned Lies, and Web Logs." *Netconnect* (Spring).

Duranceau, Ellen Finnie, and Cindy Hepfer. 2002. "Staffing for Electronic Resource Management: The Results of a Survey." *Serials Review* 28, no. 4: 316–320.

Duy, Joanna, and Eric Pauley. 2004. "Is It Working: Usage Data as a Tool for Evaluating the Success of New Full-Text Access Methods." *The Serials Librarian* 46, nos. 3, 4: 295–300.

Duy, Joanna, and Liwen Vaughan. 2003. "Usage Data for Electronic Resources: A Comparison Between Locally Collected and Vendor-Provided Statistics." *The Journal of Academic Librarianship* 29, no. 1: 476–481.

Eaton, Jonathan. 2002. "Measuring User Statistics." *Update Magazine* (September). Available at www.cilip.org.uk.

EBSCO. 2003. "Serials Prices 1999–2003 with Projections for 2004." Available at www.ebsco.com/home/printsubs/serialspriceprojec06.pdf.

Eisenberg, Bryan, Jim Novo, and John E. Shreeve. 2002. "Introduction to the Guide to the Web Analytics." *Future Now.* Available at www.futurenowinc.com.

Eldredge, Jon. 2004. "Evidence-Based Librarianship." Available at http://www.mcmla.org/meetings/2004/EBL04Keynote.pdf.

Elliott, Donald. 2003. "Cost-benefit Analysis: Return to Taxpayer Investment in Public Libraries." Available at www.siue.edu/BUSINESS/econfin/papers/Illinois%20Library%20Association%2010_03%20webfile.ppt.

Equinox. 2000. "Library Performance Measurement and Quality Management System." Available at http://equinox.dcu.ie.

Fisher, Brian. 2003. "Revisionist Early History of e-Commerce BAIT523." Available at www.cs.ubc.ca.

Flatten, Kay. 1997. "Five Things to Change First When Academic Libraries Embrace Web Access." *Information Research* 3, no. 2 (September).

Flynn, Ann. 2005. "Performance Indicators for Electronic Library Services." Available at http: //epress.lib.uts.edu.au/__data/assets/pdf_file/10665/Performance_Indicators_2005.pdf.

Franconi, Enrico. 2002. "Data Warehouse Design CS 636." Available at www .inf.unibz.it.

———. 2002. "Introduction to Data Warehousing CS 636." Available at www .inf.unibz.it.

Franklin, Brinley, and Terry Plum. 2002. "Networked Electronic Services Usage Patterns at Four Academic Health Sciences Libraries." In *Proceedings Of The Northumbria Lite Conference.* International Federation of Library Associations and Institutions (IFLA). Available at www.ifla.org.

———. 2004. "Library Usage Patterns in the Electronic Information Environment." *Information Research* 9, no. 4 (July).

Friedlein, Ashley. 2003. "Web Measurement and Analytics Understanding What it is, How to do it and the Vendor Marketplace. E-Consultancy." Available at www.e-consultancy.com.

Gaudet, Françoise, and Claudine Lieber. 2002. "L'Amérique A Votre Porte" *Bulletin des Bibliothèques de France* 47, no. 6: 70–77.

Gedye, Richard. 2001. "Notes From a Meeting to Explore the Feasibility of a Multi-agency Effort to Develop a Code of Practice for Vendor Based Online Usage Statistics." Available at www.nclis.gov/statsurv/FocusGroup4/Dec%205%20mult-agency%20meeting%20-%20RG's%20notes.doc.

Goldberg, Jeffrey. 2001. "Why Web Usage Statistics Are (Worse Than) Meaningless." (April) Available at www.goldmark.org.

Griffin, Michael P. 2000. "E-Marketing Planning: Accountability and eMetrics. White Paper." Embellix Software. Available at www.embellix.com.

Hahn, Karla L., and Lila A. Faulkner. 2002. "Evaluative Usage-Based Metrics for the Selection of E-Journals." *College and Research Libraries* 63, no. 3 (May).

Hanson, Lynn. 2003. "UI Current LIS Clips: Electronic Resources." Available at www.lis.uiuc.edu/clips/2003_04.html.

Hespos, Tom. 2001. "Spiders and Robots and Crawlers, Oh My!" Available at www.clickz.com.

Hill, B. Terry. 2004. "Using Traditional Methodologies and Electronic Usage Statistics as Indicators to Assess Campus-wide Journal Needs: Contexts, Trade-offs, and Processes." University of North Carolina at Chapel Hill. Available at http://etd.ils.unc.edu.

Hiott, Judith. 2002. "Evaluating and Applying Web Statistics: The Library Web Site." Special Libraries Association (SLA). Available at www.sla.org.

———. 2002. "Issues Still Outstanding and Future Solutions in Networked Statistic Collection." U.S. National Commission on Libraries and Information Science (NCLIS). Available at www.nclis.gov.

Holbert, Gentry Lankewicz. 2001. "Technology, Libraries and the Internet: A Comparison of the Impact of the Printing Press and World Wide Web." *E-JASL: The Electronic Journal of Academic and Special Librarianship* 3, no. 1–2 (Winter).

Holt, Glen E., and Donald Elliott. 2003. "Measuring Outcomes: Applying Cost-Benefit Analysis to Middle-sized and Smaller Public Libraries— Public Libraries." *Library Trends* (Winter).

Hunt, Steve. 2001. "Remote User Authentication." Available at http://library.smc.edu/rua.htm.

ICOLC (International Coalition of Library Consortia). 1998. "Guidelines for Statistical Measures of Usage of Web-based Indexed, Abstracted, and Full Text Resources." (November) Available at http://www.library.yale.edu/consortia/webstats.html.

Ingoldsby, Tim. 2003. "Usage Statistics: Different Audiences, Different Goals, But LOTS of Effort." American Institute of Physics. Available at www.cesse.org/MEET/2003/TimIngoldsby.pdf.

ISO (International Standards Organization). 1998. *ISO 11620 Information and Documentation: Library Performance Indicators.* 1st edition.

———. 2003. *ISO 2789 Information and Documentation: International Library Statistics.* 3rd edition.

Jewell, Timothy D. 2001. "Selection and Preservation of Commercially Available Electronic Resources: Issues and Practices." Digital Library Federation (DLF)/Council on Library and Information Resources (CLIR). Available at www.clir.org.

Jewell, Timothy D., Ivy Anderson, Adam Chandler, Sharon E. Farb, Kimberly Parker, Angela Riggio, and Nathan D. M. Anderson. 2004. "Electronic Resources Management: Report of the DLF Initiative." *Digital Library Federation.* Available at www.diglib.org.

Jones, Steve, Sally Jo Cunningham, Roger McNab, and Stefan Boddie. 2000. "A Transaction Log Analysis of a Digital Library." *International Journal on Digital Libraries* 3, no. 2: 152–169.

Jordan, Mark. 2003. "The Self-Education of Systems Librarians." *Library Hi Tech* 21, no. 3: 273–279.

Kaplan, Nancy R., and Michael L. Nelson. 2000. "Determining the Publication Impact of a Digital Library." *Journal of the American Society for Information Science* 514, no. 4: 324–339.

Kidd, Tony. 2002. "Electronic Journal Usage Statistics: Present Practice and Future Progress." In *Statistics in Practice—Measuring and Managing.*

Kiger, Jack E., and Kenneth Wise. 1996. "Auditing an Academic Library Book Collection." *Journal of Academic Librarianship* 22, no. 4: 267–272.

Kilmartin, Donna. 1999. "Technical Support Survey." (November). Available at www.sls.lib.il.us/infotech/surveys/technical/.

Kimbrough S., B. Padmanabhan, and Z. Zheng. 2000. "On Usage Metrics for Determining Authoritative Sites." Available at http://portal.acm.org/citation.cfm?id=794126.

King, Donald W., Peter B. Boyce, Carol Hansen Montgomery, and Carol Tenopir. 2003. "Library Economic Metrics: Example of the Comparison of Electronic and Print Journals Collections and Collections Services." *Library Trends* 51, no. 3: 376–400.

Klein, V. Daniel. 2002. "The Evolution of E-commerce, History Repeats Itself (Again)." Available at www.klein.com.

Kohavi, Ron. 2001. "Mining E-Commerce Data: The Good, the Bad and the Ugly." Available at http://ai.stanford.edu/users/ronnyk/goodBadUgly KDDItrack.pdf.

Kyrillidou, Martha. 2003. "E-Metrics: Lessons Learned from the ARL E-Metrics Project, Challenges and Opportunities. Association of Research Libraries." Available at http://arl.cni.org.

Kyrillidou, Martha, Julia Blixrud, Consuella Askew, and Jonathan Sousa. 2003. "Attachment 2 Performance Measures." In *Activities. Association of Research Libraries*. Available at www.arl.org.

Kyrillidou, Martha, and Sarah Giersch. 2004. "Qualitative Analysis of ARL E-Metrics Participant Feedback about the Evolution of Measures for Networked Electronic Resources." *Library Quarterly* (June).

Lafferty, Meghan. 2004. "A Comparison of Subscribed and Non-Subscribed Titles in the Springer Link Electronic Journal Package. A Master's Paper for the M.S. in L.S. Degree."

Lagier, Jennifer. 2002. "Measuring Usage and Usability of Online Databases At Hartnell College: An Evaluation of Selected Electronic Resources." Available at www.hartnell.edu.

Lakos, Amos, Jeff Shim, Charles R. McClure, Bruce T. Fraser, and John Carlo Bertot. 2001. "The ARL E-Metrics Instructional Module 1 (Importance)." Association of Research Libraries. Available at www.arl.org.

———. 2001. "The ARL E-Metrics Instructional Module 2 (Preparation)." Association of Research Libraries. Available at www.arl.org.

———. 2001. "The ARL E-Metrics Instructional Module 3 (Statistics)." Association of Research Libraries. Available at www.arl.org.

Law, Derek. 2003. "Simplifying Access to Electronic Resources: the Changing Model of Information Provision." Available at www.itsltduk.co.uk/PDF/communique6.pdf.

Lawrence, Steve, and C. Lee Giles. 1999. "Accessibility of Information on the Web." *Nature* 400.

Library of Congress. 2003. "Guidelines for the Use of Field 856." (March). Available at http://www.loc.gov/marc/856guide.html.

The Library Research Center, Graduate School of Library and Information Science, University of Illinois. 2000. "Survey of Internet Access Management in Public Libraries, Summary of Findings." Available at www.ala.org.

Lobet, Jean-Luc. 2004. *Evaluer l'Utilisation de la Collection Electronique: l'Exemple du SCD de Lyon 2*. France: Ecole Nationale Supérieure des Sciences de l'Information et des Bibliothèques.

Luther, Judy. 2001. "White Paper on Electronic Journal Statistics. Council on Library and Information Resources." Available at www.clir.org.

———. 2002. "Why Libraries Need Statistics? Informed Strategies." Available at www.nfais.org.

———. 2003. "Slippery Slope of Usage Data. Informed Strategies." Available at www.sla.org.

Mahé, Annaïg. 2002. "Usages des Revues Electroniques." Available at http://revues.enssib.fr/pdf/Usages.pdf.

Marchionini, Gary. 2000. *Evaluating Digital Libraries: A Longitudinal and Multifaceted View (Draft)*. Chapel Hill: University of North Carolina.

McClure, Charles R. 1999. "Developing National Statistics and Performance Measures for Public Libraries in the Networked Environment." Available at http://slis-two.lis.fsu.edu/~cmcclure/.

McClure, Charles R., David R. Lankes, Melissa Gross, and Beverly Choltko-Devlin. 2003. "Statistics, Measures, and Quality Standards for Assessing Digital Library Reference Services: Guidelines and Procedures." *Libraries and the Academy* 3, no. 4 (October): 692–693.

McCook, Alison. 2004. "Open-access Journals Rank Well." (April). Available at www.the-scientist.com.

McCord, Sarah, Janet Chisman, Joel Cummings, and Ryan Johnson. 2002. "One Stop Shopping (Almost): SFX Implementation at Washington State University." Available at www.wsulibs.wsu.edu/holland/sfx4onnw.ppt.

Mercer, Linda S. 2000. "Measuring the Use and Value of Electronic Journals and Books." *Issues in Science and Technology Librarianship* (Winter).

Microsoft. 2003. "Harlan Community Library. Library Reduces IT Support Costs, Increases Productivity and Communication." In *Microsoft® Windows® Small Business Server 2003 Customer Solution Case Study*. Available at www.microsoft.com/resources/casestudies/CaseStudy.asp?CaseStudyID=15038.

Miller, Rush, and Sherrie Schmidt. 2001. "E-metrics: Measures for Electronic Resources." Association of Research Libraries (ARL). Available at www.arl.org.

Moen, William, and Charles McClure. 1997. "Appendix C-6 Web Server Log Transaction Log Analysis Methodology." In *An Evaluation of an U.S. GILS Implementation*. Available at www.unt.edu.

Moen, William, Charles McClure, and John Carlo Bertot. 2004. "Making Sense of Usage Statistics for Online Databases." Available at www.unt.edu.

Montgomery, Carol Hansen. 2000. "Measuring the Impact of an Electronic Journal Collection on Library Costs." *D-Lib Magazine* 6, no. 10. Available at www.dlib.org.

Mosher, H. Paul. 2002. "Penn Library Assessment Program." Available at www.arl.org.

Mouw, James. 2003. "Linking patrons to online materials." Available at http://home.uchicago.edu/~mouw/Linking.ppt.

Mundt, Sebastian. 2002. "Sampling In-library Use." International Federation of Library Associations and Institutions (IFLA). Available at www.ifla.org.

Murphy, Jamie, and Charles F. Hofacker. 2004. "A Methodology and Investigation of an eLoyalty Metric, Consumer Bookmarking Behavior." *JCMC* 10, no. 1: Article 10.

Nagle, Ellen. 1996. "The New Knowledge Environment: Quality Initiatives in Health Sciences Libraries—Perspectives on Quality in Libraries." *Library Trends* (Winter).

NCES (National Center for Education Statistics). 1998. "Integrated Postsecondary Education Data System (IPEDS) Academic Library Survey." National Center for Education Statistics (NCES). Available at www.nces.gov.

NELINET. 2002. "Open URL Group Questions and Responses." Available at www.nelinet.net.

Nester Kresh, Diane. 2001. "Library quality reference meets the World Wide Web. International Federation of Library Associations." Available at www.ifla.org.

NetIQ. 2001. "Understanding Hits, Page Views and User Sessions." NetIQ. Available at www.netiq.com.

———. 2003. "WebTrends, Tracking Visitors' Steps. White Paper." Available at http://whitepapers.zdnet.co.uk/0,39025945,60041157p-39000589q,00.htm.

NISO (National Information Standards Organization). 1995. "Library Statistics." Bethesda: NISO Press. Available at www.niso.org.

———. 2002. "Appendix B: Measuring the Use of Electronic Library Services." In *NISO Z39.7-2002 Draft Standard for Trial Use, Information Services and Use: Metrics & Statistics for Libraries and Information Providers—Data Dictionary*. Available at www.niso.org/emetrics.

———. 2002. "Introduction." In *NISO Z39.7-2002 Draft Standard for Trial Use, Information Services and Use: Metrics & Statistics for Libraries and Information Providers—Data Dictionary*. Available at www.niso.org/emetrics.

———. 2004. "MetaSearch Initiative." Available at www.niso.org/committees/ MS_initiative.html.

———. 2004. "The OpenURL Framework for Context-Sensitive Services." Available at www.niso.org/committees/committee_ax.html.

NIST (National Institute of Standards and Technology). 2002. "Web Metrics: Technical Overview." Available at http://zing.ncsl.nist.gov/WebTools/.

Oberg, Steve. 2003. "Gold Rush: An Electronic Journal Management and Linking Project." *Serials Review* 29: 230–232.

Okerson, Ann. 2003. "The Matrix Reloaded: New Ages in Collections Development." International Federation of Library Associations. Available at www.ifla.org.

Pace, Andrew K. 2003. "Dis-Integrated Technical Services and Electronic Journals." Available at www.lib.ncsu.edu/presentations/cil2003/ disintegrated.ppt.

Pardue, Bill. 2001. "Internet Librarian 2001, Webwizard's Symposium: Using Statistics." Available at www.infotoday.com/il2001.

Pasquinelli, Art. 2003. "Information Technology Advances in Libraries. White Paper." In *Digital Library Technology Trends.* Sun Microsystems.

Perry, Beth. 1999. "Literature Review of Digital Libraries and Highlights of Activities in DOE and Contractor Libraries." Available at www.osti.gov/ inforum99/papers/perry.pdf.

Pesch, Oliver. 2004. "Usage Statistics: Taking E-Metrics to the Next Level." *Serials Librarian* 46, nos. 1, 2: 143–154.

Peterson, Eric T. 2004. *Web Metrics Demystified: A Marketer's Guide to Understanding How Your Web Site Affects Your Business.* Celilo Group Media and CafePress.

Peterson, Walker Janet. 2003. "Stretch Your Budget! How to Select Web-Based Subscription Resources." Infotoday. Available at www.infotoday.com.

Pinfield, Stephen. 2001. "Managing Electronic Library Services: Current Issues in UK Higher Education Institutions." *Ariadne* 29.

Pushpa, Ramachandran M, Ragavendra Shripad, and Kunal Turakhia. 2001. "E-customer Analytics. White Paper." Wipro. Available at www.wipro.com.

Rappa, Michael. 2003. "Web Metrics" In *Managing the Digital Enterprise.* Available at http://digitalenterprise.org.

Rappaport, Avi. 1999. "Robots & Spiders & Crawlers: How Web and Intranet Seach Engines Follow Links to Build Indexes. A White Paper." Search Tools Consulting. Available at www.searchtools.com.

Reynolds, Wil. 2003. "Your Web Metrics are All Wrong, and They'll Never be All Right!" Available at www.wilreynolds.net.

Richardson, John A. 2002. "Benchmarking Technical Solutions in Libraries." einfo Dynamics LLC. Available at www.infotoday.com/cil2002/ presentations/richardson.pps.

Roberts, Stephen A. 2003. "Financial Management of Libraries: Past Trends and Future Prospects—Financial Management." *Library Trends* (Winter).

Rodgers, Keith, and Denis Howlett. 2000. *What is CRM?: A White Paper*. TBC Research, in association with Goldmine Software (Europe) Ltd. UK: Goldmine Software (Europe).

Rousseau, Ronald. 2002. "Journal Evaluation: Technical and Practical Issues." *Library Trends* 50, no. 3: 418–439.

Rupp-Serrano, Karen, Sarah Robbins, and Danielle Cain. 2002. "Canceling Print Serials in Favor of Electronic: Criteria for Decision-Making." *Library Collections, Acquisitions & Technical Services* 26: 369–378.

Ryan, Joe. 2005. "Library Statistics & Measures." Available at http://web.syr.edu/~jryan/infopro/stats.html#top.

Saha, Sommath, Sanjay Saint, and Dimitri A. Christakis. 2003. "Impact Factor: A Valid Measure of Journal Quality?" *Journal of Medical Library Association* 91, no. 1 (January): 42–46.

Samson, Sue, Sebastian Derry, and Holly Eggleston. 2004. "Networked Resources, Assessment and Collection Development." *Journal of Academic Librarianship* 30, no. 6: 476–481.

Sane Solutions. 2002. "Analyzing Web Site Traffic White Paper." Sane Solutions. Available at www.sane.com.

Santos, Nuno. 2000. "Clickthrough Package Requirements Template." Available at http://openacs.org.

Saracevic, Tefko. 2000. "LIDA: Libraries in the Digital Age." LIDA (Libraries In the Digital Age). Available at www.ffos.hr/lida/.

Schwartz, Randal L. 1998. "Where Did They Go?" Web Techniques, Column 25. Available at www.stonehenge.com/merlyn/WebTechniques/.

Sears, JoAnn. 2001. "Chat Reference Service: An Analysis of one Semester's Data." *Issues in Science and Technology Librarianship* (Fall).

Seattle Pacific University. "Library Annual Report 1999/2000." 2000. Available at www.spu.edu/depts/library/about_library/main/annual_reports/annual_report_2000.htm.

Sen, Shahana, Balaji Padmanabhan, Alexander Tuzhilin, Norman White, and Roger Stein. 1998. "On the Analysis of Web Site Usage Data: How Much Can We Learn About the Consumer from Web Logfiles?" Available at http://opim-sun.wharton.upenn.edu/~balaji/ejm.pdf.

Shearer, Barbara S., and Suzanne P. Nagy. 2003. "Developing an Academic Medical Library Core Journal Collection in the (Almost) Post-print Era: The Florida State University College of Medicine Medical Library Experience." *Journal of Medical Library Association* 91, no. 3 (July): 292–302.

Shearer, Kathleen. 2002. "Statistics and Performance Measures for Research Libraries. Recent Research and New Developments." *CARL/ABRC.CARL/ABRC Backgrounder Series* 3.

Shim, Wonsik "Jeff." 2004. "Network Performance Measures Task Group #6." Available at www.ii.fsu.edu.

Shim, Wonsik "Jeff," Charles R. McClure, Bruce T. Fraser, and John Carlo Bertot. 2001. "Data Collection Manual for Academic and Research Library Network Statistics and Performance Measures." Association of Research Libraries (ARL). Available at www.arl.org.

Shim, Wonsik "Jeff," Charles R. McClure, Bruce T. Fraser, John Carlo Bertot, Arif Dagli, Emily H. Leahy with the assistance of Don L. Latham, Benjamin Keith Belton, and Linda Carruth. 2001. "ARL E-metrics Project: Phase Two Report." Association of Research Libraries. Available at www.arl.org.

Shim, Wonsik "Jeff," Charles R. McClure, John Carlo Bertot, James T. Sweet, and Jean-Michel Maffre de Lastens, Arif Dagli, Bruce T. Fraser. 2000. "ARL E-metrics Project: Phase One Report." Association of Research Libraries. Available at www.arl.org.

Slade, Alexander L. 2004. "Chapter 5: Electronic Resources and Services." In *Library Services for Distance Learning: the Fourth Bibliography*. Englewood, CO: Libraries Unlimited Books.

Slayton, Marc. 1997. "An Introduction to Cookies." Available at http://webmonkey.wired.com/.

Smith, G. Alastair. 2001. "What can E-Libraries Learn from E-Business." Victoria University of Wellington, NZ. Available at www.vala.org.au/vala2002/2002pdf/12Smith.pdf.

Smith, Mark. 1996. *Collecting and Using Public Library Statistics*. New York, London: Neal-Schuman.

Sorgenfrei, Robert. 1999. "Slicing the Pie: Implementing and Living with a Journal Allocation Formula." *Library Collections, Acquisitions and Technical Services* 23, no. 1: 39–45.

SourceForge. 1999. "MARC/Perl." Available at http://marcpm.sourceforge.net/.

Sterne, Jim. 2002. *Web Metrics: Proven Methods for Measuring Web Site Success*. New York: John Wiley & Sons.

———. 2003. "E-Metrics: Measuring Online Success." Target Marketing. Available at www.targeting.com.

Stoklosa, Kristin, Ivy Anderson, Elaine Fadden, Jeff Kosokoff, and Heather McMullen. 2001. "Task Force on Vendor Statistics." Available at http://hul.harvard.edu.

Strupp, Paul G. 2004. "An Introduction to Web Metrics: The National Science Digital Library." Available at http://webmetrics.comm.nsdl.org/strupp_intro.pdf.

Sullivan, Danny. 2001. "SpiderSpotting: When A Search Engine, Robot Or Crawler Visits." Available at http://searchenginewatch.com.

Summary.net. 2002. "Web Analytics Tutorial." Available at www.summary.net.

Sutherland, Alison, and Peter Green. 2003. "An OpenURL Resolver (SFX) in Action: The Answer to a Librarian's Prayer Or a Burden for Technical Services?" Available at www.vala.org.au/vala2004/2004pdfs/11SutGrn .PDF.

Tec-Ed. 1999. "Assessing Web Site Usability from Server Log Files White Paper." Available at www.teced.com/PDFs/whitepap.pdf.

Tenopir, Carol. 2003. "Use and Users of Electronic Library Resources: An Overview and Analysis of Recent Research Studies. Council on Library and Information Resources." Available at www.clir.org.

Thelwall, Mike, Liwen Vaughan, and Lennart Björneborn. 2005. "Webometrics." *Annual Review of Information Science and Technology* 39: 81–135.

Todd, Heather, and Lisa Kruesi. 2002. "E-Statistics: Are We Comparing Apples and Oranges? Getting a Grip on E-Statistics to Measure our Performance: A University of Queensland Cybrary Perspective." Available at www .library.uq.edu.au.

Troll Covey, Denise. 2002. "Usage and Usability. Assessment: Library Practices and Concerns." Digital Library Federation/Council on Library and Information Resources. Available at www.clir.org.

United Nations Economic Commission for Africa. 2003. "The Value of Library Services in Development." Available at www.uneca.org.

University of California, Academic Senate. 2003. "Memo: Contract Negotiations With Publishers." Available at www.universityofcalifornia .edu/senate/committees/ucol/aclibrarians1003.pdf.

Urban Library Council. 2000. "Impacts of the Internet on Public Library Use: Basic Fact Sheet." Available at www.urbanlibraries.org.

Useful Utilities. 2003. "Log File Analysis." Useful Utilities. Available at www .usefulutilities.com.

Van Epps, Amy S. 2001. "When Vendor Statistics Are Not Enough: Determining Use of Electronic Databases." *Science and Technology Libraries* 21, nos. 1, 2: 119–126; and *Information Practice in Science and Technology: Evolving Challenges and New Directions.*

———. 2003. "Dynamically Generated Pages Using Database-To-Web Technologies." Available at www.lib.purdue.edu.

Vigna, Giovanni, William Robertson, Vishal Kher, and Richard A. Kemmerer. 2001. "A Stateful Intrusion Detection System for World-Wide Web Servers." Available at www.acsac.org.

Wahlen, David. 2002. "The Unofficial Cookie FAQ." Available at www .cookiecentral.com/faq/.

WebTrends. 2003. "Tracking Visitors' Steps." WebTrends. Available at www .webtrends.com.

Weidman, Will. 2003. "Web Site Metrics." *WC Journal* v.

Weintraub, Jennifer. 2002. "Usage Statistics for Yale's Digital Collections." Available at http://www.acrlnec.org/sigs/itig/Usage_Statistics.ppt.

Weitz, Jay. 2004. "Cataloging Electronic Resources: OCLC-MARC Coding Guidelines." (November) Available at www.oclc.org/support/documentation/worldcat/cataloging/electronicresources/.

Winett, Bill. 2003. "Tracking Your Visitors." Available at http://webmonkey.wired.com/.

Wulff, Judith L. 2004. "Quality Markers and Use of Electronic Journals in an Academic Health Sciences Library." *Journal of Medical Library Association* 92, no. 3 (July): 315–322.

Zucca, Joe. 2001. "Building the Plumbing for Measurement."

———. 2002. "Through the Bytes Darkly." Available at http://digital.library.upenn.edu/pubs/Through_the_Bytes_Darkly.ppt.

———. 2003. "Find a Way to Make One: Strategies for Measuring and Analyzing the Use of Digital Information. Association of Research Libraries." Available at www.arl.cni.org.

———. 2004. "Plumbing and Counting . . . An Update on the Penn Library Data Farm." Available at www.libqual.org.

"Webography." 2003. Available at www.shef.ac.uk/scharr/eblib/webography.html.

"Why Homegrown is Better (for Comparing Electronic Journal Usage Statistics)." Available at www.lib.baskent.edu.tr/tez/Homegrown.doc.

INDEX

A

AACR2 (Anglo-American Cataloging Rules), 189
Access: barrier, 197; remote, 107–109, 165; restrictions, 77–78, 83, 209–210
ActivePerl, 150
Actors: project team, 162; third party, 171
ADA (Americans with Disabilities Act), 185
Alert system, 188
AMA (American Medical Association), 142
Analog, program, 122
Analyst programmer, 187. *See also* IT: personnel
ANSI (American National Standards Institute), 20–21, 24
Archival issues, 76, 85, 96, 210
ARL (Association of Research Libraries), 25; e-metrics, 26
Ask Jeeves, 91
Authentication, 39, 108–109, 197–199; as aid to e-metrics, 134–135, 145–147, 167–168, 176–178

B

Backfiles, 209–210
Bibliographic record, 97
Big Deal, 46, 90. *See also* Bundles
Bundles, 45–46, 54, 74–76, 80–81, 83–84, 90–92; title price, 161
Buzz Index, 91

C

CGI (Common Gateway Interface), 149
Circulation, 17, 56, 63, 188, 213
CLF (Common Log Format), 15, 39–41, 121, 135–136, 139, 144
Click rate, 10–12, 14
Click-through, 10–12, 14; in local e-metrics, 128; script, 130–133, 149; in TLA, 135–137
Code of Practice, 29–31, 150. *See also* COUNTER
Committee AX, 213

Computer hardware: desktop computer, 104; hub, 155; PDA (personal digital assistant), 105; print server, 168; router, 99, 155. *See also* Proxy server; Workstation
Cookie, definition, 196
COUNTER (Counting Online Usage of Networked Electronic Resources), 27–29, 41–42; benefits of, 38–39; report types, 31; short-comings, 39–40
Crawlers, 40, 141
CRM (Customer Relationship Management), 12–13

D
Database-driven. *See* Web site
Data repository, 126, 156, 211
Data warehouse, 156, 211
Date of first access, 157, 158, 159
Date of first public availability, 158
Demographics, 11–12, 44–45, 69–70, 81, 172–173, 175–176, 206–207
Disaster recovery, 112
Disk space, shared, 156
DLF (Digital Library Federation), 94
Document Delivery, 169, 212, 214
DOI (Digital Object Identifier), 134
Domain name, 99, 173

E
EBL (Evidence-Based Librarianship), 185
E-book, 94, 105, 127, 141, 212
ECLF (Extended Common Log Format). *See* CLF
E-commerce, 8–9; use of e-metrics, 10–14
856 MARC field, 131, 165, 189
E-ISSN/ISBN, 134, 186
E-ISXN, 158
E-journal, 119
Electronic Resource Management Initiative, 94
Electronic resources manager, 186
Elsevier, 31, 35, 37, 40–41
eMarketer, 212
EMIS (E-metrics Instructional System), 118, 125
ERM (electronic resource management), 94–95, 97–100, 102–104, 112; interaction with e-metrics, 189–190, 203
E-services, 125, 211–213
Excel, 126, 171, 201
EZproxy, 146

F
Federated search, 213
FSCS (Federal-State Cooperative System), 20

G
Gate count, 10–11, 46, 56–57, 62–63
Google, 91

Googlebot, 141
GPL (General Public License), 170

H
Highwire, 32, 43
Hit, 10–12; in COUNTER, 40; as measurement of use, 22–123
Hyperlink, 8, 12, 29, 100; "broken," 98–100; in TLA, 11, 131, 135

I
IBM, 65
ICOLC (International Coalition of Library Consortia), 21, 25
IFLA (International Federation of Library Associations and Institutions), 21
ILS (Integrated Library System), 165, 169–170, 193, 212
Impact Factor, 82, 158, 161
Ingenta, 31
Interlibrary loan, 7, 23, 83–85
Internet: as communication medium, 4, 89; history, 8; 101; impact on commerce, 5, 8–10, 13; impact on libraries, 22–23, 55–56, 187; impact on publishing, 22–23, 73
Interpretation. *See* Report
IPEDS (Integrated Postsecondary Education Data System), 20

ISI (Institute for Scientific Information), 158
ISO (International Organization for Standardization), 20–21
ISO 2789, 21, 26, 39–40. *See also* ISO
ISP (Internet Service Provider), 175, 196
IT (Information Technology): importance in libraries, 204; personnel, 193

J
JAMA (Journal of the American Medical Association), 194
JCR (Journal Citation Report), 158

K
Kluwer, 41–42, 43

L
Library performance measurements, 12, 21, 24–26, 45–46, 51
Licensing, 73–75, 77–78, 106–107
Linkout, Pubmed, 152
Linux, 172
Lycos, 91

M
MARC, 131, 189
MEDLINE, 35
MetaSearch, 213–214
MicroStrategy, 43

N

Nature Publishing Group, 76
NCES (National Center for
    Education Statistics), 20
NCLIS (National Commission
    on Libraries and Information
    Science), 25
Network address, 37, 61–62,
    106–107, 116
Newsmap, 91
NFAIS (National Federation of
    Abstracting and Information
    Services), 202
NISO (National Information
    Standards Organization),
    20–21
NISO Z39.7, 26, 163. *See also*
    NISO
Non-circulating, 17, 60, 77, 96

O

OA (Open Access), 206
OPAC, 22; source for e-metrics,
    26, 40, 98, 165
OpenURL, 169, 213–214
Osama bin Laden, 91
Ovid, 43, 82

P

Page view, 10–12; in COUNTER,
    31–32, 41–42; vs. gate count,
    46; in Web analytics, 121
PALINET, 126
Perl, 130, 215, 222
PHP, 131

Privacy, 44, 70, 196, 198
Proxy server, 107–109, 143–145,
    209; for authentication,
    146–147, 197, 214; as data
    collector, 165–167, 196
Public Library of Science Biology
    (PLoS), 206
Publishing market consolidation,
    101–102, 207–208, 211–212

R

Report: format, 126;
    interpretation, 127; processing,
    199; storage and preservation,
    156, 201

S

SearchIQ, 91
Session, 35; browser, 146;
    simultaneous user, 78. *See also*
    Cookie; Turnaway
SFX, 213–214

T

Taliban, 91
Targets, 130–131. *See also*
    OpenURL
TC46/SC8, 20–21. *See also* ISO
Thomson ISI, 158
TLA (transaction log analysis),
    10, 135–137
Traffic. *See* Web
Turnaway. 26, 31–32, 127. *See also*
    Session

U
Unix, 171–172
URL: global change, 164;
modified, 164; rewriting proxy,
165; target, 164
User: access management, 191;
behaviors, 153; ID, example of,
135; identity verification, 167;
intention, 11, 40, 46, 153, 196;
list or database, 176, 178,
196–199; support, 94, 99, 188,
191, 198. *See also*
Authentication; Privacy
Use studies, 17, 44, 46

V
VI, text editor, 131
Visit, 10–11, 25–26, 141; in Web
analytics, 121
VPN (Virtual Private Network),
107–108

W
W3C (World Wide Web
Consortium), 121

Web: analytics process, 121;
design, 123; metrics, 119, 124;
OPAC, 165; traffic analysis,
120; usability, 122
Web analytics, 43, 120–122, 128,
169–170
Web-driven, 187
Webmaster, 164. *See also* IT:
personnel
Web site: activity, 124; analysis,
122–123; database-driven, 132,
159; static, 203
WebTrends, 121
Workload, shift in libraries,
184
Workstation, 120, 171–172,
193
World Trade Center, 91
Wusage, 121, 123

Y
Yahoo!, 91

Z
Zeitgeist, 91

About the Authors

Both authors bring extensive experience in both libraries and information technologies to the authority of this book. Eric is a graduate of Sheffield Hallam University (UK) and Bordeaux University (France) with degrees in Information Technology. He has worked as an analyst programmer, collecting and analyzing data for molecular mechanics and ecotoxicology projects at the Photochemistry Laboratory of the National Scientific Research Center at Bordeaux University. Eric also has corporate-world experience, working for four years in the leading telecommunication company in France employed as a systems administrator at France Telecom. He now works at the Stony Brook University Health Sciences Center Library developing library e-metrics tools in addition to administering and integrating the library's management system into a statewide academic/research electronic library initiative.

Andrew has nearly twenty years of professional library experience, holding positions in circulation, technical services, and information systems administration. His education includes an MLS from Queens College and a Ph.D. from the Graduate School and University Center, City University of New York. Currently the Associate Director at Stony Brook University Health Sciences Center Library, Andrew's technical hands-on experience includes administration of thin-client network infrastructures and cost-recovery printing solutions. He has contributed articles to the *Encyclopedia of Library and Information Science*, *The Electronic Library*, and *Computers in Libraries*. Both authors have been presenters at *InfoToday*, *E-Libraries*, *Computers in Libraries*, *Internet Librarian*, and *Content-World* conferences.